Restitution of Cultural Property and the Law

This book adopts a novel approach to the social question of restitution and repatriation of sacred cultural property and heritage acquired unethically during the colonial era. It uses an approach premised on better integration of law, ethics, history, anthropology, and provenance research.

To bridge the material and the sacred world in adjudication and policy formulation, a common definition of what the 'sacred' denotes in the context of colonial legacies is adopted as a viable methodology. 'Sacred' loot in private and public collections is defined based on clues imparted by disputes which are paradigmatic of the fragmentation that envelops the material, the systems of knowledge associated with that material, the structure and method of international law, subject specialisations, and the legal frameworks in play. The book suggests that the Parthenon Sculptures dispute and the parallel transnational litigation in the Zhanggong Zushi Statue cases offer practical approaches for deconstructing hurdles and assumptions concerning historical claims in the secondary legal norms and tenets of PrIL.

It will be of interest to researchers interested in interdisciplinary work across the humanities and social sciences, including public and private international law, cultural property law, heritage law, and provenance research and practice.

Christa Roodt is Senior Lecturer in the School of Culture and Creative Arts, University of Glasgow, United Kingdom. She specialises in the provenance and restitution of cultural heritage and acts as consultant on projects designed to achieve a more appropriate international regime for the protection and return of cultural objects removed from colonial, archaeological, and Nazi-era contexts. She is a serving member of the British Committee for the Reunification of the Parthenon Marbles.

Cultural Heritage and International Law

Regulating Transnational Cultural Heritage
Diversity, Memory and Identity
Merima Bruncevic

Transboundary Heritage and Intellectual Property Law
Safeguarding Intangible Cultural Heritage
Patricia Covarrubia

Cultural Heritage, Sustainable Development and Human Rights
Towards an Integrated Approach
Edited by *Laura Pineschi*

Legal Protection of Intangible Cultural Heritage
Perspectives from Indonesia and Malaysia
Diyana Sulaiman

Intentional Destruction of Cultural Heritage and the Law
A Research Companion
Alberta Fabbricotti

Restitution of Cultural Property and the Law
Complex Colonial Histories
Christa Roodt

Restitution of Cultural Property and the Law

Complex Colonial Histories

Christa Roodt

Routledge
Taylor & Francis Group
LONDON AND NEW YORK

First published 2025
by Routledge
4 Park Square, Milton Park, Abingdon, Oxon OX14 4RN

and by Routledge
605 Third Avenue, New York, NY 10158

Routledge is an imprint of the Taylor & Francis Group, an informa business

British Library Cataloguing-in-Publication Data
A catalogue record for this book is available from the British Library

ISBN: 978-0-367-42536-4 (hbk)
ISBN: 978-1-032-93307-8 (pbk)
ISBN: 978-1-003-56531-4 (ebk)

DOI: 10.4324/9781003565314

Typeset in Times New Roman
by Deanta Global Publishing Services, Chennai, India

Contents

Acknowledgements

In 2013 I stepped away from teaching Private International Law (PrIL) and into the world of art, history, and culture. As I became more absorbed in the emancipatory potential of the 'sacred' in art and cultural heritage, the predominant modes of thought that steer the core business of PrIL became more visible to me. The deep dive I took into the practice and theory of art history, provenance, and the restitution of art and cultural heritage drew me into the histories behind those modes. Several colleagues in History of Art, The Hunterian and CREATe deserve special mention: Clare Willsdon, Debra Strickland and Sabine Wieber, Steph Scholten, Giovanna Vitelli, Andy Mills, Marta Iljadica, and Elena Cooper. I also benefited greatly from interactions on international cultural heritage law with Valentina Vadi, Lucas Lixinski, Lucie Morisset, Ana Vrdoljak, Andrzej Jakubowski, and Alessandro Chechi. The Routledge editorial team were pro-active, energetic, and accommodating. Thank you to Nicola Sharpe and Diksha Bhugra for doing so much to see the project through to fruition. Sincere thanks are also due to Shioban Poole for her share in the project prior to her departure from Routledge. A very special word of thanks is reserved for Maggie Cacot. I could not have asked for better, more sure-footed editorial assistance on this project.

I am indebted to Haoyang Zhao, who translated pertinent passages from the Buddha Mummy case exactly when I needed them. My gratitude for the indefatigable and painstaking work Andreas Giorgallis did on tables, references, research details, and indexing, knows no bounds. Andreas also contributed his energy and knowledge on my courses 'Discourses in Cultural Property' and 'Provenance and Restitution.' I was unbelievably lucky to have him in my corner for the duration of his PhD study.

Koos, your generosity of spirit enabled me to meet the challenges in the production of the text. Without the problem-solving skills you shared so freely not a single bibliography would have seen the light. Your mischievous sense of humour continues to inspire me.

The research was concluded on 2 May 2024. Errors that remain are mine alone.

Christa Roodt, Glasgow, Scotland, 2 September 2024.

Abbreviations

General

ACE	Arts Council of England
ADR	Alternative Dispute Resolution
AFFORD	African Foundation for Development
APPG-AR	All-party Parliamentary Group on African Reparations 'African Restitution'
ARPA	Archaeological Resources Protection Act of 1979
CLT	Classical Legal Thought (1850–1914)
CT	Contemporary Thought (1945–2000)
DCMS	United Kingdom Department for Digital, Culture, Media and Sport
DIVUM	Declaration on the Importance and Value of Universal Museums
DMB	Deutscher Museumsbund (German Museums Association)
EU	European Union
ECHR	European Convention for the Protection of Human Rights and Fundamental Freedoms/European Court of Human Rights
FNSCORA	First Nations Sacred Ceremonial Objects Repatriation Act
FPIC	Free, Prior, and Informed Consent
ICC	International Criminal Court
ICCPR	International Covenant on Civil and Political Rights
ICESCR	International Covenant on Economic, Social and Cultural Rights
ICPRCP	Intergovernmental Committee for Promoting the Return of Cultural Property to its Countries of Origin or its Restitution in Case of Illicit Appropriation
ICTR	International Criminal Tribunal for Rwanda
ICTY	International Criminal Tribunal for the Former Yugoslavia
ILA	International Law Association
IRS	Indian Residential Schools
NAGPRA	Native American Graves Protection and Repatriation Act
NGO	Non-governmental organisation
NMAI	United States National Museum of the American Indian
NMAfA	National Museum of African Art
OJ C	Official Journal of the European Union, Information and Notices
OJ L	Official Journal of the European Union, Legislation

PrIL	Private International Law
PublIL	Public International Law
SLT	Socially Oriented Legal Thought (1900–1968)
SWA	German South West Africa (now Namibia)
SWAC	South West Africa Company
UK	United Kingdom of Great Britain and Northern Ireland
UDHR	Universal Declaration of Human Rights
UNDRIP	United Nations Declaration on the Rights of Indigenous Peoples
UNESCO	United Nations Educational, Scientific and Cultural Organisation
UNIDROIT	International Institute for the Unification of Private Law
UNTS	United Nations Treaty Series

Table of Cases

International and Regional

European Court of Human Rights (EurCtHR)

Syllogos ton Athinaion v United Kingdom, Application No. 48259/15, First Section, 31 May 2016; ECHR 23 June 2016

Kononov v Latvia [GC], Application No. 36376/04, ECHR 17 May 2010

International Criminal Court (ICC)

The Prosecutor v Ahmad Al Faqi Al Mahdi, Judgment and Sentence, 27 September 2016, ICC-01/12-01/15; *Reparations Order*, 17 August 2017, ICC-CPI-20170817-PR1329

International Court of Justice (ICJ)

Case Concerning Right of Passage over Indian Territory (Portugal/India) Merits, 12 April 1960 [1960] ICJ 6

Land and Maritime Boundary Between Cameroon and Nigeria (Cameroon v Nigeria; Equatorial Guinea Intervening), 10 October 2002 [2002] ICJ 1

Application of the Convention on the Prevention and Punishment of the Crime of Genocide in the Gaza Strip (South Africa v Israel) Provisional Measures Merits, 29 December 2023 [2023] ICJ 1

The Legal Consequences for States of the Continued Presence of South Africa in Namibia (South West Africa) Notwithstanding Security Council Resolution 276 (1970), 21 June 1971 [1971] ICJ 16

The Legal Consequences of the Separation of the Chagos Archipelago from Mauritius, 25 February 2019 [2019] ICJ GL No 169

Inter-American Court of Human Rights (IACHR)

Barrios Altos Judgment of 14 March 2001 Series C No. 75

Almonacid-Arellano et al. Judgment of 26 September 2006 Series C No. 154

La Cantuta v Peru, Merits, Reparations and Costs, Judgment of 29 November 2006 Series C No. 162

International Military Tribunal of Nuremberg (IMT)

Nuremberg Decision 6 Federal Rules Decisions 69 (1946-1947), Trial of German Major War Criminals in Nuremberg 30 September and 1 October 1946, reprinted in Her Majesty's Stationary Office (1962) 40

Permanent Court of Arbitration

Island of Palmas (The Netherlands v USA), 4 April 1928, II Reports of International Arbitral Awards 829

NATIONAL

Canada

Cloud v Canada, (2004) 73 OR 3d 401 (Ontario CA)

Fabrique de la Paroisse de L'Ange-Gardien c. Procureur Général de la Province de Québec, Musées Nationaux du Canada et autres (1980) CS 175; *Fabrique de la Paroisse de L' Ange-Gardien* [1987] 2 RCS IX

China

Yunchun Village and Dongpu Village Committees v Oscar van Overeem, Design & Consultancy B.V. and Design Consultancy Oscar van Overeem B.V. Sanming Intermediate People's Court, 2015 San Min Chu Zi No. 626, 4 December 2020

Oscar van Overeem, Design & Consultancy Oscar van Overeem B.V. v Yangchun Village and Dongpu Village Committees, Fujian Province Higher People's Court, 2021 Min Min Final No. 302, 19 July 2022

France

Hopi Tribe v Néret-Minet and Estimations Ventes aux Enchères, Tribunal de Grande Instance de Paris, Interim Order, 12 April 2013, No. RG 13/25880; Interim Order, 6 December 2013, No. RG 13/59110; Interim Order, 27 June 2014, No. RG 14/55733

Germany

BVerwG NJW 2001, 1878

BVerwGE 69, 366

Italy

Associazione nazionale Italia Nostra Onlus c. Ministero per i beni e le attività culturali et al., Tribunale Amministrativo Regionale del Lazio (Sez. II-Quarter) Case No. 3518, 28 February 2007; Consiglio di Stato, Case No. 3154, 23 June 2008

Netherlands

Amsterdam District Court, Village Committee of Yangchun and DongPu v Oscar van Overeem et al., No. ECLI:NL:RBAMS:2018:8919, 12 December 2018

The Hague Court of Appeal, Children of Executed Men in South-Sulawesi v The Netherlands, Case No. 200.243.525/01 (1 October 2019)

The Hague Court of Appeal, Heirs Java Torture Victim v The Netherlands, Case No. 200.247.634/01 (1 October 2019)

Namibia

Swartbooi and Another v Speaker of the National Assembly High Court of Namibia Case No. HC-MD-CIV-MOT-REV-2023/00023, Founding Affidavit (20 January 2023)

United Kingdom

Athanasios Sophocleous & Ors v Secretary of State for the Foreign and Commonwealth Office & Secretary of State for Defence [2018] EWHC 19 (QBD); [2018] EWCA Civ 2167

Attorney-General of New Zealand v Ortiz [1982] 3 All ER 432 (QBD and CA); [1983] 2 All ER 93 (HL)

The Case of the Hottentot Venus (1810) 13 East's Reports of Cases Argued and Determined in the Court of King's Bench 195, 104 ER 344

Government of the Islamic Republic of Iran v The Barakat Galleries Ltd. [2007] EWHC 705 (QBD); [2009] 1 QB 22 (CA)

Her Majesty's Attorney-General v Trustees British Museum [2005] Ch 397

Kamidian v Holt and Others [2008] EWHC 1483 (Comm)

King v Earl of Crewe (1910) AC 588

Walker v Innospec Limited and others [2017] UKSC 47

United States

Autocephalous Greek-Orthodox Church v Goldberg and Feldman Fine Arts Inc 717 F Supp 1374 (SD Ind 1989) aff'd 917 F2d 378 (7th Cir 1990)

Doe v Nestle USA Inc 766 F.3d 1013 (9th Cir. 2014); *Doe II III IV VI v Nestle USA* Docket No: 17-55435 USCA (9th Cir 2018); *Nestle USA, Inc. v Doe et al.* Certiorari to the United States Court of Appeals for the Ninth Circuit No. 19–416, 17 June 2021

Deadria Farmer-Paellmann and Restitution Study Group v Smithsonian Institution, No. 1:22-cv-3048, D.D.C 7 October 2022

Hilton v Guyot 159 US 113 (1895)

In re Flamenbaum 2013 NY Slip Op. 7510 (NY 2013)

In re African-American Slave Descendants Litigation, Appeals of Deadria Farmer-Paellmann et al., and Timothy Hurdle et al. 471 F.3d 754 (7th Cir 2006)

Na Iwi O Na Kupuna I Mokapu v Dalton 894 F Supp 1397 (D Haw 1995)

Rukoro et al. v Federal Republic of Germany 363 F Supp 3d (436 SDNY 2019)

Rukoro et al. v Federal Republic of Germany 976 F3d 218 (2d Cir. 2020)

The Herero People's Reparations Corporation, et al., v Deutsche Bank, A.g. and Woermann Line, D/b/a Deutsche Afrika-linien Gmblt & Company 370 F.3d 1192 D.C. Cir. 2004

Hereros v Deutsche Afrika-Linien GMBLT & Co Case No. 06-1684, 232 F.App'x 90 (3rd Cir. 2007)

United States v A 10th Century Cambodian Sandstone Sculpture Currently Located at Sotheby's in New York, New York, Stipulation and Order of Settlement, No. 12 Civ 2600 (GBD) (SDNY 13 December 2013)

Table of Legislation

Bilateral Agreements

Agreement between Germany and Maharero, the Paramount Chief of the Hereros (21 October 1885)

Agreement between Germany and Samuel Maharero of Okahandya (6 December 1894)

Agreement between Germany and Hendrik Witbooi of Gibeon (15 September 1894/16 November 1895)

Draft Joint Declaration/Reconciliation Agreement 'United in Remembrance of our Colonial Past, United in our Will to Reconcile, United in our Vision of the Future', signed by the Federal Republic of Germany, May 2021

Joint Declaration on the Return of Benin Bronzes and Bilateral Museum Cooperation (signed by Germany and Nigeria) 1 July 2022.

Treaty of Friendship, Partnership and Cooperation between the Great Socialist People's Arab Jamahiriya and the Republic of Italy of 2008, Law no. 2 of 1377 FDP/2009 AD

Conventions

Articles of Capitulation proposed by Abdoullah Jaques Francois Menou, General in Chief of the French Army now in Alexandria, to the Generals Commanding the Land and Sea Forces of His Britannic Majesty, and of the Sublime Porte, forming the Blockade of Alexandria, 30 August 1801 (text reprinted in Robert Thomas Wilson, *History of the British Expedition to Egypt Vol II*, London: C. Roworth 1803)

Convention on the Suppression and Punishment of the Crime of Apartheid, 30 November 1973, 1015 UNTS 243

Convention on the Prevention and Punishment of the Crime of Genocide, General Assembly Resolution 260, 9 December 1948, 78 UNTS 277

Convention on the Non-Applicability of Statutory Limitations to War Crimes and Crimes Against Humanity, 26 November 1968, 754 UNTS 73

Council of Europe, Convention on Offences relating to Cultural Property, signed 19 May 2017, CETS 221

Council of Europe, European Convention for the Protection of Human Rights and Fundamental Freedoms, 4 November 1950, ETS No. 005

Council of Europe, Protocol 1 to the European Convention for the Protection of Human Rights and Fundamental Freedoms, 20 March 1952, ETS No. 009 as amended by Protocol No. 11 ETS No. 155

Definitive Treaty of Peace and Amity Between his Britannic Majesty and his Most Christian Majesty [of France], Paris, 30 May 1814, London, 1984 (First Treaty of Paris 1814)

Definitive Treaty between His Majesty [Great Britain] and his Most Christian Majesty [of France], Paris, 20 November 1815; and other Conventions and Documents (*Second Treaty of Paris 1815)*

Final Act of the Congress of Vienna *of 25 March 1815 ('Treaty of General Alliance')*

Geneva Convention for the Amelioration of the Condition of the Wounded and Sick in Armed Forces in the Field (First Geneva Convention or GC I), 12 August 1949, 75 UNTS 31

Geneva Convention for the Amelioration of the Condition of Wounded, Sick and Shipwrecked Members of Armed Forces at Sea (Second Geneva Convention or GC II), 12 August 1949, 75 UNTS 85

Geneva Convention relative to the Treatment of Prisoners of War (Third Geneva Convention or GC III), 12 August 1949, 75 UNTS 135

Geneva Convention (IV) relative to the Protection of Civilian Persons in Time of War (Fourth Geneva Convention or GC IV), 12 August 1949, 75 UNTS 287

Geneva Conventions Additional Protocol of 12 August 1949 and relating to the Protection of Victims of International Armed Conflicts (Additional Protocol I), 1125 UNTS 3

General Act of the Berlin Conference, 26 February 1885, C 4361 1885 ('*Congo Act*'/'*Berlin Act*')

Hague Convention (II) Respecting the Laws and Customs of War on Land with Annex of Regulations, 29 July 1899, TS 403

Hague Convention (IV) Respecting the Laws and Customs of War on Land with Annex of Regulations, 18 October 1907, TS 539

Hague Convention for the Protection of Cultural Property in the Event of Armed Conflict and First Protocol, 14 May 1954, 249 UNTS 215

Hague Convention for the Protection of Cultural Property in the Event of Armed Conflict and Second Protocol, 1954, 26 March 1999, 2253 UNTS 172

Hague Convention on Choice of Court Agreements, 30 June 2005, Hague Conference on Private International Law (www.hcch.net)

International Covenant on Economic, Social and Cultural Rights, 16 December 1966, 993 UNTS 3

International Covenant on Civil and Political Rights, 16 December 1966, 999 UNTS 171

Manual on the Laws of War on Land, adopted at Oxford, UK, on 9 September 1880 5 Annuaire de l'Institut de Droit International (1881–1882) ('*Oxford Manual*')

Peace Treaty between Great Britain, France, the Ottoman Empire, Sardinia and Russia, Paris, 30 March 1856 *(Treaty of Paris*)

Peace Treaty between the Allied and Associated Powers and Germany, Versailles, 28 June 1919, including the Covenant of the League of Nations, Part I, UKTS 4 (Cmd. 153)

Project of an International Declaration Concerning the Laws and Customs of War (Brussels Declaration) adopted by the Conference of Brussels, 27 August 1874, American Journal of International Law 1907 1(S2) Supplement: Official Documents 96-103

Red Cross Convention on the Amelioration of the Condition of the Wounded in Armies in the Field, 22 August 1864, TS 377 (superseded by the Geneva Conventions)

Treaty and Supplementary Treaty No. 7 between Her Majesty the Queen and the Blackfeet and other Indian Tribes (the Siksika (Blackfoot), Kainai (Blood), Piikani (Peigan), Stoney-Nakoda and Tsuut'ina (Sarcee)), at the Blackfoot Crossing of Bow River and Fort MacLeod, made 22 September and 4 December 1877, Reprinted from the Edition of 1877 by Roger Duhamel, FRSC Queen's Printer and Controller of Stationary Ottawa, 1966

UNESCO Convention on the Means of Prohibiting and Preventing the Illicit Import, Export and Transfer of Ownership of Cultural Property, 14 November 1970, 823 UNTS 231

UN General Assembly, Rome Statute of the International Criminal Court, adopted on 17 July 1998 by the United Nations Diplomatic Conference of Plenipotentiaries on the Establishment of an International Criminal Court (last amended 2020)

UNESCO Convention for the Safeguarding of Intangible Cultural Heritage, 17 October 2003 UNTS 2368, 3

UNIDROIT Convention on Stolen or Illegally Exported Cultural Objects, 24 June 1995, 34 ILM 1330

Universal Declaration of Human Rights, adopted and proclaimed by General Assembly resolution 217 A (III) of 10 December 1948

European Union

Commission Communication, 'Towards an Integrated Approach to Cultural Heritage for Europe' COM(2014) 477

Council Directive (EU) No 2014/60 of 15 May 2014 on the return of cultural objects unlawfully removed from the territory of a Member State and amending Regulation (EU) No 1024/2012 (Recast) [2014] OJ L159, 28.5.2014

Council Regulation (EC) No 44/2001 on jurisdiction and the recognition and enforcement of judgments in civil and commercial matters OJ L 12/1 16.1.2001

Council Regulation (EC) No 1215/2012 of the European Parliament and of the Council of 12 December 2012 on jurisdiction and the recognition and enforcement of judgments in civil and commercial matters (recast) OJ 2012 L351/1, 20.12.2012

European Parliament Resolution on Fundamental Rights of People of African Descent in Europe, 26 March 2019 (2018/2899(RSP))

Regulation (EC) No 864/2007 of the European Parliament and the Council on the law applicable to non-contractual obligations ('*Rome II*') OJ L 199/40 31.7.2007

Treaty on the Functioning of the European Union, 9 May 2008, OJ C 115/47

African Union

African Union Model Law on the Protection of Cultural Property adopted at the Fortieth Ordinary Session 20 January-3 February 2022 Addis Ababa, Ethiopia, EX.CL/1309(XL) d

Organisation of American States

American Declaration on the Rights of Indigenous Peoples, 15 June 2016, 46th Session, Santo Domingo, Dominican Republic AG/RES.2888 (XLVI-O/16)

United Nations

Charter of the United Nations and Statute of the International Court of Justice, San Francisco, 26 June 1945

Resolution 2249 (2015) of 20 November 2015 (Terrorist attacks Islamic State in Iraq and the Levant (ISIL))

UN Declaration on the Rights of Indigenous Peoples ('*UNDRIP*') A/RES/61/295, 13 Sep 2007

Belgium

Projet de Loi Reconnaissant le Caractère Alienable des Biens liés au passé Colonial de l'État Belge et Determinant un Cadre Juridique pour leur Restitution et leur Retour 28 September 2022 No. 2022042012, Le Moniteur Belge 28 September 2022, No. 2022042012

Canada

Act to Amend the Indian Act SC 1920 c 50

Constitutional Act 1982 ch 11 (RU), Annexe B

Cultural Property Export and Import Act, Consolidated Statutes of Canada, Chapter c 51 RSC 1985

Historical Resources Act of 1973

Indian Act of 1876

Indian Act of 1880

Indian Act of 1884

First Nations Sacred Ceremonial Objects Repatriation Act F-14 RSA 2000

First Nations Sacred Ceremonial Objects Repatriation Regulations 96/2004

Royal Proclamation (1763 R.S.C. 1985, App. II, No. 1)

China

Law on the Protection of Cultural Relics of the People's Republic of China, No. 76 of 1982 (as amended in 1991 and 2013)

France

Loi relative à la restitution par la France de la dépouille mortelle de Saartjie Baartman à l'Afrique du Sud, Journal officiel de République française, Loi n° 2002-323 du 6 mars 2002 parue au Journal officiel de République française N° 56 du 7 mars 2002

Heritage Code (*Code du Patrimoine*) of 20 February 2004

Germany

Civil Code of 1 January 1900

Greece

Law on Scientific and Technological Collections, on the Discovery and Conservation of Antiquities and the Use Thereof, Act of 10/22 May 1834, OJ 22 of 16/28 June 1834

Civil Code of 1946

Italy

Civil Code adopted by Royal Decree No. 262, 16 March 1942

Namibia

Namibian Constitution, 21 March 1990

Netherlands

Burial Act of 1991

Civil Code of 1992

Cultural Property Originating from Occupied Territory (Return) Act of 2007

Heritage Act of 2016

Ottoman Empire

Antiquities Law of 1874

South Africa

National Heritage Resources Act 1999

United Kingdom

British Museum Act 1753
British Museum Act 1963
Charities Act 2011
Charities Act 2022
Holocaust (Return of Cultural Objects) Act 2009
Museums and Galleries Act 1992
National Heritage Act 1980
National Heritage Act 1983
National Heritage (Scotland) Act 1985
Parthenon Sculptures (Return to Greece) Bill 2016
Private International Law (Miscellaneous Provisions) Act 1995
Public Libraries and Museums Act 1964
Return of Cultural Objects Regulations 1994
Sale of Goods Act 1979

United States

Alien Torts Statute 28 US Code 1350 (1948)
Archaeological Resources Protection Act of 1979, 16 US Code 470aa–470mm
General Orders No. 100: Instructions for the Government of the Armies of the United States in the Field of 24 April 1863 (‘*Lieber Code*’)
Native American Graves Protection and Repatriation Act of 1990, 25 US Code 3001–3013
Native American Graves Protection and Repatriation Act Systematic Processes for Disposition or Repatriation of Native American Human Remains, Funerary Objects, Sacred Objects, and Objects of Cultural Patrimony, 13 December 2023
Regulations for Repatriation of Native American Ancestors and Objects 2024, 43 CFR Part 10, 88 FR 86518 of 13 December 2023
Safeguard Tribal Objects of Patrimony Act, 21 December 2022 (Public Law No 117-258)
Smithsonian Institution, National Museums and Art Galleries, 20 US Code 41–80j (1976)

1 Introduction

1.1 Plunder for 'viewing pleasure'—a mutilating ambition

Nationalist rivalries between the empires of Europe played out through looting, manipulation, and corruption. Europe's colonial powers leveraged power imbalances to garner the dignity and status they believed they lacked. The symbols of this power—Africa's art and heritage—have been hung in homes and museums across Europe since the 18th century. The English, French, Germans, Italians, and Portuguese were interlocked in a European–African confrontation that profoundly changed the nature of law and justice in the colonies over a short period between 1875 and 1914. Their compulsions compromised their colonies' long-term development and the fashioning of capable institutions. The Benin Kingdom managed to maintain its independence but was defenceless against the predations that led to the losses of their heritage and royal treasures, and the devastation of its Royal Palace. Germany was the first to undertake efforts to right the wrongs of the taking of these treasures in 2022.

Attempts to gain power through the objects that had been taken are evident in the competition between Britain, France, Malta, and the Ottoman Empire for the famed adornments of the Athenian Temple that was constructed nearly 2,500 years ago on the Acropolis. The removal of the adornments occurred when the conditions were right for the corrupt men in Lord Elgin's party to commit the historical theft behind the enduring issue of ownership (Titi 2023: 82). His colonial networks in the Ottoman Empire facilitated their extraction to multiply the marble ornaments in Broomhall House, his ancestral home in Scotland. The Parthenon Sculptures point to what human custody of the manifestations of the subtly interconnected biosphere at the vulnerable 'heart' of a culture can accomplish or deny. Having abandoned any notion of further legal recourse in 2015, the Greek government nevertheless continues to raise the issue at every opportunity. The Greek state's first official demand for Elgin's loot came in 1836 and claims followed in 1890 (Titi 2023: 125, 128). Senior officials in the Foreign and Commonwealth Office in Britain supported the return of the Parthenon Friezes, the Caryatid, and the column from the Erectheum when Greece and Britain joined forces against Hitler in 1941. The Foreign Office accepted the return to Greece in principle, in a gesture of friendship, after the war. It was not intended to be an acknowledgement of a principle that antiquities should be returned to their place of origin (Vrettos 1997:

DOI: 10.4324/9781003565314-1

205–211). The British Museum advanced feeble objections. Soon after, however, it was decided that their return would not be allowed (Robertson 2019: 23). An official demand against the UK government came in 1983. During the 1990s the return campaign gathered steam (Vrettos 1997: 211–212). The UK government restated its uncompromising position in 2021 (Hansard HL Deb. vol. 834, cols. 1992–2006, 14 December 2023). The dispute about continued ownership of the Parthenon Sculptures pervades cultural property argument (Audi 2007: 141). If occupation granted the Sultan the right to sell or give away the sculptures to foreigners, the argument could be extended to the authority of occupying powers to own the cultural heritage of territories they occupy. If the Sultan had no right to permit foreigners to take their pick, however, any number of museums in Britain and elsewhere are not at liberty to hold such items in their collections (Chamberlain 1983: 8). The discourse about law and legality is entirely circular and self-serving but the detached and scattered Parthenon Sculptures stoke debate about the return of dispersed and fragmented collections more broadly while the far-flung individual fragments and pieces are admired as sterile, individual works of art. The dispute prompts museums in Europe and North America to rethink their ethnographic and anthropological collections.

Colonial greed and ruthless self-interest combined with pietist commitment to bring civilisation to the barbarians and forestall the imminent extinction of colonised societies. The competition for collecting skulls and bones deriving from communities believed to be on the verge of extinction was savage and ghastly. Bodies and skulls were exhumed from their resting places, ravaged on battlefields, and funnelled into museum and university collections in Europe and the United States as trophies and objects for research (Hubert 1992: 105). These museum trophies are displayed not to honour the cultures they belong to, but to glorify and serve as 'educational' tools and provide viewing pleasure for the groups who stole them. It was preferable to bury information that could shed light on origins but heaped shame on the collectors and the institutions that benefited from their collections (Clegg 2020: 122–123).

For primary legal rules to change, the political will must exist to enact new instruments (Thielecke and Geißdorf 2021: 162). The social, economic, and political costs will vary with every statute promulgated, and the weight accorded to the values and principles considered pertinent will be different in every case (Zeidler 2016: 19–25, 26, 52). Law tends to be time and space specific. The values that determine the normative horizon, legitimacy, and political authority of law, guide its reform and are open to debate (Muir Watt 2016: 389). A moral shift in confronting the part a state played in the colonial project and the legacy of injustice it has created, may prompt legislative change. Some commentators prefer normative change in restitution of colonial-era collection items at the museum level and in policy guidelines that form part of national frameworks alongside common principles, over a new convention on repatriation and return of looted art (Stahn 2023: 513, 519; contra Robertson 2019: 226, 229ff).

If repatriation processes are co-opted for political gain, future collaboration may be imperilled. The unknown African man whose half-naked, stuffed body was on display in Europe for tourists to gawk at for 170 years, provides ample warning that action must retain credibility. Everything about 'El Negro'—from the abhorrent acquisition of his dislocated remains, their treatment and display, to his repatriation and reburial—mirror a racist European mindset incapable of recognising his common humanity. The lack of a name, known date of birth or death, community or state of origin, any information whatsoever about his person and personality, reflect an utter failure to remember the colonial past (Westerman 2004: 16). Every available opportunity to rehumanise him was missed. The mounted body was put on display at the Palais d'Industrie in 1872, and in 1880 the Catalonian, Francesco Darder, bought it. He displayed it in Barcelona in 1888. The inscription 'Bushman of the Kalahari' was added to the pedestal in the Darder Museum in Banyoles in 1916, but the display followed that of the other wildlife specimens in the museum. Spanish anthropometrics and DNA testing in 1995 identified the body as 'negroid, with features of an African Bushman' (Westerman 2004: 8–9). Notwithstanding the evidence put forward by journalists and scholars that confirmed El Negro's South African origin among Cape Hottentots, Spanish politicians and bureaucrats decided 'Bechuanaland' was where his remains had to go. Botswana's Ministry of Foreign Affairs offered reburial. South Africa never advanced a claim, however, and by the time the Darder Museum pleaded to halt the repatriation, museum officials had already scraped the skin from the bones and removed non-human additions (Woodhead 2002: 345). Only the skull and a few bones arrived in Gaborone in an unvarnished wooden packing case. There was no body and no casket. The Christian reburial in a community playground in Botswana was an undignified affair. The Spanish Ambassador insisted that Spain deserved absolution for taking the body and declared that it had done more than enough having returned it (Parsons and Segobye 2009: 397). No research records, including the DNA analysis, were ever returned. An entomological journal not previously digitised, the *Annales de la La Société Entomologique de France*, has since confirmed that the Verreaux brothers searched for fauna specimens in the Cape Colony, and never set foot in Botswana. The unknown man was from Tulbagh in the Western Cape. Prioritising political mileage over decency sent him to Botswana, further dislocating his remains and compromising the dignity of Southern African societies. It constituted a new wrong.

Provenance refers to the original location and chain of ownership of art and artefacts, documents, photographs, and parts removed from buildings. Provenance research may be undertaken to 'map' the history of ownership to determine whether a museum is justified in keeping collection items. Restitution requires that rightful ownership and custody is established to determine who has the authority to lend and borrow, duplicate, and digitise. Ownership as an idea accommodates various combinations of legal relations that shift in meanings in relation to land, chattels, bodies and ideas, and the contexts in which they function (Waldron 1988: 29). However, the idea of ownership hardly fits sacred objects and human remains. An uncritical reading of simple transactions records that list owners omit the inherent function, significance, and histories of sacred objects invite construction of 'new' meanings from histories that suppress the intended sacred functions of the objects for the people they were made for. Research based on written records alone misplaces the focus from the objects' lives in their communities to the limitations imposed on their participation in social life. Provenance research may manage to retrace an object's origins and identify to whom it should be returned, but ultimate repatriation decisions and issues of procedure are not automatically resolved if the place and function of an object in a spiritual tradition is not understood. Institutions in possession of ethnographic material may consider it less costly to maintain a state of injustice than to devise large-scale property transfers on a systemic level (Zeidler 2016: 121).

The broader debate about dispossession of land in colonial law and land reform is connected to dispossession of Indigenous peoples' resources and cultures, which gave rise to reparation claims and restitution claims. 'Colonial international law' made claims of universality and primacy but European powers made unfounded jurisdictional claims over others. Imperial Germany claimed that their colonisation of South West Africa (SWA) between 1884 and 1890 transferred sovereignty to them by occupying a so-called *terra nullius*. However, they did not meet the *terra nullius* requirements in international law because Indigenous peoples exercised sovereign powers over their land prior to colonisation (Goldmann 2024: 588, 592).

As the law became instrumentalised and legal fictions were created, non-discriminatory measures, e.g., remuneration for expropriated land, were prejudicially applied. The fiction that, because the land was uninhabited prior to Europeans' assertion of sovereignty, the territory was vacant and 'ownerless' enabled Europeans to establish a right of occupation (Koskenniemi 2017: 3–4). This mechanism supported claims of effective administration of land through a doctrine of discovery that was made to fit.

Britain annexed land in North America by *Royal Proclamation* (1763 R.S.C. 1985, App. II, No. 1). Aboriginal titles in Canada are founded on this Proclamation, the Common Law, and the 1982 Constitutional Act. The Crown's obligations to Indigenous peoples in Canada have become clearer after many years of political and legal conflict (Hance 2020b: 172–173, 176). Tribal authorities were rarely part of negotiations between colonial powers, not even when treaties established borders that divided their land. Policy decisions that determined the US–Canadian border eroded the livelihood and future of Indigenous peoples, but they had no say in them (Stark et al. 2011: 5). Oral history indicates that First Nations people believed Treaty 7 at Blackfoot Crossing (one of several signed from 1871 to 1921 between First Nations and Queen Victoria) to be a peace treaty in preparation for the peaceful settlement of what is now Alberta (Treaty and Supplementary Treaty No. 7 Between Her Majesty the Queen and the Blackfeet and other Indian Tribes, 22 September and 4 December 1877). The First Nations signatories were unaware that the government intended to dissolve their rights of possession to enable Euro-Canadian settlers to gain ownership of the land. They unknowingly surrendered their rights and subjected themselves to European control and oppression (Treaty 7 Elders and Tribal Council 1996: 323).

First Nations peoples had a mystical relationship with land and the natural environment where its supernatural powers dwell. However, the formal authorisation to determine Indian communities' land base and who qualifies as Indian lodges in the Canadian government. The Indian Act of 1876 was designed to assimilate a diverse population into Euro-Canadian settler culture and to establish governing structures to control the exercise of rights to practice culture and traditions. The authority to regulate and administer the affairs of registered First Nations and reserve communities belongs to the Canadian federal government under the Indian Act but Indigenous communities cannot afford to surrender their rights in the unique historical constitutional relationship between the Indigenous communities and the State and have no choice but to live in bondage.

The displacement that accompanied settler colonialism contributed to rapid impoverishment and the disintegration of communities (Zimmerer 2021: 97). Colonialism made objects of peoples and sanctioned expeditions to take ownership of their bodies, their grave goods, and what they considered sacred. So-called friendly, peaceful, or diplomatic expeditions turned 'punitive' when their true purpose came to light. Opportunities to remove cultural, historical, and religious objects abounded when the slave trade was in full swing, and human remains of Africans who were removed from illegal Portuguese slave vessels in the 19th century were offloaded and quarantined in places such as the island of St Helena, a British Overseas Territory, during British abolition efforts. The improper acquisition, display, and sale of their human remains creates painful intergenerational histories of indignity (Human Rights Council Report 2020: 95).

In the 19th century, the US Federal Government forced the removal of thousands of Native Americans and transferred more than a billion acres of their land to private owners to profit from the extraction of resources and from the taxes they paid. Coinciding with Indian territorial dispossession, between 1819 and 1969 the US Federal Government forced the cultural assimilation of American Indian, Alaska Native, and Native Hawaiian children through its Boarding School Initiative (Federal Indian Boarding School Initiative Investigative Report May 2022). Euro-Canadian settlers took away children from their homes and families, placed them in foster homes, changed their names, and put them up for adoption by white families from across Canada and the United States (Moran 2019: 421–427, 444–446). Children were placed in abusive Indian Residential Schools (IRS) run by Roman Catholic priests and nuns. To 'civilise' them through forced religious conversion they were punished for practising their own spiritual beliefs and sacred traditions, and the use of their languages and stories were forbidden (*Cloud v Canada*, 73 OR 3d 401, para 12 (Ont CA)). The connection which the children had with their lineage and origins was systematically stripped away and their contact with their families weakened to the point where many parents were not even notified that their children had died (Moran 2019: 439–442). The IRS policy disrupted the link between the cultural heritage and education of children and erased the culture of the youngest and most vulnerable carriers of the Indian heritage. The IRS abuses highlight the complex role which law has assumed in relation to bigotry and racism. An Act to Amend the Indian Act SC 1920 mandated the taking of the children without parental consent and offered defences that prompted the courts to reject reparative claims (c 50).

The cultural and spiritual attachment to a specific territory counts among the strongest indicators of 'indigenousness' (Gilbert 2011: 253–254). Diminishing rights over territory impacted on self-governance, including the capacity to institute claims for repatriation and restitution. Living Native American and First Nations communities in North America and Canada, treat sacred medicine bundles as their children and as living beings who are their equals (Human Rights Council Report 2020: para 8). The bundles are wrapped collections of sacred items which are central in communal rituals. The simplicity of the fur pelts, feathers, roots, and herbs gathered into bundles belie the complex, primordial role as the communities' ancestors and the intricate rules of usage and protocols that govern their treatment. The medicine bundles are gifts from the gods to human ancestors. They express appreciation for the earth and its creatures and carry the teachings of the elders. Bundles can only be protected or cared for by different keepers, who provide them with food, shelter, songs, and prayers, which are unique and integral to the cultural identities and social structure of their communities (Simpson 1996: 123). The transfers of bundles and their constituent power from one keeper to another connects communities with their ancestry, environment, and landscape. It allows for the sharing of this knowledge, connection, and sense of identity with the community (Champagne 2012: 31, 47).

The threat faced by Native American bundle culture and the loss of that culture permeated the spaces and the land in which bundles were formed and used. Countless rituals and stories that would otherwise have been transmitted to the young, were lost when ceremonies and spirituality of Native Americans and First Nations people were restricted in a misguided effort to encourage their acculturation. Bundles were given up, pawned, or sold at prices far below their actual value. Numerous bundles ended up in the private collections of outsiders who had stolen them or acquired them from thieves. Museums were sometimes requested to take care of bundles because the communities were themselves unable to. Components of sacred bundles would enter public and private collections through sales and donations that separated the materials from the traditional knowledge they carry. The dispersal and destruction of the bundles impoverished children's cultural experiences and diminished their hopes for the future (Cash Cash 2001: 139). When medicine bundles started to be returned in the 1970s more youngsters took an interest in traditional knowledge and language; their sense of community and responsibility was renewed. Evidently, the renewal of traditional cultural and spiritual values improves physical and mental well-being (Human Rights Council Report 2020: paras 94–96). The effect is understandable, as the relationship of the people to their bundles is shaped by their belief that they possess spiritual potency and a life-force that is activated in ceremonies (Kreps 2003: 3; Simpson 1996: 135). The complex role of the material in ceremonial or spiritual contexts renders even a collective decision to trade the material a breach of protocol. Whereas the gods may repossess the gifts they have given, human beings cannot give them away but it is incumbent upon those who received these gifts to pass on the benefits of the powers that emanate from them (Godelier 1996: 122; Conaty 2015: 60).

Colonial expansion was expected to enhance the great economic power of European states, and colonial power was seen as a marker of 'success' in sociological terms. Imperialism facilitated informal profiteering from ill-gotten gains, but colonialism made formal claims to colonial territories to control people's wealth—to what they produced, how they produced it, and how it was distributed (wa Thiong'o 1986: 16). Imperial centres succeeded one another in an interminable effort to outdo and dominate (Koskenniemi 2017: 4). As competition intensified over the course of more than 600 years, the law became increasingly instrumentalised. To maintain dominance over their colonies, colonial powers capitalised on the propensity of law to 'totalise.' A great unevenness took hold in European–African relations. Equality and non-discrimination were shoved aside. One system of law gave way to another as western ideas and practices overtook those in the colonies.

To exploit its valuable resources, break open the potential for trade, and 'civilise' its people, European powers competed for title deeds to African territory. Semi-nomadic forms of land use were deemed inferior. In British Columbia they were criminalised (Bhandar 2018: 3). The late-20th century saw dramatic shifts in land rights, but the perpetuated dispossession of land remains a fact of life for many Indigenous communities in many parts of the world, including in Namibia (Koot and Hitchcock 2019: 55).

Restitution and repatriation claims are typically brought by nation states or emanate from communities and individuals whose rights over territory extends to cultural property and heritage produced in it, and the right to designate, classify and control its movement. Legal processes and concepts frequently ensure that voiceless Indigenous peoples become invisible and remain silent about the violence that enabled the formation of public and private collections from their cultural and spiritual resources purchased on the European art market. This poses a significant question for erstwhile colonisers and their museums. The importance of systematising knowledge in this field is underlined by a potential confluence between restitution, repatriation, and reparation claims;international restitution and repatriation claims in respect of sacred cultural material may overlap with claims for reparative justice.

Collection mania, economic exploitation, and social denial of the individual and collective worth of minoritarian communities have had an incalculable human cost. What was trafficked under colonialism included material categorised as sensitive and/or restricted. Restrictions on the viewing and interaction with sacred and secret objects, and confining knowledge of their power and meaning to initiates alone, have an important function in their communities of origin. Removal makes this knowledge less accessible. Since no respectful treatment is possible if unrestricted public access to museum collections continues, the restitution and return of these materials is the only sensible option.

Western museology and art history tend to relate the 'sacred' to objects that are religious in use or iconography. Religious historians frequently assume that 'sacred' places and artefacts are central to people's religion but unessential to their lives. Similar assumptions are evident in law and jurisprudence (e.g., Case of the Treasures of l'Ange Gardien, *Fabrique de la Paroisse de L'Ange-Gardien c. Procureur Général de la Province de Québec, Musées Nationaux du Canada et autres* (1980) CS 175; *Fabrique de la Paroisse de L' Ange-Gardien* [1987] 2 RCS IX). Domestic courts lack the mechanisms to consider how essential religious heritage or spiritual property and the knowledge systems associated with the material are to the survival or flourishing of disposed people. Conceptual fragmentation at the level of the material object affects the conceptualisation of ownership, belonging, and return of this type of cultural material. There is no multilateral treaty on the protection of sacred places or artefacts and the standards to apply. The issue remains obscure and as yet unsolved. To achieve a fuller understanding of the resonance between different cultural conceptions of the 'sacred' in the debate about ethics, a more systematic treatment that takes account of the central concern posed by ethics and the fragmentation that occurs at the level of ethics, is needed. It is important to know what return means for all the communities that cannot honour their cultural obligations to care for the dead and for sacred objects (Human Rights Council Report 2020: para 14).

Histories saturated with scientific racism and stained by violence and unfair trade harden and imprint on the colonised culture. As the political philosopher Franz Fanon put it, they become fixed in their colonial status by the cultural mummification of those 'caught in the yolk of oppression.' Individual thinking becomes mummified, not unlike a mummified object adopting the body structure and form of the corpse (Fanon 1964: 34). The exaggerated beliefs or distorted truths we hold about others carry over into arrested, fixated representations. The quest to 'understand' the sacred rituals of the colonised continues. However, race relations are tarnished by learning from unethically collected human remains and looted materials in European museum collections. Pursued under the guise of a great desire of colonial powers to 'learn from' the colonised 'Other,' learning is an imposition of power. Everyone is not educated equally. Moreover, legal and non-legal obstacles conspire to keep racial inequality hidden from view, while the quest for knowledge transforms people into things by depriving them 'of the spiritual nourishment that is the foundation of [their] humanity' (Sarr and Savoy Report 2018: 8). The quest for collecting and collecting practices have interfered with the thriving of societies. The hoarding and scattering of the bones and belongings of communities across jurisdictions and institutions for public enjoyment make provenance research arduous and expensive. The law has taken inordinately long to process the removal of cultural material during the colonial era.

Empires have always forced ever-larger diverse ethnic and cultural groups together within flexible borders under a unified 'political umbrella' (Harari 2011: 212). What was different in the colonial era, however, was the potential for scientific discoveries and the pressure exerted by a European vision of cultural worth imposed on the artefacts being traded transnationally. Disciplinary boundaries drawn in a European context promoted study of the natural world and human cultures by scientific method, which was considered both universally valid and neutral in its determination of what was 'real.' A view that denies that the spiritual is 'real' relieves cultural and educational institutions from any responsibility to acknowledge the spiritual dimension of culture, and from the responsibility to prioritise the societal bonds that sacred cultural property and heritage construct and sustain. The sacred meaning embodied in the objects may be discounted in decisions concerning access. The significance and purposes of 'potent' artefacts may remain unknown (Brown 2014: 3). The task of restoring the law for the restitution of sacred cultural property and heritage has scarcely begun.

1.2 Colonialism, competition, and force

Social envy manifested as the desire for art and antiquities for glamorous collections. The French plundered the libraries of the University of Louvain upon invading the Netherlands in 1794. Moving to Italy in 1796, their craving intensified to the point where Raphael's frescoes were removed from the Vatican's walls. The competition between France and Great Britain over access to the 'resources' of the great civilisations of antiquity precipitated the removal of the Parthenon Marbles. This long-standing dispute became the cause célèbre of the larger debates around cultural heritage and restitution now taking place (Herman 2023). The competition between Great Britain and colonial Germany culminated in a genocide. Rogue colonisers with ownership rights under predominant colonial law were free to neglect or destroy possessions (Eaton 2018: 32). Foreign rule has come to be seen as no better than enslavement and a breeding ground for force—which is how the Parthenon Sculptures and frieze fragments were detached from their architectural setting. Whatever the mores or mood of the time, official permission to vandalise the Parthenon is unthinkable.

1.2.1 Competition and mimesis: from glamorous antiquities to genocide

At the height of its power the Ottoman Empire controlled most of the Balkan region, and it occupied Athens from 1458. European archaeologists were captivated by the allure of archaeological sites in Egypt, the Aegean coast, and the Mediterranean region. Networks comprising officials, diplomats, and state entities plundered and transported archaeological materials. They would have made a clean sweep had the Ottomans not opened their own museums and put in place laws to restrict the export of antiquities (Greenhalgh 2019: 556–557).

The colonial mimetic competition between France and Great Britain is a strong point of orientation in the historical narrative of the Parthenon Sculptures. In 1784, the French ambassador to the Ottoman sultan assigned promising French artist Louis-François-Sébastian Fauvel to make drawings and casts of Greek antiquities. Four years in, the ambassador urged Fauvel to plunder all he could from the Acropolis. Fauvel's personal ambition to become an antiquarian in his own right blossomed when the ambassador fell out of favour with the sultan. His energetic looting was matched only by that of Scottish nobleman Thomas Bruce, the Earl of Elgin and Kincardine and British Ambassador to Constantinople (Istanbul today). Lord Elgin arrived in Constantinople in November 1799. Napoleon had already invaded Ottoman Egypt by this point, but victory was not yet ensured. Elgin assisted the united forces of Great Britain and the Ottoman Empire in Egypt to defeat France in 1801. The Ottoman Empire ruled Greece as a foreign power until

Greek revolutionaries instigated the War of Independence (1821–1830). Greece won its independence, but not without staggering losses and the Acropolis littered with bones. The London Protocol of February 1830 recognised Greece's status as an independent state. On 15 July 1840, the Ottoman Porte or central government of the Ottoman Empire in Istanbul finally acceded to a convention signed by Austria, Great Britain, Prussia, and Russia (Wheaton 1866: paras 69–70).

The early years of the 19th century saw Britain and the Ottoman Empire among the few places in Europe that remained free from Napoleon's control. The antagonism between the British and French Empires was palpable and spilt over into their propositioning of the Parthenon Sculptures. The Ottomans depended on Britain for military support in Egypt and were keen to demonstrate their gratitude to the British and Lord Elgin after success was achieved (*Report from the Select Committee of the House of Commons on the Earl of Elgin's Collection of Sculptured Marbles* (*HC Report*) 1816: 47–48). Whereas the Ottomans had long denied the French access to the Parthenon Sculptures, at a time when Elgin became the main ally of the Sultan in foiling the French advances in Ottoman Egypt, British officials could easily manipulate the Ottomans to deliver Greek heritage to them. Having achieved the status of the most influential foreign representative in Constantinople, Elgin expected public concessions to be made to him (*HC Report* 1816: 47–48).

Elgin's compatriots had mimetic desires which they only expressed privately. The shrewd clergyman Reverend Philip Hunt, Lord Elgin's chaplain and secretary between 1801 and 1802, confided in his father his deep desire to amass a 'splendid' and 'independent' fortune (Stockdale 2023: 32). Under instruction to reassure Ottoman officials of British support and stave off French collaboration, Hunt asked the governor of the city, the Voivode, for permission to remove one loose metope from the Parthenon. Hunt's wish was granted. The ease with which permission was secured induced Elgin to request permissions to remove sculptures from the Acropolis (*HC Report* 1816: 142). To date, the translation of a 'lower category' official letter that lacks legal standing because it does not bear the Sultan's seal, is the only one on record. The original is nowhere to be found.

Hunt later produced a note detailing Elgin's main objectives, namely the making of measurements, casts, and drawings, which, he suggested, he had drawn up when he advised Elgin to obtain another permit to excavate and '*take away any sculptures or inscriptions which do not interfere with the works or walls of the Citadel*' (as cited in Hunt's memorandum dated 1 July 1801; after Smith 1916: 190). Elgin's expectation was that no harm come to the Greek sculptures, but Hunt's keenness to dismantle the Parthenon Temple was shared by the Neapolitan painter Giovanni-Battista Lusieri, whom Elgin recruited and sent to Athens to act as his agent and to lead a team of artists to draw, document and mould antiquities. Lusieri and Hunt nurtured strong desires to outdo the French (De Lathuy 2018: 18). Since the Grand Vizier was in Egypt to re-establish Ottoman control over the territory and Egyptian victory was still uncertain, his Deputy issued an official letter about the work of Elgin's artisans in Athens in July 1801, addressed to the Chief Judge and the Governor of Athens (Titi 2023:

65). It refers only to entry, sketches, and picking up stones on the ground and making moulds for copies to be made. Lusieri asked Elgin to secure a firman from the Ottomans that would not make removal so difficult (Kakaounaki 2024). Hunt then set his sights on obtaining permission from the Sublime Porte to do more than the Deputy's letter authorised, specifically to permit Lusieri's team unrestricted access to the Acropolis to not only measure the ruins and excavate their foundations for inscriptions, but also take 'the particular objects I pointed out to him' (*HC Report* 1816: 140–141). Lusieri had access to the Acropolis for three years before his team was blocked from entering the site. Under his charge, Elgin's artists proceeded to haul down the first of the high-standing sculptures on the 31 July 1801. This inaugurated the stripping of the Parthenon. Elgin's men hacked off a 247-foot section of the north and south frieze panels and shipped them off. The Frieze is a 525-foot band of relief sculptured around the top of the building's interior colonnade high up on the exterior wall of the inner chamber. A total of 79 frieze panels out of 111 survive and are dispersed throughout Europe with the majority implaced in the British Museum (Hitchens 1997: 117–125, Appendix 1). The figures were carved directly into the building, produced under the building programme of the temples on the Acropolis which Perikles initiated and oversaw c 447–432 BC, and yet most are on display in the Duveen Gallery of the British Museum. Elgin's team also carried off 17 free-standing pedimental figures and 15 sculpted panels. The number equates to nearly half of the adornment of the Parthenon temple and its structure.

When Lord Elgin testified about the difficulty with obtaining permissions from the Ottomans to the Select Committee, he mentioned the historic efforts of the French government to obtain permission to remove the Sigean Marble from the Acropolis (*HC Report* 1816: 39). Hunt testified that he insisted on a literal translation of a permission that had already been given and that he had this permission in his possession, but also disclosed that he never saw a translation of this letter and could not produce it (*HC Report* 1816: 143). His excuse was that he had left it in Bedford but testified that the Porte had granted 'the most extensive permission to view, draw, and model the ancient temples of the idols and the sculptures upon them, and to make excavations, and to take away any stones that might appear interesting to them' (*HC Report* 1816: 141). Hunt subsequently provided an English translation for the Parliamentary Report, which reads: '*when they wish to take away some pieces of stone* (qualche pezzi di pietra') *with old inscriptions, or figures thereon, that no opposition be made thereto*.' Rigorous trawling of the Ottoman archives in recent years has not yielded the original Ottoman document (Titi 2023: 71). Neither Elgin's nor Hunt's testimony resolved the discrepancies and gaps in this narrative. The question has been framed in terms of 'whether it appears, on a balance of probabilities, that authorisation to remove the Marbles had indeed been given' (Herman 2023: 43, 51). Given the ambiguity of the meaning of the authorisation and the certainty of the personal plans and ambitions of Elgin and Hunt, the legality of the removal deserves to be questioned. Whether the proposed evidential standard is suitable to the circumstances of the case also deserves closer scrutiny.

The principle of state ownership, which has applied to antiquities in the region since 1453 (the year of the Fall of Constantinople) precluded the unauthorised removal of fragments from the temples on the Acropolis. Concern for their sacred heirlooms meant that the fledgling Greek state was anxious to deter the exportation of antiquities. By 1825 there was a decree regulating the collecting of antiquities. By 1827, a decree forbidding sale and transfer of antiquities outside Greece was in place, but two years later, when the National Assembly of Argos confirmed the export ban, it exempted 'antiquities contributing to the archaeological research of a scientific establishment of any Government' (Voudouri 2008: 125). In 1836 an independent Greece confirmed state ownership in a decree to the effect that all Hellenic antiquities existing in Greece are considered the property of the nation (Act on Scientific and Technological Collections, on the Discovery and Conservation of Antiquities and the Use Thereof of 16/28 June 1834 s 61). The provision was enacted in the same year that the Parthenon was inaugurated as an ancient monument as part of a plan to declare the entire Acropolis hill an archaeological zone. This would restore the area as the Sacred Rock that founded the political rebirth of Greece, where all the sculptures of Greece belonged.

The scramble for the glamour of prestigious objects spurred the Ottoman Empire to introduce regulations on a project-for-project basis, mirroring the tightening of the Greek legislative framework. When the Imperial Ottoman Museum was established in Constantinople in the late 1860s, exportation of excavated finds was no longer permitted. The Ottoman's change of tack exasperated the Europeans. Excavators who were unable to obtain renewals of firman made elaborate plans to circumvent the new regulations.

The Ottoman Empire lasted close to 600 years. The treaties that were signed as part of the Versailles Peace Settlement in 1920 and 1923 solidified the western sentiment that collections need to be kept together in universal museums and that any attempt to break them 'would be a great loss to the world's cultural heritage.' Post-conflict reparations between states were excated by other peace treaties that redrew territorial boundaries, relocated populations, and reallocated cultural objects. The provisions on specific items of cultural heritage evolved into more general provisions, but the European powers never applied them when the colonial era formally ended (Byrne 2015: 10). The ideological and political dimensions of exportation have continued to gather global interest (Voudouri 2008: 125). The victors of the First World War reinstated partage for their own benefit (Greenhalgh 2019: 548–551). A lot of plunder continues in the face of export regulations.

The colonial mimetic competition between Germany and Great Britain undermines the view that German colonial rule was an insignificant episode of colonial history; this view has become thoroughly discredited (Biskup and Kohlrausch 2016: 1, 12). Up until 1871, Germany was reluctant to risk conflict with established colonial powers because it lacked a colonial tradition that could compare to the overseas expansions of Britain, France, the Netherlands, and Spain. However, with the formation of the German Empire in 1871, the foundation of the framework for its colonial aspirations were fundamentally changed. By the time the

Berlin Congress took place in 1884–1885, Germany had come to possess the fourth largest colonial empire.

German SWA and the Cape Colony had been uneasy neighbours since 1884. The rivalry between them played out in the border region between the Cape Colony and SWA (Dedering 2000: 43). Thousands of African contract workers were drafted in the Cape to work for the German authorities in SWA under harsh and exploitative conditions. Movement of African resistance fighters across the colonial borders proved a constant source of concern for the German military command, who suspected they were smuggling arms and ammunition. Border skirmishes engendered strife. German war efforts relied on the collaboration of the Cape authorities, but British control of the Walvis Bay harbour in SWA made it difficult to bring goods purchased abroad into SWA. The economic colonial ties that bound Germany and Britain were knitted together more closely by the SWA Company 'SWAC.' The company had German stockholders but was founded by Cecil John Rhodes. British directors were in charge (Lyon 2015: 68–70). Rhodes became Prime Minister of the Cape Colony in 1890, during the Second British Empire (1775–1945). Rhodes secretly intended to use the SWAC to take over the colony, co-opting a state institution for private enrichment. The worst evils of British colonialism were palpable in his 'Confession of Faith' (1877):

> Africa is still lying ready for us it is our duty to take it. It is our duty to seize every opportunity of acquiring more territory … [for] the Anglo-Saxon race [*sic*] … the best the most human, most honourable race the world possesses
> (Flint 1974: 248–252)

The Germans were utilising British financing in SWA but this model did not deliver financing to the German colonial administration. German national involvement in the SWAC reached its zenith in the lead up to the First World War. The Germans blamed British foreign influence when things did not go to plan (Lyon 2015: 2, 6).

Both sides treated the Nama and Herero people as property. Cape workers received poor treatment in SWA while Nama refugees were mistreated in the Cape Colony (Dedering 1999: 4). Hendrik Witbooi (c.1834–1905), chief of the Nama, had trekked with his people from the Northern Cape Province of South Africa further northward. In the mid-1880s they encountered the Herero. Armed clashes ensued. Both groups were seeking to set out the normative premises of their relationships with other groups including the increasing numbers of Europeans (Goldmann 2024: 588, 593). Witbooi wrote to the Paramount Chief of the Hereros, Captain Maharero Tjamuaha (1820–1890), in his capacity as a military auxiliary of German rule, beseeching Maharero to grant the Namas free passage through Herero land in search of a new dwelling place where they could settle in peace (letter dated 27 June 1884; Bosman 2011: 337). Aware of the threat that German colonial rule posed to the traditional lifestyle, autonomy, and resources of African communities, Witbooi rejected the offer of the German authorities to conclude a protection treaty in 1892. Aspiring to end white supremacy, he entered into a peace agreement with the Hereros. The spiritual relationship between these communities and their ancestral lands bred resistance against the commodification of the land (Goldmann 2024: 597). The Hornkranz Massacre of 12 April 1893 subdued Witbooi into signing the protection treaty with the Germans, but it revived and intensified the rivalry with the Herero.

Anglo-German tensions were at a high point when the Second Boer War (the 'South African War') ended in 1902 (Bachmann 2018: 30, 35). The Germans perpetually compared themselves to the British and their struggle to exercise effective control over the territory of SWA did not allay their insecurities. What had started as economic emulation deteriorated into a rivalry. German troops located Herero settlements at night, drove them out by day, and confiscated their property. Women and children were targeted for extermination. In January 1904 the Germans faced a drawn-out Herero uprising. Twenty thousand Namas in the south of the colony severed their alliance with the Germans and staged a revolt in October that year (Dedering 1999: 4). The German military commander, General von Trotha, ordered German colonial troops (the *Schutztruppe*) to encircle and shoot on sight all Herero within the German borders whether armed or unarmed (letter to the Ovaherero dated 2 October 1904, German Federal Archives, Berlin). Survivors were driven into the Omaheke desert, where springs were poisoned. To contain revolts from survivors, concentration camps were set up in the same way the British did in South Africa. Men, women, and children were subjected to forced labour on meagre rations and women had to scrape clean the skulls of their family members for race science research in Germany (Theurer 2023: 1148).

It is uncertain that the October 1904 extermination order issued by von Trotha against the Herero had been authorised. It contradicts the protection treaty concluded between the Reich and the Maharero in 1885. Consequently, its validity under German law is in dispute (Goldmann 2024: 600). General von Trotha's superior, Graf von Schlieffen, wrote to German Imperial Chancellor Count von Bülow on 23 November 1904 pledging support for von Trotha's assessment that the Herero had to be annihilated but von Bülow expressed his concern to the Emperor, as he deemed the extermination order contrary to Christian precepts and a crime against humanity (letter dated 24 November 1904, German Federal Archives, Berlin). By the time the order was lifted, on 9 December 1904, tens of thousands of Herero had already died. The genocide of 1904–1907 claimed the lives of an estimated 65,000 Herero and 10,000 Nama. White settlers, the colonial administration, the *Schutztruppe*, and commercial enterprises benefited financially and in terms of the percentage of land owned. After the Herero defeat, the settler community called for retributions against the African population and for stricter colonial policies. Tellingly, however, Germany was forced out of SWA in under 30 years. The brutality which German colonial authorities used against the Herero and Nama violated the 1864 Red Cross Convention and amounted to war crimes under the 1899 Hague Convention (II). Imperial Germany acted in violation of its duties under international law which, in 1904, formed part of its domestic law. Germany's occupation of SWA was illegal and the genocide violates rules of international law but contemporary German international legal scholarsinsisted that the genocide did not constitute a violation of international law at the time and advanced numerous arguments to support this interpretation. One of the arguments was that the Herero and Nama communities lacked legal subjectivity and the capacity to raise a claim against Germany based on the Hague Convention. Another was that only German domestic law applied and at the time it did not provide a basis for reparation claims. The German Civil Code (Section 839) was considered inapplicable because civil servants were under no official duty to protect the inhabitants of the colonies against inhumane treatment. Any protections owed to the Indigenous populations in the colonies under Article 6 of the Final Act of the Berlin Congress were deemed to apply exclusively between the signatory states and would not give rise to rights and obligations on the part of third parties. They also maintained that the 1864 Red Cross Convention did not find application to colonial wars (Goldmann 2024: 597–598).

German military doctors dissected the bodies of deceased African prisoners of war and shipped them to the Berlin Anatomical Institute for 'racial anthropological research' (Förster 2020: 103). Berlin was the centre of academic humanism in the first imperialist period, during the colonialist expansion of Imperial Germany (1870s to the early 1900s). The intensified anthropological support for colonialism shown since the 1890s co-incided with a rising interest in the science behind evolution and human origin. A host of pseudo-academic fields sprang up to prove the superiority of some people over others based on their physical characteristics. Researchers were empowered to pursue eugenics. Human and biological sciences became more extreme in Germany after 1900. Biological-racist arguments cultivated a sense of superiority that increased intolerance and promoted exploitation (Zimmerer 2021: 95, 99). By the end of the 19th century anthropological studies were closely aligned with natural sciences, but theoretical humanism was not a subject for study. During the imperialist period, anthropology joined hands with ethnography to determine the value of races, and anthropology and ethnology shared the same interest in racial anthropometrics. As a 'method' used to find evidence of supremacy, the measuring of human heads required numerous samples from a wide range of individuals. Human remains were sought after. The heads of several prisoners who did not survive the Nama concentration camp on the uninhabitable Shark Island were sent to the Berlin Anatomical Institute; anthropologists vied to recover evidence of culture-specific characteristics of a 'disappearing' race. Human remains collections in museums expanded rapidly to support the racial research that continued until after the First World War (Stoecker and Winkelman 2018: 19). Berlin remained at the centre of academic humanism during the 'second imperialist period' from roughly the 1920s to 1945, when 'Nazi expansionism' was at its height. Seventy-five years later the Namas and Hereros were specifically excluded and sidelined during the early days of Namibia's struggle for independence (Förster 2020: 116). They were also prevented from participating in the organisation of repatriation events in 2014.

The experimentation on Herero and Nama captives and the extermination between 1904 and 1907 were the products of a state machinery that converted racism into genocidal impulses. Mimetic collection practices bolstered white European supremacy. European society's indulgent comparisons of cultural traits found expression in hopes to improve humankind through selective breeding for racial purity; neither the doctors in the colony nor the researchers in the metropole deemed individual data important for racial science research purposes. Ethnic identity was the chief identifier for scientists who exploited violent colonial circumstances to create anthropological collections in Europe. Most of the human remains that can be dated to 1904–1908 remain unidentifiable, but commendations were bestowed on military leaders who were able to supply precise dates of seizure and violent details of removal Herero objects—not to highlight the physical trauma suffered by the Herero, but to emphasise the value of what was described as 'collected,' 'found,' 'war loot,' and 'what we plundered' (Grimme 2020: 55, 58–60).

Colonialism in SWA formally ended in 1919, but the after-effects continue to linger (Steinmetz and Hell 2006: 148, 150, 153). The Ambassadors of European states congregated in late September 1814 at the Congress of Vienna to reorganise European borders and agree a long-term plan to create the foundations for a lasting peace and the reconstruction of Europe in the Treaty of Paris. The 1815 Congress of Vienna secured a peace that lasted for almost a hundred years, but the 1919 Versailles Treaty set in motion Germany's financial and economic crisis (Williams 2014: 96). The Versailles Treaty unleashed a mimetic dynamic that culminated in the Second World War. The Treaty included the covenant to form the League of Nations, which was established in 1920, but the members did not have equal rights. Cultural protection was embedded in colonial discourses of civilisation or guardianship (Stahn 2023: 349–350). Keen to secure control over SWA at the end of the First World War, the South African government presented Germany as unfit to exercise control over colonies. Article 22 of the Covenant of the League of Nations placed communities formerly under German colonial rule under mandate administration as 'peoples not yet able to stand by themselves under the strenuous conditions of the modern world.'

The term 'colony' might refer to the relationship between former metropoles and colonies subject to the territorial sovereignty of the colonising State in a narrow sense of the term (Lubina 2009: 138). The term also encompasses different types of dependent territories such as overseas territories, protectorates, mandate, and trust territories. The classic law of nations regarded such territories as subjects under international law governed by the principle of the 'sacred trust of civilisation.' The European transferee held certain acquired rights as trustee for the community, and the community retained beneficial interest and the capacity of reversion to the enjoyment of these rights when European rule ended (Alexandrowicz 1973: 126). Understandably, Protectorate States and mandated territories raised special challenges for the conflict of laws system. Different jurisdictions and a plurality of laws call for a conflict of laws system with legal doctrines and methods intended to find a way through the jungle of normative pluralism. Mandatory Powers were supposed to administer colonial territory in trust for the peoples under their control until they returned to the universal Family of Nations where the rule of law prevailed between nations (Institute of International Law meeting Cambridge 1931; Alexandrowicz 1973: 112–113). These traditional legal notions of statehood faded away during the colonial era. A certain 'provisional racism' applied in mandated territories, akin to the notion that individuals in colonised territories could achieve 'civilisation.' Novel ways were sought to solve conflicts arising between incompatible territorial claims and principles in former German and Ottoman colonial territories distributed under the mandate system of the League of Nations after the First World War (Steinmetz and Hell 2006: 148). One such mandate for trusteeship was the territory of SWA. The League of Nations transferred control of the territory of SWA to Great Britain in 1920, and Britain conferred its responsibility on its South African colony (Steinmetz and Hell 2006: 165). The territory of SWA was a Class C Mandate territory, retaining the status of a League of Nations Mandate until the League's collapse in the Second World War. In its capacity of functionary of the international community charged to administer the territory, British-ruled Union of South Africa exercised mandatory power over SWA. At the same time, SWA existed as a 'buffer state' between independent Africa and Apartheid South Africa. It was located somewhere 'betwixt colony and nation-state' in terms of its status (Berman 2019: 31, 48). German SWA eventually gained independence in 1990, through terms established by the ICJ in the Hague, which is the primary judicial organ of the UN.

Mimetic theory offers a handy aid in describing the competitive behaviours that shaped museum collections in Europe. For instance, the German Empire wanted to surpass other colonial powers. Coveting the role of a world power, it turned the violent dehumanisation in its colonies onto the European continent. It deprived people of their freedom of choice, turned people into things, and established an illegitimate 'ownerhip of human flesh' (Little ed. tr. 2003: 14, 27–28). The Nama and Herero are expected to make peace with the dehumanisation of their ancestors whose body parts and skulls remain in western cultural institutions.

1.2.2 The proliferation of fragmentation

The ideology of National Socialism, which derived from a combination of Darwinism and völkisch traditional religious themes, provided Western European countries with the methods of conquest and domination that deprived colonised people of their past (Little ed. tr. 2003: 110). Shocking regulations aimed not only to dehumanise and eradicate the Jewish populations, but also profit from their oppression. Nazism also elevated genocide and euthanasia to normative aspects of state policy (Hartman 1997: 126). A striking facet of the genocide was the 'normalising' bureaucracy within which it was enshrined. Bureaucratic form is refined, expanded, and rationalised over time. Knowledge becomes more insular as specialisations increase. Legal theorist and philosopher Pierre Schlag (1988: 961) cautions that the heightened instrumentalisation which cultural symbols and values undergo provokes proliferation of complexity and fragmentation:

> In this sort of world … substance offers little (if any) resistance to form … [a]nd … form becomes cannibalistic.

The power dynamics of trade during the colonial era are preserved by bureaucratic form and the premium which the modern world places on on the rationalisations of capitalism which bureaucracy sustains. The inescapable trappings of financialisation and economic capitalisation of stolen culture keep the collections of public museums and private collectors going. The inherent political and economic value of the Parthenon Sculptures makes the restrictive control exerted under an outdated legal framework a highly convenient narrative. The 'salvage mentality' and 'rescue' narratives recounted as justification of the removal of cultural objects during the colonial era provide the oil for the machine that drives complexity and fragmentation. The ideology of the 'Enlightenment' and the culture of collecting in the 19th century promoted saving and preserving material artefacts in Europe. The 'salvage mentality' in the preservation of cultural material is the product of the conviction that those who do not preserve the culture they produce should not be permitted to possess it. However, swamped with cultural artefacts, museums could not properly catalogue and inventory them. Objects remained 'illegible,' 'ad hoc' and semi-discarded (Dudley 2018: 39, 44, 47; Eaton 2018: 37). Neither did the natural life cycles of cultural material fit with museological routines that put physical preservation first. Spurious classifications of collections as 'material culture' or 'artefact' effectively stripped the material of their ability to challenge ways of thinking. These museological and collecting practices were oblivious or indifferent to what others considered 'sacred' (Vrdoljak 2008: 119).

The salvage mentality fosters excuses for retention, e.g., that pieces are fragile and will be damaged if returned. The rescue ideology also brings on 'contradictory protectionist practices' in museums that harbour the stereotype of the saviour. A self-congratulatory narrative of having 'rescued' the Parthenon Marbles shaped their collecting history but was somewhat dented when the patina of the west frieze, exposed in Athens, turned out to be better preserved than the patina on the frieze fragments that had been subjected to a 'cleaning' stint in London in 1937–1938.

No legal obligation to return objects taken from former colonies arose as they did for returns to European states. In fact, the diplomatic meetings of the Congress of Vienna set up different categories of states in 1814—the winners, the defeated, and the excluded (the Ottoman Empire). Crude, unethical, and incomplete legal frameworks were constructed around correlative constellations of rights and duties.

The documents of the 30 May 1814 First Peace of Paris were silent on the question of art restitution. There was scope for an interpretation of 'to the victor goes the spoils,' with a legal position resembling the 'Roman right of conquest' (Sandholtz 2008: 113). War booty that had not been allocated to the social elites was made available for purchase ever since the 2nd century BC. Title was divested from the original owner with immediate effect and transferred to the captor (Miles 2002: 30). In the 17th century, whether a conqueror was obligated to return wartime booty after the war was determined by the distinction between 'just' and 'unjust war.' A 'just war' was fought by a party who had suffered a serious grievance which the other side refused to redress. Lacking a justification to wage war or misconduct during the war rendered the war unjust. However, a policy of pillage was set up in France in 1794 by the Convention Nationale as a means of paying off war debts. Given the issues caused by the French Revolutionary Wars and the fate of Napoleon's loot, questions concerning the recovery of looted cultural objects arose. During the Ministerial Conference in Paris (12 July–21 September 1815), France was agitating for a clause that would permit the retention of looted European property on the basis that the law had permitted a 'right of conquest' for 'all nations in all times.' The Duke of Wellington, whose army defeated Napoleon and prevailed in all the Peninsular campaigns, maintained that the Allies had a duty to facilitate the return of the art treasures to the places they were torn from, and to return spoils of war. His view was that, even in a 'just' war, confiscation and coercion during European campaigns were not a valid means of property acquisition (open letter to Viscount Castlereagh, Paris, 23 September 1815, reprinted in Gould 1965: 131ff). Decisions taken in the duke's capacity as head of the army of occupation had the force of law despite his lack of formal legal training (Miles 2011: 38, 40). The French protested that the First Paris Treaty of 1814 set a precedent for a provision in the Convention that would permit retention of looted art as war booty but Allied representatives refused to permit Napoleon's attempts to legalise the transfer of cultural objects in peace treaties to stand. It was resolved that stolen art could be repossessed without diplomatic negotiations and that the looted artworks were to be returned to the states from which the French had taken them. A precedent was thus set for art and cultural property returns. Objects held in public collections other than the Louvre were retained, as well as objects held in public collections which, after the rearrangement of the map of Europe, no longer fell on French territory but international law scholars refused to recognise the requisitioning and spoliations under the cover of treaties. They insisted that France return to moral, peaceful conduct. Wheaton wrote, for instance, that Napoleon's ornamental spoils could no longer be regulated in accordance with an ancient mode of property transfer that had enjoyed legitimacy for centuries. The 'only guide[s] to justice' were the principles of property regulated by the claims of the territories from whence the art had been taken (Wheaton 1866: paras 354, 359, 398). Many French citizens desirous of maintaining a competitive edge destroyed items they considered rightfully theirs to avoid restitution.

Double standards continue to persist regarding the protection of cultural property, where universalist arguments are upheld only in relation to the so-called civilised nations (Stahn 2023: 29). The steps taken by several Western European states and their museum sectors to establish dispute resolution fora for Nazi spoliated art claims have not been replicated for restitution of the spoils from beyond Europe. Former colonising states have routinely denied the accusation that the African material in Europe's museums had been stolen or that the taking inflicted an injury for which compensation was due (Prott ed. 2009: xxi–xxii). Historians and politicians focused on the legacy of Nazism. Germany's colonial past was ignored for decades. Nazi spoliation, requisitioning, and destruction concerns artworks and cultural objects taken from Europeans by Europeans. According to the Best Practices for the Washington Conference Principles on Nazi-Confiscated Art of 2024, the principles relate to what was:

> looted, confiscated, sequestered, and spoliated by the Nazis, the Fascists and their collaborators through various means, including but not limited to theft, coercion, and confiscation, and on the grounds of relinquishment, as well as forced sales and sales under duress, during the Holocaust era between 1933–45. (Sub 'B')

Colonialism drew more attention in the post-war period, but the failure to identify the golden thread that connects the racism of Germany's colonial empire, its Nazi ideology, the politics of annihilation in Africa, and the violence that beset Europe during the Second World War creates risks (Biskup and Kohlrausch 2016: 13). Ascribing normative effect to mimesis counts among the most significant risks. If normativity is ascribed to arbitrary force international law is fragmented by the inequality among nations. In addition, there are states that do not reliably provide law and order in the post-colonial era, leaving a vacuum in which there is scope for wealthy private actors to perpetuate injustices in many industries and commodities markets.

1.3 Private enterprise in colonialism

Colonialism was not just a state enterprise. Private individuals and business corporations laid firm foundations for colonial rule and actively sustained it. Their involvement tainted both the public and the private spheres (Spitra 2021: 142).

Missionary colonialism is the first type that springs to mind. Missionaries and priests were the 'rogue colonisers' of the colonial era who, along with tradesmen, diplomats, and military officers, were encouraged, under Article 6 of the Congo Act of 1885, to bring 'the blessings of civilisation' to the 'natives' in occupied territories. Many missionaries believed that proselytising imbued the imperial project with moral authority. Christian missions and churches were often closely identified with the workings of the state and its imperial aspirations (Oh 2018: 422–423). The expansion of Empire was facilitated by special protections granted to religious, scientific, or charitable institutions and undertakings, and missionaries, scientists, explorers, and their 'followers, property and collections' acted on them. Missionary colonialism legitimised the rhetoric of 'converting' the local peoples from idol-worship and enabled the extraction of material proof of idols from temples and shrines (Cummings 2017: 198–199). Countless objects were burned during the first missionary campaigns in the early modern period in Africa, whereas exportations to which local people never agreed or consented accompanied scientific missions (Effiboley 2020: 74).

The desire of the colonial masters to 'describe' went hand in hand with the civilising efforts undertaken by western governments and missionaries. Large concentrations of African heritage languish in storerooms overseas. For instance, the historical collections of cultural artefacts from Namibia are being kept in Germany and Finland (Silvester and Shiweda 2020: 32). Finnish missionaries in German SWA categorised the material culture of the Aawambo (plural for Owambo) as 'heathenism.' The Aawambo considered sharing religious customs with outsiders a taboo, but conversion obligated them to relinquish the relics of 'heathenism' (Harju 2019: 79). In object lessons taught by Christian missionaries, 'wrong' artefacts caused idolatry and 'right' artefacts provided the solution. The spaces that used to be filled by the 'heathen' idols were to be filled with the latter. The control exerted by the missions rendered a multitude of 'sacred' objects obsolete. 'Idolatrous objects' were frequently destroyed to achieve missionary aims. Missionary zeal indicated devotion. The rhetoric of idolatry was deeply self-contradicting, espousing pastoral care while despotically policing people (Eaton 2018: 33–35). The 'civilised' version of expansionism indoctrinated more than helped local populations, but still there were nomadic groups that chose to settle with missionaries for reasons of ease of access to provisions.

A broad typological shorthand of colonisation highlights trade colonialism, settlement colonies, military enclaves, and exploitation colonies, in addition to missionary colonialism (DMB *Care of Collections* 2021: 96–98). Trade colonialism is identifiable by the *gratis* or cheap labour provided by local ethnic groups and farmers, drifters and imported slaves which made a colony's economy sustainable. Many colonial territories and overseas dependencies were 'producing parts of a wider economy' (Greaves 1954: 1). The production surpluses they created in capitalist markets benefited the coloniser's market (Bachmann 2018: 34). The Netherlands conquered expansive stretches of territory in the 17th century in the Dutch East and West Indies, for instance. Dutch trade colonialism in the Dutch East Indies (now Indonesia) and British trade colonialism in India saw commodities of all kinds produced for what was never intended to be 'free trade' exchange in a context of political integration. To ensure that the metropole accumulated capital for colonisers' benefit, it was vital to obtain cheap raw materials and gain access to new markets for European products. Smuggling at the hands of European merchants was not policed effectively (Fanon 1986: 108). For instance, the British East India Company benefited from a profitable trade in opium with Chinese suppliers. When the Qing government banned opium imports from British India for public health reasons, British merchants resorted to smuggling to get the drug into the country. A series of wars were fought to protect British interests in the opium trade and sustain the forcible illegal smuggling and exportation of opium from the Indian subcontinent to China. In parallel with the trafficking of goods extracted in the colonies, resources were exploited for tax revenue and tariffs.

Settler-colonialism was based on 'implanting' European settlers who had emigrated *en masse* and needed land to sustain a living. Compared to native populations, settlers were frequently part of the dominant culture of government, media, and academic institutions that benefited from considerable public investment, technological innovation, and infrastructure. The migration and settlement of Euro-Americans frequently imposed colonial borders that either clustered Indigenous communities together in alien and hostile newly created states or tore them apart. Displaced Indigenous populations were dispelled from their land and pushed into conflict with other communities (Zimmerer 2021: 97). Their existing socio-political and legal structures came under considerable pressure (DMB *Care of Collections* 2021: 23–24). The imperialist territories that were undergoing economic and industrial progress looked down on other less progressive territories. The dominant culture also facilitated the collection of human remains, whether from war, genocidal annihilation, or stolen from their place of origin and repurposed as artefacts. Ancient human remains and objects made of body parts have been traded and commodified since European travellers reached the furthest shore. There was a prevalent and unregulated culture of collecting artefacts in the Edwardian and Victorian periods. New museums were established across Europe to cater to Western societies' fixation with 'exotic' tastes and foreign cultures (Coody Cooper 2008: 61). In Germany, most of the human remains and sacred cultural material in the restitution debate are in the possession of publicly owned museums and collections but legal claims and complaints are also bringing to light the hidden transactions sustaining private collections.

The exploitation of labour and land for commercial gain left imprints on infrastructural development as well as on collections of ethnographical specimens and sacred cultural material. Settler colonialism perpetuated systems that undermined the protection of Indigenous lives, cultural knowledge, histories, and values through the suppression of their spirituality and ritual practices. It gave rise to the proliferation of disease, starvation, and loss of land. In Germany's colonial empire, its only settler colony SWA became a German Protectorate on 24 April 1884. Less than 15,000 people settled there before the First World War. The settlers received logistical, financial, and military support from the German state in exchange for maintaining German territorial control of SWA, but a customs border remained in place between Germany and its colonies and customs tariffs continued to be paid until 1914. Despite having a colonial masterplan to increase trade and improve infrastructure, the settlers never benefited from industrialism in Germany. The tensions between German leaders and the ethnic groupings in SWA prevented the integration of the local people into a larger German market. A larger intra-German market was never achieved (Bachmann 2018: 30, 35). The normative hegemony which capitalism demands creates tension with capitalist pressure. This dynamic continues to be overlooked today (Ruiz Abou-Nigm 2019: 384).

Exercising informal power to increase their profit margins in global market exchange, private actors and business corporations interact with the public ordering effected by lawmakers and judiciaries. When multinational corporations are held to a lower standard of care and responsible for a lower damage quantum in the law of the place in which they operate compared to the law of the place of incorporation, lower standards are applied even when they committed atrocious violations against civilian populations and depleted the natural resources of developing countries (Banu 2013: 302; 2022: 386). When multinational corporations focus solely on increasing their profit margin through exchange in global markets, pressure points arise in adjudicating claims for compensation in transnational contexts—access to justice, social responsibility, and compliance with moral standards. Private international law (PrIL, or the 'conflict of laws' as this branch of law is commonly called outside of the United States) is making little headway in relation to corporate complicity in child slavery, for instance. Driven to obtain the cheapest cacao possible in the chocolate industry, farmers use children as slaves, but they retain their position in the global production and supply chains of powerful multinational corporations (*Doe v Nestle USA Inc* 766 F. 3d 1013 (9th Cir. 2014); *Doe II III IV VI v Nestle USA* Docket No: 17-55435 USCA (9th Cir 2018); *Nestle USA, Inc. v Doe et al.* Certiorari to the United States Court of Appeals for the Ninth Circuit No. 19—416, 17 June 2021). These private actors protect and maintain their financial dominance in the food market when exercising power beyond state lines.

A similar trend has long been afoot with collectors of ethnographic material (e.g., African and Oceanic) who exercise power beyond the confines of the state, with telling examples in market states on the demand-end of the trade in ethnographic material (*Attorney-General of New Zealand v Ortiz* [1982] 3 All ER 432 (QBD and CA)). The scope for laundering title to cultural objects through various jurisdictions is an undeniable result of the fragmentation imposed by rules of PrIL on the validity and lawfulness of transfers of property, which incentivises the illicit trade in cultural objects (*Republic of Iran v The Barakat Galleries Ltd* [2009] 1 QB 22 (CA); Campfens 2024: 153). These cases highlight adjudicators' approaches to normative clashes and overlaps between different legal systems—and therefore also different legal cultures—when disputes contain foreign elements. The litigation fora of both cases are in market states on the demand-end of the trade in ethnographic material. If the law of the court is expected to govern questions about the validity of colonial era takings, the political and social justice questions presented by studies in imperialism and colonialism may go unchallenged. PrIL adjudication makes it necessary for states to adopt a policy in relation to the outside world, whether implicit or explicit. PrIL adjudication might reveal the propensity of a court to default to its own law, justify cultural imperialism, or halt the smuggling and title laundering of certain cultural material and secure their return to source. In the case against Barakat Galleries Ltd, for instance, Iran pursued the recovery of 4th millennium BCE carved chlorite bowls, jars, and cups allegedly excavated and unlawfully exported from cemeteries in the Jiroft region in 2001. Iran claimed conversion and asserted title in accordance with the requirements of PrIL (para 154). Barakat Galleries disputed the origin of the objects. The parties agreed that the law of the place where the antiquities had been found and where they were when title was created, had to apply. It was held at first instance that the 1979 Legal Bill regarding Prevention of Unauthorised Excavations and Diggings constituted a foreign penal law that was unenforceable in England (*Government of the Islamic Republic of Iran v The Barakat Galleries Ltd.* [2007] EWHC 705 para 81). This ruling was overturned on appeal with the Court of Appeal considering the proprietary provisions in the 1979 Legal Bill as the basis of Iran's claim. The claim in conversion was held to be tenable. Iran was owner, not an accidental finder, and had extensive personal rights to the antiquities (Roodt 2018: 209). The CA declared in an aside that it would be contrary to public policy to shut out a claim to recover national heritage (*Republic of Iran v The Barakat Galleries Ltd.* [2009] 1 QB 22 (CA) paras [151]–[154]). It was acknowledged that the 1995 UNIDROIT Convention on Stolen or Illegally Exported Cultural Objects and other provisions, while not directly affecting the outcome of the appeal, confirmed the international acceptance of the desirability of protection of the national heritage (para [163]). The CA marked the conclusion reached by the court at first instance 'regrettable' because it overlooked the UK's ratification of the 1970 UNESCO Convention on the Means of Prohibiting and Preventing the Illicit Import, Export and Transfer of Ownership of Cultural Property in 2002. PrIL's connectivity enabled the ethical standards set in conventions and the legal standards set in a foreign public law to be upheld in this case. Its governance strategies are more than positive law and systematic legal doctrine, for they draw on bundles of rules, roles and relationships that define the social practices of state and non-state actors interacting on issues (Kennedy 1997: 594 n4). PrIL's political character is tied to its co-ordination function and capacity. PrIL sees subject-matter, processes and methods interact with public values (Lixinski 2018: 22). Moreover, PrIL is also concerned with ethics, for if law regulates the behaviours of role occupants, and the law is a servant of society, then how courts treat foreign law is in many ways asking how it treats people (Michaels 2019: 15). Will the discipline sidestep the great questions of our time in international civil litigation, or will it integrate those public values in complex colonial contexts, and in contexts of extreme unethical human behaviour?

As an instrument of governance the nature and function of PrIL has been shaped by dominant modes of legal thought (Neidhardt 2018: 35). The scope it is given may differ depending on location. In some countries its subject-matter is confined to identifying the applicable law alone, but many others include international civil procedure, which covers all questions of jurisdiction of the national courts and the procedure of recognition of foreign judgments and other instruments made by foreign officials. In some jurisdictions its scope encompasses the treatment of citizens of the realm and of foreigners, and of foreign bodies corporate (Struycken 2009: 189–190). These national differences notwithstanding, PrIL's range and diversity of responses to international problems gives it capacity to promote peaceful co-existence. The educational remit of the *Hague Academy of International Law* was set up to promote peace through law (Michaels 2019: 13). The *Hague Academy* is a centre for high-level education in both public international law and PrIL.

PrIL retains its relevance when special legislative frameworks have been devised or restitution mechanisms put in place (Labadie 2021: para 16). Adjudicators may deploy PrIL's secondary legal norms to co-ordinate and determine the scope and application of primary rules in cross-border disputes about ownership and restitution. Secondary legal norms are concerned with the introduction, extinction, and modification of primary material legal norms or rules. The extent to which they may extend recognition to rights that existed in erstwhile colonies while reining in unqualified forum dominance in the name of distributive justice considerations deserves further investigation (see 1.6.2 below).

Secondary norms and the obligations they engender in restitution claims highlight PrIL's space time dimensions. The results of their application may be fragmented because events are spread out over years and span multiple jurisdictions with legal frameworks containing diverse provisions on the validity of the transfer of stolen goods in the hands of new possessors (Campfens 2024: 148; Roodt 2024: 561ff). Pertinent international treaties clearly set the norm that looted cultural objects should be returned, but losses that predate their adoption are outwith their purview and much depends on the quality of implementation on the national level to ensure that effect is given to the principle (e.g., Article 15 of the 1970 UNESCO Convention; the 1995 UNIDROIT Convention's restitution provisions are applicable only to objects stolen from the territory of a Contracting State after its entry into force for that State (Article 10) although past illegal transactions are not legitimised nor are states precluded from seeking remedies outside the conventional framework). Cultural property and heritage conventions do not offer clear international standards for cross-border disputes concerning the removal of cultural material during the colonial era. Uniform law is uniform only in content. The scope, or the delimination of the scope of uniform law may differ depending on the law of the signatory state. To confer 'legal protection status,' they may use a variety of mechanisms or special regimes in domestic administrative, constitutional, private, intellectual property, and criminal law. So-called 'sacred' material that is culturally sensitive is 'lumped in' with pre-determined categories of material that forms part of the cultural heritage of each state (e.g., 'objects of ethnological interest' in Article 1(f) of the 1970 UNESCO Convention, or 'cultural property acquired by archaeological, ethnological or natural science missions, with the consent of the competent authorities of the country of origin of such property,' which is recognised as forming part of the cultural heritage of each State in Article 4(c)). 'Sacred' material is not specified in Article 2 of the 1995 UNIDROIT Convention, which permits Contracting Parties to define cultural objects in their domestic law but provides that 'cultural objects are those which, on religious or secular grounds, are of importance for archaeology, prehistory, history, literature, art or science.' This provision refers Contracting Parties to the 'categories listed in the Annex,' which reflects the same categories as in Article 1 of the the 1970 UNESCO Convention. Article 3(8) is the only provision that refers to 'a claim for restitution of a sacred or communally important cultural object belonging to and used by a tribal or indigenous community in a Contracting State as part of that community's traditional or ritual use.' However, this provision regulates time limitations (Jagielska-Burduk and Fincham 2024: 555). The formulation 'traditional or ritual' is not helpful. Courts in signatory states of the 1995 UNIDROIT Convention are expected to issue an order for return when illegal exportation of an object impairs its ritual use by a tribal or Indigenous community (Article 5(3)(d)) or when an Indigenous community has made an object for its ritual use (Article 7).

The 1970 UNESCO Convention shapes domestic law in the signatory states in respect of cultural property stolen from museums or secular public monuments in another State Party to the Convention. While illicit trafficking of cultural objects post-1970 drew more attention than it did prior to 1970, the return mechanism in the 1970 UNESCO Convention is narrow in scope. Article 7(b)(i)–(ii) provides for the requesting state to pay compensation to the innocent purchaser or one with valid title to the object. The 1995 UNIDROIT Convention endeavours to harmonise the private law instruments of return, restitution, and compensation across domestic legal systems. It creates a framework for stolen cultural objects as well as for illegally exported objects, extending its reach to undiscovered objects which the States Parties have not specifically designated or registered as cultural property and items that have been clandestinely excavated (Van Woudenberg 2016: 125). The 1995 UNIDROIT Convention limits the protection available to possessors of stolen cultural objects in good faith in civil law systems so that legal protection is available only for possessors who meet a clear due diligence test and who can discharge the burden of proof. The person or institution who acquires an object must prove that they have verified its provenance. This reversal in the burden of proof applies in respect of stolen cultural objects, and a museum located in a signatory state may offer proof of its efforts to verify the provenance of a collection item when it was acquired. These two instruments have largely 'failed to recognize the wrong of cultural removals or exploitation in the colonial encounter or to address its ongoing effects' (Stahn 2023: 347).

When conventions do not qualify to apply or adjudicators do not invoke them, a national legal system will stand in. However, the identification of which legal system applies poses challenges. Divergent national interpretations raise the spectre of the re-appearance of the problem of conflict of laws (Struycken 2009: 113, 115). The notion of community is central in the intangible cultural heritage framework but is not legally defined in the 2003 UNESCO Convention for the Safeguarding of Intangible Cultural Heritage. Communities, groups, and individuals designate a population in relation to intangible cultural heritage (Négri 2020: 44ff). The definition of 'community' assumes a crucial role in litigation seeking recognition of intellectual property rights and when invoking common rules of evidence to prove the existence of a traditional practice based on the customs of the heritage and shared by a cultural community (Hance 2020b: 177).

To systematise the analysis in this study, the parallel proceedings in the international civil case brought by the two Chinese village committees for the return of the Buddha statue in the Zhanggong Zushi case serve as a baseline. The litigation concerns the artefactual human remains of a medieval self-mummified monk from the Song Dynasty smuggled into the West via Hong Kong in 1994–1995 (*Amsterdam District Court, Village Committee of Yangchun and DongPu v Oscar van Overeem et al.*, No. ECLI:NL:RBAMS:2018:8919, 12 December 2018; *Yunchun Village and Dongpu Village Committees v Oscar van Overeem, Design & Consultancy B.V. and Design Consultancy Oscar van Overeem B.V.* Sanming Intermediate People's Court, 2015 San Min Chu Zi No. 626, 4 December 2020; *Oscar van Overeem, Design & Consultancy Oscar van Overeem B.V. v Yangchun Village and Dongpu Village Committees*, Fujian Province Higher People's Court, 2021 Min Min Final No. 302, 19 July 2022). The monk lived and died during the Song Dynasty and for centuries, his mummified remains were revered as an ancestor and the deity Zhanggong Zushi in temple rituals in South-eastern China. A sculpture casing was made for the ancestor more than a hundred years after the completion of a self-mummification ritual that lasted approximately 7 years. The casing dates from 1292, seemingly made to preserve the ancestral remains. The casing depicts a partially bald monk bedecked with a Chinese-style robe under a monastic shawl (Bruijn et al. 2015: 337–342). The statue was kept in the Puzhao Temple Hall. It was jointly owned and cared for by the villagers of Yangchun and its neighbouring village DongPu. Locals noticed a van travelling through Yangchun in December 1995 that had a seated figure covered with a blanket in the rear seat but claim not to have realised then that they were witnessing the theft. They reported their mummy stolen in December 1995 (Liu 2017: 222). In 2014 the statue was found in the possession of a Dutch private collector of Chinese antiquities, Oscar van Overeem. Van Overeem claimed to have bought the mummy from a Dutch buyer called Rustenburg. He disclaimed links in the mummy's chain of ownership, maintaining that Rustenburg had acquired the encased mummy from a Chinese artist in Hong Kong at the at the end of 1994 or the start of 1995 (Liu 2017: 222). When negotiations with van Overeem failed to reach a settlement and diplomatic efforts went nowhere, the village committees representing the group's interest of the villagers who had the mummified monk under their care until it was stolen instituted a claim based on a property right in Fujian and in Amsterdam. The case is the first of its kind as earlier claims in respect of dispersed Chinese heritage did not involve human remains nor other sacred cultural material and relied on diplomatic channels or buy-back.

The transaction occurred during the final years of Britain's 99-year lease, when Hong Kong was a British colony (1841–1997) and had semi-autonomous status in China, before formally reverting to Chinese rule. China was never colonised and was not subject to formal colonial rule at the time of the export or acquisition of the mummy. The artefactual remains of the ancient monk do not possess an imperial provenance, therefore. Nonetheless, the reamins fell victim to cultural trafficking when the final phase of colonialism played out in Hong Kong. Furthermore, the informal influence of colonial powers continued when the mummified monk was exported. The Buddha Mummy links aspects of colonialism, such as the control which former colonial powers exert over global trade, with the post-colonial illicit trade in antiquities.

A secondary legal norm may constitute a rule that indicates which jurisdiction's courts are competent to hear the case. If a court in one jurisdiction has already issued a judgment in a transnational case, a court in another jurisdiction may be asked to recognise its decision. Recognition and enforcement of the Chinese ruling and the Chinese public law that regulates the status of cultural objects was not pursued in this instance. Instead, parallel proceedings had been lodged, which compounds uncertainty in sales of cultural objects to private collectors. Legal techniques to control competing judgments if parallel proceedings are instituted include rules of priority, consolidation of related proceedings, party autonomy election and waiver, and discretion to decline jurisdiction or control parallel litigation (McLachlan 2009: 59–72). Mechanisms that prevent contradictory judgments from being reached based on the same facts diminish the likelihood of such contradictions by suppressing judicial discretion. Parallel proceedings cannot always be effectively reined in, however, because the legal mechanisms designed to prevent contradictory judgments in competing jurisdictions may not have global application or be entirely unlimited in spatial terms. For instance, the inappropriate forum doctrine cannot find application to prevent parallel proceedings in these cases because it does not operate between courts in EU Member States and third states such as China (Council Regulation (EC) No. 44/2001 of 22 December 2000 on jurisdiction and recognition and enforcement of judgments in civil and commercial matters OJ L 12/1; Council Regulation (EC) No. 1215/2012 of the European Parliament and of the Council of 12 December 2012 on jurisdiction and the recognition and enforcement of judgments in civil and commercial matters (recast) OJ L351/1, 20.12.2012).

Parallel proceedings can facilitate an appreciation of the facts from more than one vantage point (Bollée 2019: 346–347). A plurality of legal interpretations and legal viewpoints shaped courts' interpretations in the case of the mummified monk. Reaching contradictory judgments in parallel international civil litigation does not necessarily suggest that one court decision is correct whereas the other is 'wrong' or that one interpretation of the governing law is the only appropriate one. Diversity creates contestation in a dynamic process yielding more than a single right idea (Mills 2009: 98).

The historical, ethnological, sociological, and anthropological significance of the mummified monk statue for the Chinese villagers is apparent but for legal purposes, however, it was necessary to determine whether the claimants had standing to sue for its recovery (*locus standi*). The classificatory complexities underpinning the simplified dichotomy in PrIL between matters of substance governed by the *lex causae* and matters of procedure governed by the law of the court provide instruction on what needs to change to surmount them.

For art history and anthropology, 'local' is a situational construct. In PrIL, 'localisation' is synonymous with finding the connecting factor between a dispute and a jurisdiction after the dispute has been 'classified' as relating to property, contract, delict/tort, or some other category. This enables the dispute to be heard in a court located in that jurisdictional territory and the connecting factor to be used in a proprietary conflict rule (*lex situs*) or delictual conflict rule (*lex loci delicti*) to identify the governing law by which the legal question is to be resolved.

Ascertaining the character or nature of the legal relationship is the foundational guideline in PrIL's choice-of-law method (Struycken 2009: 233). PrIL disputes may require the law governing a particular legal question to be determined with reference to the choice-of-law rules that indicate which substantive body of law should be selected to apply. Should the law of the court (the forum) be applied as a matter of principle, with the international aspects considered of secondary importance, or should adjudicators employ secondary rules to help them choose between potentially applicable laws? Choice-of-law owes its very existence to the fact that there is no world-wide system of private or public law. Conflicts rules operate in many domains of private law where the international dimension is given primary status based on the premise of territoriality or geographical delimitation. Van Overeem claimed that the Dutch Civil Code should be applied to settle the claim, whereas the village committees claimed that Chinese law applied. No agreement was reached. The Higher Peoples' Court of China determined that Chinese law should apply, by which title never passed to the Dutch collector (Min Min Final 2022: sub 'On issues concerning the applicable law'). Interpreting the law in accordance with the 1995 UNIDROIT Convention, despite the case not arising under it, made it possible for the court to rein in an unfettered good faith standard and apply a more universal notion of justice, which is ensconced in the more demanding due diligence standard in the convention. This specialised approach to the application of the choice-of-law rule of PrIL protects the interest of the source community, but 'legitimate owners' in civil law countries that have not ratified the convention resist the application of this standard (Campfens 2024: 150).

Adopting the perspective that the application of foreign law to individuals requires justification, the high level of embeddedness of a private law relationship within a community, based on analysis of both geographical connecting factors and the policies of the laws regulating the respective private law relationships, provides such a justification (Banu 2018: 292). If private law relationships are understood in the context of extra-legal social expectations, legal analyses can benefit even more.

The quest for justice for the cultural depletion caused by international law of the 19th and 20th centuries has led to investigations of material justice, along with human rights, *jus cogens*, and the underlying ethic of international law itself (Glenn 2011: 270). Public international law (PublIL) makes available arguments framed around cultural rights, the right to self-determination, the sovereignty of cultural communities, religious freedom, identity, and morality. The property argument cannot be neglected, however. For instance, 'missionary colonialism' had virtually unlimited opportunities to gather collections from local people forced to abandon their indigenous religions. Missionary museums in Europe were filled with them. The language of ethics and global justice is increasingly invoked as an alternative normativity in the international context (Spitra 2021: 143–144; Mills 2009: 300–301).

Principles of property and contract closely aligned with the commercial decisions of *de facto* sovereigns to invest in the colonies. International law was law made by and for states at the normative and practical levels. Empire and corporations wielded it as an instrument of power (Koskenniemi 2017: ix). Sales and leases of large tracts of land to companies transmitted the rights to the natural resources, as well as control of the lives of those living on the land. During the latter half of the 19th century, small village communities in Africa were concentrated into viable units within the Family of Nations, which described the community of sovereign states between which the rules of international law applied. African kingdoms were split into small tribes with government-appointed chiefs responsible to district commissioners and provincial administrators, and the traditional authority of chiefs was nullified. The various types of African land tenure did not count as private ownership. Land farmed by Africans became state property. It was up to the government to set aside reserves for the exclusive use of Africans with the supposed aim to safeguard traditional ownership, but only if there were no competing interests from companies or whites. Foreign public and private agents acquired title to vast tracts of land. In 2001 the Herero became the first ethnic group to seek reparations for the slave labour and confiscation of land and tribal property under the legal definition of genocide along with an official apology. Approximately 125,000 claimants launched a class action against Germany on behalf of members and descendants of the Ovaherero and Nama peoples. Their claims were dismissed but they illustrate the entanglement between property and sovereignty in international law. One of the allegations was that the German treasury had benefited from the seizure, sale and lease of land, livestock, and other personal property, as well as fees, customs, tariffs and taxes on exports, mining, railway construction and other business ventures in German SWA, and that it had used co-mingled funds to purchase real estate in New York City and enter into service contracts in respect of those properties. Germany refused to submit to the jurisdiction of the US state and federal courts, resulting in lack of subject matter jurisdiction (*The Herero People's Reparations Corporation, et al., v Deutsche Bank, A.g. and Woermann Line, D/b/a Deutsche Afrika-linien Gmblt & Company* 370 F.3d 1192 (D.C. Cir. 2004)). The causal effect between atrocities and tort liability was held unproven and 'judicially discoverable or manageable standards' were deemed non-existent (*Hereros v Deutsche Afrika-Linien GMBLT & Co* Case No. 06-1684, 232 F.App'x 90 (3d Cir. 2007) 8–10). Actions based on the Alien Torts Statute (28 USC para 1350), federal common law, and the Law of Nations, failed to oblige the German government to include the Nama and OvaHerero as participants in the negotiations with the Namibian executive and to receive reparations for enslavement and genocide between 1885–1909 and property expropriated by imperial Germany (*Rukoro et al v Federal Republic of Germany* No. 17 CV 62-LTS (SDNY 2019)).

The Germans deployed private property openly to serve and consolidate their primary interests in SWA. The contractual relationships established with and by the private sector directly supported the achievement of the standard required for 'effective' territorial control, which was a prerequisite condition of statehood for German sovereignty. The relationship between private economic actors and the government resembled a form of 'state capitalism.' The structures and policies of the colonial period created the networks, framework, and methods that facilitated the collection practices of European museums, even after the end of formal colonial rule (DMB *Care of Collections* 2021: 24, 26). Employees, company shareholders, transporters, colonial military, and administrative agents all had a stake in the colonial economy. They were at liberty to take collection items back to the metropole where they could be sold or given as 'gifts.' Priceless antiquities and 'curious' ethnographic objects were absorbed by the markets of Europe. The purveyors of these markets considered them 'resources' of ancestral lands alongside ancestral remains. The procurement of tangible objects proceeded by means of fieldwork and patronage or through gift and bequest. The chain of custody of objects with religious, sacred, or spiritual significance was bound to consist of clandestine or forcible removal even when benevolent donors passed these objects to museums. Because the definitions, legal norms, and standards for repatriation for these materials still bear the marks of this history, the relationship between normativity, ethics, law, and justice is a potential minefield and nuanced expression of the position is achieved only with sustained observation.

1.4 Normativity, ethics, normative conflicts

The 'normativity' of law (as primary legal norms) lodges in its concern for social behaviour. 'Hard law' gives people reasons to act (or not act) in a particular way by its direction to act (or not act) in that way (McBride and Steele 2018: 31). The law's normative claim as a legal system or domain extends to the machinery of its creation and application. Its normative effect derives from the inherent capability of a system of law to guide action by generating practical reasons with special status. A 'legal norm' sets a standard of behaviour. Rules are norms that require specific conduct. The judge is the authority that confirms the normativity of a rule (Van Roermund 2013: 247). Principles set the aims and limits of these rules that guide adjudicators in their decision-making function.

Standards for behaviour are not only set through individual legal provisions or rules. Adjudicators weigh up the interests in claims for return; policymakers assess the criteria and procedures set out in policies, guidelines, and 'soft law' (rules with normative qualities in political-moral terms without constituting legally binding norms, or that have 'relative normativity' because they possess strong power to persuade) (Chechi 2014: 247–248). Examples include provisions in non-binding texts; provisions of international agreements that either do not impose obligations or require low levels of obligation and thus cannot be enforced; imprecise provisions; or provisions that do not delegate control to a court, arbitrator, or organisation (Shelton ed. 2000: 292). Resolutions adopted by an international organisation are 'binding' when capable of creating obligations for their addressee(s).

Soft law and softer policy frameworks aid the interpretation of hard law. Formal and informal sources of law affect conceptions of rights, obligations and responsibilities in cultural property and heritage, thus it is preferable to consider public policies, moral tenets, ethical guidelines, social trends, as well as soft law. French President Emanuel Macron committed to repatriating African heritage removed between 1885–1960 in a speech delivered at the Ouaga I University, Ouagadougou, Burkina Faso, 28 November 2017. He commissioned economist Felwine Sarr and art historian Bénédicte Savoy to prepare a report on cultural restitution to former African colonies. In a brave response to the strong interest of many African states to protect their cultural heritage by retaining the material manifestations of their culture, and recovering artefacts that were removed during the colonial era, the report denied that there was any valid, sustainable, unconditional justification for African heritage to remain in private collections and European museums (Sarr and Savoy Report 2018: 29). The report recommended that the large-scale return of African objects—75% of the 88,000 objects in French ethnographic collections—be achieved by a series of bilateral agreements, some of which will be ratified by the French Parliament. Those operating at the supranational level will override domestic heritage and public law principles. These agreements would make provision for committees to monitor requests; the completion of inventories of qualifying cultural objects in French public collections; and renewable research programmes to determine the provenance of the items claimed. The report has executive impetus but does not constitute a legislative enactment, executive order, administrative rule, nor a judicial determination. It brought restitution into the mainstream political debate and has the weight of government policy. It is particularly notable because it encourages ratification of the 1995 UNIDROIT Convention as 'the lone juridical tool capable of … establishing a common law for restitution as well as ensuring the permanence of the process undertaken for the cultural objects stockpiled during the colonial period' (Sarr and Savoy Report 2018: 85).

Norms articulated in law may interact as part of a system (e.g., constitutional provisions; primary sources of law such as statutes and regulations; multi-level legislation and legislation adopted by sub-national levels of government; unwritten customary law, legal principles, regulations adopted by independent authorities; and written soft law at the boundary of—or outside—the sources of law). While legislation is a particularly significant element in contemporary legal discourse, the normative phenomena that support claims for return within moral and historical frameworks are not confined to legislation. Legislation on repatriation of Indigenous objects such as the US Federal Native American Graves Protection and Repatriation Act (NAGPRA) requires repatriation of human remains and sacred (ceremonial) items to Indigenous peoples. The NAGPRA incorporates return criteria that combine moral ideas with common principles in relation to provenance research and acknowledge the wrongfulness of past cultural takings affecting societies of origin. The frame and the method of this legislation can be typified as 'victim-centred' (Stahn 2023: 420). The catalyst for the promulgation of the NAGPRA was the discovery of nearly 18,500 human remains in a Smithsonian Institution warehouse in 1986 by representatives from the Northern Cheyenne tribe (Trope 2013: 24). The binding structure of the NAGPRA renders the role of law in restitution reasonably straightforward, but there are shortcomings. More than 200 tribes do not enjoy federal status and are excluded from its operation. Information flows are not always optimal and tribal representatives did not participate in claim review discussions until recently.

Article 38(1) of the ICJ Statute instructs the court to apply the 'teachings of the most highly qualified publicists.' These are the most eminent experts in the field. Judicial decisions and opinions of jurists given to their own governments constitute formal yet subsidiary means for determining the rules of PublIL. Whether 'general principles of law recognised by civilised nations' are those of PublIL proper or of comparative domestic law that applies at state level, remains to be settled (*Right of Passage over Indian Territory (Portugal/India)* [1960] ICJ). Some commentators include secondary laws of international governmental institutions, soft law, and the International Law Commission's codifications of international law under the formal sources of PublIL (Kaczorowska 2010: 25ff).

In antiquity, a distinction was drawn between 'mores,' systematic reflections on what constitutes acceptable conduct, and 'ethos,' beliefs, common expectations, and traditional customs. The two differ in normative effect. Morality or mores encapsulates principles, attitudes, practices, and motivations by which what is right, good, or appropriate may be identified. Several perspectives are available: whether the act itself is right, wrong, or permissible; whether the consequences of the act are good, bad, or neutral; whether the character of the actor is virtuous or vicious; and whether the will or the motive is good or evil. Mores may be judged based on ethos, such as a person's culture, or ideology. Ethics is more generally understood as the structure that enables reflection on 'human action.' Ethics govern the intentional behaviour of autonomous individuals with the capacity to follow principles that direct their conduct towards others when pursuing their own goals. Ethics have normative effect. Ethical norms derive from principles of social co-existence or an inner sense of duty that assume certain imperatives and prohibitions (Zeidler 2016: 47, 109, 111). Crucial information on the practice of repatriation and the recognition of cultural rights is to be found in codes of ethics and de-accession policies (Byrne 2015: 47).

In the Inter-American Court of Human Rights, Indigenous and Afro-descendant culture is recognised and protected. Specific rights and safeguards operate in respect of ceremonial activities, languages, arts and rituals, practices in connection with nature, and customary law. Their 'specific way of being, seeing, and acting in the world' is considered to have developed based on their close relationship with their traditional territories and the resources therein, but drawbacks to a normative approach marked by the protection of indigenous groups and their cultural identity, and the static, romanticised view of their identity, remain topical (e.g., David 2020: 162–163).

A disconnect arises frequently between the values of Indigenous communities and the professional codes of ethics and institutional norms that cause hesitation over requests for repatriation (Conaty 2008: 252). Professionalisation introduced hurdles for restitution when the 1963 British Museum Act was promulgated to alter the composition of the Trustees. To protect and conserve artefacts is a large part of a museum's responsibility. Returning sacred cultural material to communities who will use or 'damage' them by letting them return to the earth, may be seen by many as unethical. The damage that stolen or looted material may incur during a return journey to their communities of origin will not necessailry discourage communities from agitating for reactivating their connections with the invisible spirits of their ancestors. Museums cannot consider the ethical implications of keeping objects such as sacred medicine bundles, using only their professional codes, but must also balance requests for return against what would produce the best outcome over-all. The disconnect prompts a search for solutions outside law's strictures (White, Campbell, and Thomas (eds.) 2019). Meanwhile there is scope for cultural rights to evolve and shift the balance in favour of peoples for whom their cultural heritage is a way to assert their identity, spirituality, and history. New narratives that enable the values and ethics of cultural heritage, and take account of the post-colonial situ-ation, may find their way into law without attempting to regulate 'technical details of restitutions' nor 'other critical fields of the administration of culture' (Spitra 2021: 144). 'Narrative norms' count among the non-binding principles that may be taken into consideration for interpretation and construction of legal texts relevant to claims for return and the broad spectrum of practices and ethics associated with restitution (Jayme 2005: 943ff). Narrative norms may strengthen the moral orientation of new primary legal norms, helping them to recover their 'international authority.' They may also inform secondary legal norms and principles, as well as the normativity of value judgments regarding such norms in claims concerning the colonial past of sacred cultural heritage.

Restitution claims straddle legal and moral norms. A restitution claim that is not supported by either the legal norms presently in force in a country or the imperial laws of the colonial era, may find support in moral norms that create expectations and demands for regulation of the sphere of social life that has hitherto gone unregulated. Wood connects law's expansive growth to religious decline and the replacement of the certitudes of religion by political beliefs. In the post-colonial era, irrational impulses play out in the political arena as organised religion loses its hold. He theorises that law is now the most important ideology societies have at their disposal to ensure their survival. He predicts that legal recourse will become more frequent in the future as law expands; the number of lawyers grows; and the role they play in policymaking increases in scope (Wood 2016: 179ff; 226).

1.4.1 The mission to civilise

The empires of Europe organised the Berlin Congress on West Africa 1884/85 to avoid the outbreak of armed conflict between rival colonial powers. In an attempt to 'manage' the ongoing process of colonisation in Africa all major colonial powers, including the United States, ratified the General Act of the Berlin Congo Conference on West Africa (the Congo Act of 26 February 1885). There was no African representation at the Berlin Conference.

The Congo Act established the formalities required to recognise newly occupied territory in Africa. It prepared the way for European powers to conclude transactions with African rulers and to assume official guardianship of African communities (Alexandrowicz 1973: 5, 115). The conference was presented as an effort to introduce the African continent to the Family of Nations, which would allow for higher political and social status. States on the outside could gain entry to the exclusive club in different ways, including by attaining the standard of European 'civilisation' or by concluding protectorate agreements and treaties (Anghie 1999: 35–36). No definition of 'civilisation' was ever agreed on, and it came to mean whatever satisfied the whims of Europeans. 'Legal colonialism' was practised through treaties. If treaties could not be achieved, war was inevitable. Inter-European rivalry peaked after the conclusion of the Berlin Congress as the competition for title deeds to territory intensified. The challenge was to obtain titles to territory without manipulating treaty provisions. Instead of waging treaty wars with other European powers to achieve the titles for ceded territory, it was quicker to conclude treaties of protection with African Rulers, to organise colonial territories internally and achieve vassalisation directly. There was no need for protracted negotiations and inter-European discriminatory treaty clauses to make African states relinquish their sovereignty under international law (Alexandrowicz 1973: 54–55, 58, 80). The European powers were eyeing titles to territory whilst claiming to further 'the moral and material well-being of the native populations' and create conditions for 'the development of trade and civilisation.' The scramble for territorial control set Africa on a path to underdevelopment. Foreign occupation erased its sovereignty while PublIL sanctioned the property rights doctrines that validated this erasure (Amin 2023: 3). In a strange and converse reasoning, occupation was set up to erode sovereignty, with the intention to acquire territory from the African ruler, absorb it, and to lord over the vassal. Classical PublIL also started to qualify 'universalisation.' Becoming a colony of a European state could not advance the status of states outside the community of states and international law, because the norms of the 'civilising laws of war' only applied among civilised states and not to their relations with colonies (Spitra 2020: 329–235). Unsurprisingly, no true international community came into being.

The 'scramble' for collective arrangements involving protectorates lasted two short decades. In the original definition of protectorates in traditional international law, sovereignty was split and shared. Protected states were members of the Family of Nations that represented African states. Rights of external sovereignty vested in the Protector while rights of internal sovereignty and powers of administration continued in the protected entity. The external sovereignty of African rulers was restricted by undertakings not to conclude treaties, maintain diplomatic relations, go to war with other powers, or to cede territory to them (Alexandrowicz 1973: 123). Germany concluded 34 treaties with rulers and communities in Africa, including the Hereros in SWA. Some treaties establishing protectorates charged the German government with the mediation of disputes between the contracting ruler and other chiefs. The 1885 treaty concluded between Germany and Maharero, chief of the Herero, to establish a German SWA Protectorate gave assurances that military protection would be forthcoming against groups such as the Nama-Oorlam (Goldmann 2024: 600). The treaty followed the original blueprint, with undertakings not to cede territory or to conclude treaties without the consent of Germany. Treaty stipulations agreed between Britain and several African Rulers between 1887 and 1901 contained similar obligations (Alexandrowicz 1973: 61–62, 64–65).

Compared to the other European colonisers, Germany's conception of its colonies was more disordered. It could not decide whether its colonies were German possessions or foreign territory. The earlier protection treaties that Berlin had concluded with the Nama and Herero in SWA made it seem that Germany acknowledged these communities as subjects of international law, but Germany would only consider them subjects of international law if it recognised their sovereignty. Meanwhile, the colonies were bound by German constitutional law. By the logic that prevailed at the time, only relations between existing states could be regulated by means of treaties and only states could conclude them (Bachmann 2018: 35, 328). The conclusion of treaties with the leaders of inhabiting communities was an anachronistic aspect of Germany's relationship with its colonies and of their legal status. Treaties with the 'non-civilised' concluded in an earlier age were to be disregarded because they were not compliant with legal requirements. There was no scope for victims to claim that a humanitarian minimum standard applied to them because of the contradictory classifications given to protection treaties, as well as the uncertainty surrounding the principle of humanity (Goldmann 2024: 598, 601).

Originally the principle of effective occupation did not apply to the protectorates, for the African rulers would never have agreed to occupation. Later effective occupation assumed significance. On the face of treaty texts, there was nothing to indicate an intention to annex and absorb the protectorates, and any such intention was *contra legem*, but over time African rulers forfeited the benefits and advantages stipulated by them in the treaties. This happened because the signatories to the Berlin Congress granted each other *carte blanche* to interfere with the internal sovereignty of protected African entities, use them as springboards to annexation, and absorb these protected states in 'colonial' protectorates. European powers took the opportunity to fence some territories in and cut their commercial and political ties with the outside world. Treaty clauses started excluding 'all other' European competitors, not just one competitor in particular. Rulers would be retained in the annexed territories to maintain the illusion of control to their communities so that foreign domination would not be seen as national humiliations. The protectorates lost the power of legislation, administration and judicial ruling, and the traditional regime of real property collapsed. As colonial protectors absorbed the African continent any semblance of homogeneity of the law gave way and European municipal laws took the place of international law. The metamorphosis of the traditional protectorate into a juridical phantom 'colonial' protectorate undermined the ethos and edifice of international law, and international law effectively disappeared (Alexandrowicz 1973: 62–70, 80–81, 111, 124–127). If the plan succeeded the territory would be annexed and the sovereignty of the ruler eradicated, and the treaty of protection was treated as terminated. If the ruler resisted and the plan failed, the treaty of protection was treated as broken. Eventually, the main characteristic of the African protectorate became the prohibition of all foreign relations except those permitted by the protecting state (*King v Earl of Crewe* (1910) AC 588). Alexandrowicz (1973: 82) emphasises that the positivist interpretations that effective occupation was within the law, were *contra legem* or contrary to a legal obligation in international law.

Those who expect the law once and for all to resolve historical problems created by social behaviours think in positivist terms that conceive of the law as the sum of all binding legal norms. If law is 'a closed system of application-specific rules' and legal norms contained in commands and orders, it can exist independently of the moral merit of those rules (Habermas 1996: 209). Legal-positivism's preference for a definition of cultural property and heritage as having economic value that renders it amenable to export and trade enables instant, ready-made answers. However, legal idealism would much rather view the normative aspect of the production and use of cultural heritage as an identifier of membership. Sacred cultural heritage is indicative of who belongs to the society that produced or 'received' this heritage. Instantaneous answers are not available.

From 1850 onwards Classical Legal Thought (CLT) shaped and informed the positivist intellectual currents that predominated in international law (Alexandrowicz 1973: 6). Between 1850 and 1914, the proponents of CLT opposed the idea of a universal law of nations that was binding upon humanity. Their systematisation efforts bolstered the colonial project with the classification of the 'Other' as one outside of civilisation and of history (Kennedy 2010: 830). Legal idealists recognise that law uses a multitude of conceptual means to realise its aim. The aim of law is considered paramount and its form but a secondary concern in service to the objective of a law. They resolve the tension between the principle of legal certainty and a claim to a legitimate application of law by putting rightness first, whereas positivists resort to certainty over rightness (Habermas 1996: 202). The tension between positivism and idealism manifests in contemporary debatesabout the definitions employed in ownership contests for cultural property and heritage. Arguably, 'ideal law' brings justice, certainty, and purposefulness into balance (Zeidler 2016: 206). Balance among the three elements is not every adjudicator's aspiration, however. In transnational cases the law that can be established with certainty is typically preferred because of the ready availability of information about its content, application, and interpretation. If the aspiration to bring various elements into balance is present, the idea of moral evaluation of legal rules as advanced by the German legal scholar Gustav Radbruch (1878–1949) would require adjudicators to abstain from applying an unjust rule that would cause the decision to fall foul of justice and equality (Radbruch 1946: 1ff; Bix 2011: 45–57).

By the late-19th century, the criteria that defined the category of 'civilised states' were sufficiently relaxed to include states that had achieved sovereignty in fact (Kennedy 2010: 835). By 1914, African nations were placed under the rule of European powers except for Liberia and Ethiopia, which had been admitted into the Family of Nations. Nonetheless, for the most part, international law protected the superior status of the colonisers. Its racist construction denied the application of international legal standards to colonial wars and cemented the structural inequality in the application of PublIL (Stahn 2023: 300). African artefacts held in museums and libraries in the Global North did not remain unaffected by a Eurocentric international law. It legitimised dispossession, failed to recognise the legal personality of territories inhabited by Indigenous peoples and lumped Africa's peoples into the 'unadvanced' category along with those who did not qualify for full membership of the international community (Fagbayibo 2021: 480).

The cultural certainty of the mission to civilise readily manifests as racial exceptionalism and cultural superiority. Determining which peoples were 'savages' and which were 'civilised' was left to social constructs and perceptions. No legal criteria were developed (Waschefort 2016: 605). In the general European project of colonialism, the British were at the top of the racial hierarchy in Africa. The Germans aspired to the same status. The Boer republics of the Zuid-Afrikaanse Republiek were ruled by whites who could claim European ancestry, but on the racial hierarchy, the Afrikaners were below Europeans as people of mixed race were. The colonial state struggled to contain the discontent simmering below the surface of public discourse, but German observers were intrigued by the peculiar position of the Afrikaners in the hierarchy of civilisation. From a European vantage point, the Boers displayed features of an African lifestyle and lacked 'civilised' cultural attributes but were not at the level of Africans, nor were they elevated to the level of European metropolitan representatives (Botha 2007: 12). Questioning racial purity made it possible to disapply 19th century codifications of the laws and customs of war and the constraints on warfare to certain classes of people and to resort to appalling violence in appropriating their land. Peoples of colour who had organised themselves in non-state societies before the arrival of Europeans were at the bottom of the racial pyramid. By the early 20th century, the 'bushman' had become a subordinate category of labour. No amount of assimilation through association, mixed marriage, behaviour, or switching of political loyalties, could make integration into the in-group possible.

Based on blood, the ideology of the racial hierarchy can be implemented through bureaucratic ancestor-screening. This matrix of racial classification makes for a 'sliding scale of justice' on which sides can be switched and flipped in accordance with the politics of the day. Depending on who is in power, Indigenous Africans may find themselves at the top of the hierarchy or at the bottom. At the top, ethnonationalism stokes the popular conviction among groups that their children can take their rightful place only when other ethnicities are eliminated, or that they are '"the chosen people" of their gods.'

1.4.2 Mimetic competition garners normative effect

Law is more than power politics or the sum of enforceable legislation; otherwise, the ruling classes would have total control of cultural property and heritage. It is a central tenet of this study that, since 'law' is not synonymous with 'power,' the legal position of claimants is not defined by 'might is right.' Imperial law was used to justify imperial expansion to different audiences but claims resonating with ethical norms and frameworks can strengthen the law to effectively resist the normative effect of the brutality of imperial power.

When law and legality are made to depend solely on who holds power, 'might' determines 'right.' English philosopher Thomas Hobbes (1588–1679) enunciated many of his political ideas in *Leviathan* (1651) and political theories that pointed to 'the will to power' were attributed to him by his contemporaries. The precepts of 'Hobbism' include that the unrestrained actions of men are violent and ruthless, 'savagely disregarding the persons and property of his fellows' to preserve himself 'by gaining power over others.' The precept that there is no real distinction between moral right and moral wrong derives from a Hobbesian conviction that moral distinctions are arbitrary conventions which rulers and princes foist upon their subjects. Such artificial suppositions have no validity beyond the frontiers within which those rulers exercise control. Going further still is the precept that no *de facto* ruler can be immoral since the rulers are themselves the source of morality; their commands are *ipso facto* the criterion of right and wrong for those whom they are strong enough to command (Lamprecht 1940: 32–33).

Efforts to legitimise the will to power perpetuate competition. An example of this occurred when, in 1894, the Director-General of the Imperial Museum in Japan, Kuki Ryūichi (1852–1931), instructed public officials and military officers to collect Chinese and Korean treasures during imperial warfare, to make good use of the opportunities to collect objects which armed conflict provides (Stahn 2023: 304). If occupying forces have the right to sell the heritage found in occupied territory, the ethos that 'might makes right' is consolidated. Recognising the right of the victorious to collect enemy property to enhance its power and prestige is tantamount to granting normative effect to mimetism. When the removal of imperial artefacts is deemed legally and ethically justifiable at the time of their removal, and the contemporary law then treats the acquisitions as legitimate, ruthless self-interest is legitimised, and 'civilisation' is reduced to a superficial veneer (Fitzmaurice 2017: 373). It is a short step removed from the use of force ultimately determining political autonomy, economic self-sufficiency, state security, and territorial integrity.

Assumptions that the power struggle for dominance is the ultimate determinant for truth, or that 'truth' coincides with what the victor in a 'contest of wills' asserts it to be, will turn fact into norm. If the fact of imperial brutality becomes a norm that directs behaviour, disputants will be expected to conform with a standard that should not be assumed to be valid.

When normative uncertainty prevails mimetics garner a normative thrust which is discernible in restitution discourses and practice. Uncertainty is created by policy gaps, blind spots, unwarranted legal distinctions and dichotomies, lack of impartiality, inequality and discrimination, or inadequate criteria and procedures. Since Elgin's team never sought the consent of the Greeks, normative uncertainty became inevitable, and gave scope to the British Museum to place inordinate weight on the permission ostensibly given by the Ottomans to remove the Parthenon Marbles (Rudenstine 2002: 449ff). This garnering of a normative effect is also evident in the extraction of sensitive cultural assets from weaker states by more powerful states—cultural material such as ancestral remains, artefactual human remains, sacred objects, and object-beings. Restitution claims based on the find-spot or provenience of an artefact must frequently contend with uncertainty about state ownership of archaeological material. One of the problems with collections that contain cultural material removed during the colonial era, is that the dates of commencement of signatory states' obligations differ. The leeway in interpretation also gives scope for erroneous understandings, e.g., that artefacts should have a documented provenance as of the entry into force of the 1970 UNESCO Convention (24 April 1972). This interpretation prevails among auction houses, the art trade, and museums. It creates a 'time lock' that serves as a 'proxy to legality,' for if outside the country of origin before that date, the requirement of documented provenance does not apply (Campfens 2021: 191–192). Best practice standards use the date of the source country's state ownership rule as the benchmark (Crennan 2021: 9ff; 2021 National Gallery of Australia Provenance Assessment Guidelines). A state ownership law provides the baseline in space and time that acts as a legal, ethical, and practical benchmark for deducing where ownership resides. Efforts to legitimise illegal transactions that took place in the past couch colonialism as an insurmountable *fait accompli*.

Neither mimetic competition nor the modalities of racism are confined to skin tone, but cultural superiority does not hesitate to make arbitrary judgments about skin tone (Lagardien 2022: 55). The material mapping of cultural evolutionism convinced Europeans of their own historical perfection and the arrested progression of non-Europeans. To them it was clear that the 'Hottentots' (the Khoi and San peoples of Southern Africa) belonged at the bottom of the European human hierarchy (Van Niekerk 2007: 149). When the British Governor extended his guardianship over the Hottentot nation to the British Administration at the Cape in 1809, he did so 'by reason of their imbecile state' (*The Case of the Hottentot Venus* (1810) 13 East 195, 104 ER 344).

Hierarchical thinking allowed for human circuses to flourish and profit from the degradation of humans on display. Sarah Baartman (1789–1815) was born into a Gonaquasub group of the Khoikhoi, a pastoral Indigenous community in South Africa. She became a displaced person. Her Khoikhoi name was never recorded. A Dutch surname was foisted upon her before being put on show in England as an 'ethnopornographic' freak. After her death her remains were kept in the collections of the Musée de l'Homme, the former anthropological section of the National Museum of Natural History in Paris. Labelled 'Hottentot Venus' her remains were presented as scientific evidence of the perfect specimen of the 'African Hottentot.' Scientific and anthropological interest kept museum displays like this alive. Plaster casts made of her body and her remains continued to be displayed even after her remains were claimed in the 1940s. They were placed in the museum's reserves in 1974. Claims for the return of her remains intensified after apartheid's demise in South Africa in 1994.

The norm concerning the inalienability of public collections has been a founding principle for the French heritage code—*Code du Patrimoine* of 20 February 2004—since the 16th century. It originated in the context of royal estate. It allows museums to collect and study objects from different cultures because the collections are inviolable and non-transferable. Royal collections and other public collections in national museums are immune to repatriation and, consequently, special mechanisms and procedures are necessary to effect de-accession. The principle has evolved into a complex set of rules, including that special statutory exceptions are required to enable return of objects that are 'inalienable' in the eyes of French law. When an administrative decision to reverse the status of inalienability of Sarah's human remains proved unavailable, she became the face of the 'African victim of colonialism.' By the time Nelson Mandela issued a formal request for the return of Sarah's remains in March 2002, a private member's bill consisting of a single article authorising de-accession was ready to be introduced in the French Parliament. A brief window of opportunity opened to return Sarah's remains. The socialist government in power mustered the political will to pass the required legislation based on the French Constitution, which outlaws the ownership of bodies. After promulgation of the *Loi relative à la restitution par la France de la dépouille mortelle de Saartjie Baartman*, Sarah's remains were decommissioned from their status as public cultural heritage. The repatriation was completed in May 2002. The French state did not attempt to make amends for an historic injustice but presented the remains as an act of generosity (Vigneron 2020: 322–323).

The legal categorisation of human remains in physical anthropology collections has never been stable. As scientific specimens, they are inalienable heritage objects, but as human body parts, the idea of ownership or commodification cannot apply where bioethics legislation imposes such constraints. The way in which curators engage with cultural property law affects these decisions. Legal systems approach the difficulty of defining what is at once inalienable, but ultimately not fully possessable, in divergent ways, and may also change categorisations. There is no counterpart in English law to 'inalienable cultural heritage' as found in French law, but National Museums in the UK have used the 'foundational purposes of the museum as an institution,' and their role to civilise, educate and elighten, to amplify the interpretation and effect of the restrictive legislation (Jenkins 2011: 2). The scientific educational and research focus of the museum's mission to protect material in perpetuity from political and financial pressures for the sake of education and research is embedded in UK cultural law.

A Jewish lineage has frequently invited oppression. The genealogical records of Jews have been particularly vulnerable to destruction during times of revolutionary upheaval. It seems that, for populations outwith Europe, distinctions were made along the 'colour line' with skin tone being the criterion, but when the national belonging of the racialised other was questioned from within Europe, other somatic characteristics were employed (Virdee et al 2021: 33). On one interpretation, justifications for the superiority of Europeans preceded and outlasted formal colonial rule, and it precipitated the Holocaust and the ethno-nationalism that culminated in the genocide of the Jews. On another interpretation, the first modern racial subjects were the Slavs, Jews, and Catholic Irish in Europe; the peoples of Africa, Asia, and South America followed. Fanon reasoned that the colonial context enslaves certain people to their appearance, and that Black people are 'overdetermined from without.' He differentiated their position from that of the Jews, whose conduct 'is perpetually overdetermined from the inside.' White members of the Jewish population can escape being recognised for their Jewishness. Whereas Jews are vulnerable to the 'idea' others have of them, they can only be traced if they behave in a way that makes others notice their Jewishness (Fanon 1986: 115–116, 122).

The definition of racism supplied in 2003 by the European Commission Against Racism and Intolerance acknowledges the width of racism's ambit: the devaluation of certain people based on their race, colour, language, religion, nationality, ethnic origin, or other cultural characteristics, or based on the belief that their competence and character are determined by these aspects, or on the conviction that one's own race, colour, language, religion, nationality, ethnic origin, or other cultural characteristics are superior. Restitution law and policy for unethical removals, especially during the colonial era, may only start to evolve once the thread between the differentiated impact of racism, antisemitism, and fascism is revealed and acknowledged, in discourse and in practice.

Theorising the connection between racism, colonialism, imperialism, and genocide has led to a degree of hope that Germany's efforts to come to terms with its Nazi past could benefit in its relation to its colonial past, and that the state would admit guilt and assume responsibility (Steinmetz and Hell 2006: 157). The German–Namibian process has fallen short of achieving progress with attempts made to decolonise European international law and German colonial law. Germany commenced with the adoption of a Parliamentary Motion in October 2006, followed by an interparliamentary forum that had the support of the Namibian government between 2007 and 2011. Interstate negotiations were held in 2015. Between 2016 and 2021 repeated rounds of talks were held but the German government insisted it will only negotiate with the democratically legitimate Namibian government and not with the representatives of the Nama and Herero. In May 2021 the Federal Republic of Germany signed a Joint Declaration or Reconciliation Agreement ('United in remembrance of our colonial past, united in our will to reconcile, united in our vision of the future'). Germany officially acknowledged its historical responsibility for the genocide (as opposed to its legal responsibility) and pledged 1.1 billion euros in development aid over the next 30 years, to be paid voluntarily and not as official 'reparations' (Goldmann 2024: 581). The Namibian Parliament withheld ratification of the Joint Reconciliation Agreement, however, and issued a demand in November 2022 that it be renegotiated. Namibian lawyer Patrick Kauta filed an application in 2023 to review and set aside the Joint Declaration adopted by Germany and Namibia before the Namibian High Court (*Swartbooi and Another v Speaker of the National Assembly High Court of Namibia* Case No. HC-MD-CIV-MOT-REV-2023/00023, Founding Affidavit (20 January 2023)). Kauta avers that the conduct of international relations is subject to Namibian constitutional control, and that the draft Joint Declaration is inconsistent with several constitutional obligations in Namibia and the 2006 Parliamentary Motion. The affidavit urges the Namibian National Assembly, Cabinet, Attorney General, and Namibian Executive to oppose racist content that replicates colonial bias in any agreement. This is the first time in the history of a former colony that its judiciary has an opportunity to counter the normative effect of colonial injustice and colonial crimes (Theurer 2023: 1168).

The request to designate the draft Joint Declaration unlawful and prevent its implementation may provide an opportunity to review and dissect interpretations of the doctrine of intertemporal law. The principle of intertemporality in PublIL holds that juridical facts must be assessed under the standards of the law contemporaneous with those facts and appreciated in the light of the law contemporary with it, so that the (il)legality of an act can only be judged by the law in force at the time the act occurred. It may preclude a ruling on the substance of the dispute. The intertemporal character of PublIL is frequently relied upon to suppress legal claims to repatriate or restitute cultural property in museum collections (Taşdelen 2016: 91–93). The doctrine is rooted in the colonial era. Max Huber, the sole arbitrator in the famous *Island of Palmas* case, suggested that past events must be judged by the law of that time, and not by the law in force when a dispute arises or as it stands when an arbitrator must decide a case (*Island of Palmas (The Netherlands v USA)* II RIAA 829 (Perm. Ct. Arb) 4 April 1928, 854). Supposedly agreed upon by European powers to ensure legal certainty and predictability, the doctrine safeguarded their interests. Neither Sub-Saharan Africa nor South-East Asia participated in the formation of the rule of intertemporality (per Al-Khasawneh J, separate opinion, in *Land and Maritime Boundary Between Cameroon and Nigeria (Cameroon v Nigeria; Equatorial Guinea Intervening)* [ICJ] 2002, 196 para 5).

The principle of intertemporal law has been given selective interpretation in international civil proceedings. Germany acknowledgement of moral responsibility but denied that a legal obligation exists to pay reparations (Goldmann 2024: 580, 581). The principle of judging legally relevant circumstances according to the law contemporaneous to them disproportionately contributes to the hegemony of past and present powers in a quintessentially colonial dispute, according to Gruber. The legal assessment of closed questions like the creation of rights, is fixed in time, but the legal assessment of open questions concerns the continuing existence of rights or legal relationships, which evolve as the law evolves (Gruber 2019: 95). Huber made his pronouncement with regards to the law on territorial acquisition. Arguably, extending it to other contexts is justifiable only if international peace can be maintained. The principle of intertemporal law reproduces and fortifies colonial racism inscribed in European international law, but international law is less constricted on this point.

1.4.3 Cultural property protection in the shadow of a logic of brute force

What we know as cultural property today has been pivotal to war since ancient times. Cultural property and heritage are increasingly being promoted as a force of good, yet their capacity to become entangled in conflict is extraordinary. No region of the world remains unaffected by illicit traffic in cultural objects. Cultural property and heritage encompass large national and international sectors, emphasising the value of identity and belonging. Sacred places and relics frequently fall victim to religious bigotry, which fetishises, infantilises, vilifies, or degrades their associated cultures, or attempts to erase them from memory. When experienced as a direct attack by persons and groups on the place of belonging of the cultural property, its destruction can incite outrage (Rosén 2017: 14–15). Exceptionally strong identity-forming function may be assumed on the personal and community levels as was evident in respect of Timbuktu's manuscripts and mausoleums of the saints in Mali. Ahmad al-Faqi al-Mahdi led the destruction of key Muslim shrines inscribed as world heritage sites (*The Prosecutor v Ahmad Al Faqi Al Mahdi, Judgment and Sentence*, 27 September 2016, ICC-01/12-01/15 para 79). In 2012 militants damaged and removed the sacred door of the 15th century Sidi Yahya Mosque which was built for the ancient city's patron saint. The belief that the opening of the mosque door would herald the end of the world forms part of the Sufi-influenced form of Islam practised locally. The assault on the mosque was calculated to degrade the culture. Restoration was completed in September 2016, and in 2017 the ICC issued a reparations order (*The Prosecutor v Ahmad Al Faqi Al Mahdi, Judgment and Sentence*, 17 August 2017, ICC-CPI-20170817-PR1329).

Heritage has also come into sharper focus at the national level for its importance in collective memory and community identity. Nonetheless, issues of identity and the identity politics of the debate do not necessarily supply a conclusive explanation for conflict. René Noël Théophile Girard (1923–2015), French historian, literary critic, and philosopher of social science, wrote extensively on imitation as the initial and essential means of learning. He warned that while positive imitation may inspire identity, it may still cause extreme irresolvable conflict. 'Positive' mimetism cannot guarantee non-conflicting identity (Girard 2010: 44–45).

Globally, norms, laws, institutions, and the nature of conflict and war have superimposed new dimensions on the old patterns and frameworks. Preservation policies are increasingly firmly integrated into the bureaucracies of many modern states. Several NATO countries have invested big sums in the cultural sector and a plethora of international and non-governmental institutions have become involved in cultural property protection (Rosén 2017: 14). The UN General Assembly has adopted resolutions on the return or restitution of cultural property to the countries of origin, and the UN Security Council have started to address cultural property caught in the crosshairs of conflict and the looting and trafficking of antiquities as a source of terrorist financing. Chapter VII resolutions with respect to threats to peace, breaches of the peace, and acts of aggression constitute a new regime of norms that bind all nations. Resolution 2249 (2015) on terrorist attacks perpetrated by the Islamic State in Iraq and the Levant (ISIL) serves as an example. The developing global consciousness of their substantive themes lends normative and affective power to the urgency of cultural property protection. Unfortunately, the system of protection lacks balance. The Resolutions override the approaches which could have been unlocked if international criminal law and international humanitarian law had been used. The UN Charter confers primordial responsibility on the UN Security Council for the maintenance of international peace and security on behalf of a true international community, but the veto power is abused to permit members to wage war. The UN Charter contains no procedural guidance or an institutional exit point when the mandate and responsibility of the Security Council remain unfulfilled. Since the UNhas primary, but not exclusive, responsibility for international peace and security, states must act in coalition or take recourse to a regional platform. However, the inbuilt threat of blocking change by means of the veto exacerbates the wilful paralysis of the Security Council in the face of humanitarian crises and human rights emergencies. If the UN Charter is to fulfil its purpose of preventing a return to the 'Age of Empires,' a way must be found to rein in permanent members of the UN Security Council that subscribe to a 'might makes right' ethos. Arguably, when the intentional targeting of cultural heritage during armed conflict threatens peace and security, a moral responsibility arises to break out of an impossible legal framework.

UNESCO, a specialised agency of the UN, promotes culture and heritage as important sources of wellbeing and social cohesion in sustainable development. UNESCO's development projects are focused on generating jobs in heritage tourism to reduce poverty. Longer-term qualitative research on the diverse impact of heritage on wellbeing in development is considered less urgent. Recent philosophical discourse on heritage ethics engages with questions relating to norms and standards in the administration of culture in international law (e.g., Matthes

2017). Several empires disintegrated when independence movements emerged in the wake of the Second World War. Colonial situations did not necessarily cease when instruments of government were handed over and former demarcations were erased. On occasion, agreements on a process of transformation were reached between the rulers and the ruled, but for the most part, transitions were marked by protracted internal strife and violent revolutions. New historical narratives about the administration of culture in PublIL highlight that, even after newly independent countries joined the UN, problematic structures remained in place. No legal framework has emerged to address cultural property seizures (Spitra 2021: 138ff). Article 1 of the 1970 Convention on the Means of Prohibiting and Preventing the Illicit Import, Export and Transfer of Ownership of Cultural Property lists elements of artistic or historical monuments or archaeological sites which have been dismembered, antiquities more than one hundred years old, and objects of ethnological interest. Unfortunately, historic removals of cultural property are outwith its scope (Greenfield 2007: 369).

A crisis of violence erupted with acts of destruction against heritage considered 'idolatrous' by the Taliban, Daesh, and Ansar-Dine. International concern for the Bamiyan Buddhas (Afghanistan 2001), the Timbuktu Shrines (Mali 2012), and the Nabataean temples in Palmyra (Syria 2015/2016) multiplied and protective initiatives followed. Sadly, the publicity spurred non-state groups to weaponise the cultural heritage they associate with the international community as a provocation (Rosén 2017: 17ff). Counter-strategies kindled the interest of belligerents in the destruction of monuments and heritage. Discussion of the value of cultural property and the importance of protecting it motivate armed groups and terrorists to target it. For example, after the international community of states had raised the alarm over the invasion of Palmyra through various UN and UNESCO organs and committees, Daesh's propaganda material started referring to ancient sites that were being earmarked for attack. Sectarian iconoclasm does not provide a full explanation for the behaviour. Shifts in the Taliban's narrative about the Bamiyan statues made it difficult to pinpoint the real motive. Detonating explosives so heavy-handedly over several weeks seems to suggest that the desire to inflict damage became stronger as protective measures intensified.

The destruction of mosques, temples, sacred monuments, and museums is an aspect of extreme dehumanisation in non-international and international conflicts. States may exhibit a desire to deploy culture as an object of war, as the Russian invasion in Ukraine in 2022 demonstrates. Russia declared martial law and issued a special measures decree to confer the decorum of legal removals during its war of aggression on Ukraine. This crime is not yet part of the Statute of the International Criminal Court (ICC) and Russia is not a state that is party to the ICC Rome Statute. The conflict threatens museum collections in Ukrainian regions annexed on 30 September 2022. Russia and Africa are joining hands to 'complete the decolonisation process in Africa and ensure compensation for the economic and humanitarian damage inflicted on African States by colonial policies, including the restitution of cultural property displaced in the process of colonial plundering' (Declaration of the Second Russia–Africa Summit, 28 July 2023: para 14).

Russia's use of restitution of African cultural heritage to expand its influence in Africa can only accelerate global destabilisation.

The phenomena under discussion can be explained by the dynamics of mimetic competition. Law is bound up with war as much as it is with the process of peace. Girard theorised that the drive to get even has the status of a 'planetary principle'—it is literally consuming the planet (Girard 2010: 18, 39–44). Outbreaks of violence plague peaceful conditions, whereas the occasional ceasefire interrupts persistent conflicts only sporadically. He observed that the line between war and peace used to be clearly codified and 'ritualised' but became increasingly blurred after the French Revolution in 1789. Differentiating between war and peace becomes harder as regression festers and the legitimacy of the international community of states and organisations to contain the deepening crisis of violence in the world fades. Girard highlighted the immense ground mimetism has gained since 1945. Regardless of whether the world is hovering on the brink of a New Cold War, and Age of Unpeace, or slipping into another Age of Empires—mimetism is what fuels these conflicts. Mimestism gains normative significance whenever the 'logic of brute force' prevails over the rule of law.

1.4.4 The rule of law

The right or capacity to bring an action or to appear in court is 'a critical component of every litigation.' Access to justice and effective legal remedies are important building blocks in securing justice and respect for the rule of law. The essence of the rule of law in the Code of Hammurabi in Mesopotamia, which can be traced back to 2000 BC, was that the power of the ruling elite needed curbing and any ruler should be held accountable according to objective legal standards (in general Kowalski 2002: 29).

The 'rule of law' refers to basic constitutional and human rights principles that cover, for example, freedom from arbitrary arrest, torture and state killings, freedom from uncompensated expropriations, and freedom from state-sponsored arbitrary violence (Wood 2016: 53). Like the doctrine of the separation of powers, the rule of law supplies valuable background and context for the specific roles of the legislature, the executive, and the judiciary (in general Habermas 1996: 188–193). Approximating a universal idea, the rule of law has more appeal than a 'rule of restitution' as a demand for the rectification of historical injustice (Zeidler 2016: 97).

During the colonial era, the rule of law came to designate the rule of white settler governments in the interest of the white settlers. The very structure of international law presented opportunities, at central and decentralised levels, to influence the function of local law and the role assumed by domestic law. CLT contrasted law and morality along a 'rational' and 'non-rational' (religious) divide, effectively driving a wedge between law and morality in Europe. CLT's systematisation of the law was apparent in the distinction which British Indian colonial policy drew between the local law of domestic relationships, which were shown 'qualified respect' because it was perceived to be 'religious' law, and 'the law of the market,' for which they adopted a strongly interventionist policy that replaced the local traditional law and customs with the 'universal' law of the market (Kennedy 2010: 813, 838–839; Neidhardt 2018: 220). The distinction between law and morality was correlated to the basic dichotomy that derived from the primary division within private law, that is between patrimonial law, or the 'law of the market' governing economic relations, and family law governing domestic relations. Family law was a spontaneous social (moral) order that reflects the *Volksgeist* or spirit of the people. Most of the content of family law was considered not a matter of free will. Nominal respect was paid to the local family and religious law in the colonies of Great Britain, France, the Netherlands, Belgium, Germany, and the United States. When the courts in those states were asked to enforce precepts of family law, laws that would be different in every state would apply as 'exceptional' laws. Contrastingly, a firm insistence prevailed as to the universal private law of the market. The entire content of the law of contract was considered to derive from the abstract conception of a law of freedom (Kennedy 2010: 815–817, 836, 839).

The model of the 1998 Washington Conference Principles on Nazi-Confiscated Art is frequently upheld as an appropriate point of orientation for the restitution of colonial era cultural objects. Forty-four states expressed their commitment to reach 'fair and just solutions' (US State Department 1999). A handful of European states have established national committees and advisory panels on Jewish property spoliated during the Holocaust to implement these principles—Austria, France, Germany, the Netherlands, and the UK—and Germany is switching to an arbitration processes. According to the 2024 Best Practices for the Washington Conference Principles on Nazi-Confiscated Art, to enable restitution of art and cultural property that remains in state-owned collections and private hands, exceptions need to be made to barriers such as regulations against de-accessioning from state collections, statutes of limitations, market overt, usucapion (mode of acquiring title to property by uninterrupted possession for a definite period), good faith acquisition, and export bans (sub 'K'). The fragmentation in the legal framework that prevents any approach from one specific field of law, or one category of contested cultural objects, from providing the intended overview, led researchers to case-based approaches. Campfens' 2021 study on new directions for cross-border claims to cultural objects adopts Nazi-looted art as its point of focus because of the long-standing international practice this case study offers compared to the categories of archaeological material and material removed during the colonial era.

Restitution practice stems from the moral and ethical need to make repair because the legal provisions are found to be wanting (Labadie 2021: paras 28, 29). This does not mean that the 1998 Washington Conference Principles is a suitable ethical model to follow when it comes to the restitution of artefacts looted as colonial takings. Developments in respect of restitutionary claims for colonial era takings should take the rule of law and the complications it raises into account. More specifically, the role of secondary legal norms in regulating normative conflicts and market behaviour deserves more focused attention.

1.4.5 Normative conflicts in a context of ingrained inequality

In a long-standing ancient tradition, European merchants enjoyed special status under the institute of jurisdictional restrictions, concessions, and privileges granted by Asian countries to foreign merchants to pursue their way of life and govern themselves by their own law under the jurisdiction of the settlement head. By granting such concessions, the receiving country demonstrated hospitality, as these merchants were granted access to their markets without being forced to accept the territorial regime of the receiving ruler. Jurisdictional concessions used to be negotiated on an equal footing and on a reciprocal basis when African states were members of the Family of Nations. In the 19th century, however, such concessions and privileges started to be embodied in bilateral treaties. The 'capitulations' crept into the treaty provisions and the colonisers started to conceive of jurisdictional provisions that limited the sovereignty of the ruler as a signal of jurisdictional inferiority rather than the receiving country's hospitality. Jurisdictional provisions increasingly mirrored the prevailing (in)equality and the states of the Asian and African contracting parties. A wholesale takeover of jurisdiction marked the end of independence (Alexandrowicz 1973: 83, 91, 125).

Every time normative conflicts arose between western law and the Indigenous law in force in colonised territories, the impact of the capitulations would surface. Initially they functioned to balance the African customary law and tradition against the Eurocentric law but this function disappeared in due course. Some French treaties left it to the African rulers to decide mixed trade disputes (purchases and sales). The treaties of protection between Germany and Rulers in SWA went further, introducing mixed courts for mixed disputes (e.g., 1885 Treaty with Maharero). Colonial courts also had the option of referring disputes to the ruler for decisions that were subject to an appeal to higher European authority (the European consul or governor had jurisdiction over civil and criminal disputes between Europeans in African states). Consular courts were competent to hear cases involving foreign parties sharing the same nationality, and the nationality of the defendant or accused determined their judicial authority (known as the *actor sequitur forum rei* principle). When western states were unwilling to accept the jurisdiction of ordinary local courts over their nationals who had to defend their interests or plead their innocence, an alternative to consular jurisdiction had to be found. For example, mixed courts could function with the assistance of local adjudicators and assessors when legal conflicts brought before them were not exclusively related to one local or foreign resident population, but as soon as the 'foreign' element of a dispute was defined broadly, jurisdiction would overlap. European powers were averse to the risk of a potentially destabilising effect on their interests, and consequently they were reluctant to apply African law in commercial cases. They were uncertain whether doing so would expand commerce in their favour (Alexandrowicz 1973: 85–90).

Colonial interpretations of normative conflicts between western law and customary law differentiated law and morals. CLT accommodated the odious notion that the validity of law did not depend on its being moral, but rather on its being readily identifiable. If the sole requirement for law is that a formal test must be met for the establishment of a rule by a government elected by the people, any precepts lending legitimacy to conquest, dispossession, the expansion and internationalisation of the colonial territories, their exclusion and their nonrecognition, could also constitute law. The commissioners and consultants who worked on the transformation and codification of the legal systems in the colonies were the leading thinkers of their day. Sir Henry Maine (1822–1888) was one of the commissioners tasked with codifying the Indian legal system. The text that distinguished him as a leading comparative jurist and historian was *Ancient Law*, published during the Victorian era (Maine 1861). The differentiation between the 'rational' and the 'religious' manifests in Maine's adherence to the East India Company's approach of leaving religious and family law unchanged unless they contravened 'natural justice.' The position was very different in commercial, contract, criminal, and procedural law, which was codified based on the general categories of the will theory (i.e., based on either private law or public law; Kennedy 2010: 838). To consolidate the system of colonial subordination and facilitate the implementation of their colonial objectives, many colonial legal systems operated on selectivity *ratione personae* and *ratione materiae* (Schuerch 2017: 43). The rigorous, highly advanced taxonomies developed by German legal scholars contributed in distinctive ways. However, the relationship between the national (or 'internal') and international (or 'external') spheres in which legal disputes arise now calls for study beyond the parameters of western conflict of laws systems alone.

The simplification of the methods used in an internal conflicts context caused injustices in Europe and America, bringing into view the pressure points which internal conflicts (of law) create for material removed during the colonial era. The status of Indigenous societies can go entirely unacknowledged in internal normative conflicts of law if their claims are considered a threat to the interests of an erstwhile colonial power. For instance, the genocide in German SWA succeeded in rendering irrelevant the customs and law of the cultural communities whose voices were silenced. In the official 1918 British report about German colonial rule in SWA, *Union of South Africa: Report on the Natives of South-West Africa and their Treatment by Germany*, which contained evidence of German treatment of the local population in the 20th century, it was intimated that '[i]t is not necessary to deal with Berg-Damara customs and laws, as they were not a ruling people at the time of the German annexation and made no protection agreement…' (Silvester and Gewald 2003: 184). The 'Blue Book' report of recorded testimonies of Africans depicting graphic evidence of German abuses during the war of 1904–1908 compounded Germany's humiliating defeat (Botha 2007: 14). Its re-issue in 2004 after a long history of suppression was criticised as a deficient historical methodology that would only serve to inflame passions and unravel relations that were reconstructed in the post-1950 period between Germans and Herero (Botha 2007: 45).

States manage the complex relationship between culture and the state in distinctive ways. A pluralist paradigm readily garners support if national human rights charters recognise culture as a constitutional right and provide protection of the culture of vulnerable groups. A cultural rights paradigm avoids debates over the legality of past takings that draw on the doctrine of intertemporal law and the principle of non-retrospectivity (Stahn 2023: 390). Rules that are 'gatekeepers to the past' are found in cultural heritage conventions, international human rights instruments, in PublIL and PrIL. The hurdles posed by the time factor manifest in the non-retrospectivity principle and the intertemporal rule, which establish distance between past and present and form a legal barrier between them (Stahn 2023: 347, 362). Prominent among these rules are the non-retrospective nature of international instruments in the domain of cultural heritage so that cultural property and heritage conventions cannot be applied to an act committed before they came into force. Such rules are readily selected for application in international civil litigation. Invoking these rules and doctrines that regulate the effect of time on a claim and limits law's reach in time enables courts to skirt around the problem posed by old wrongs. Uncritical, romanticised ideas about pre-colonial law and Indigenous world views are not constructive, but counterpoint arguments inform one's reading of the law as it relates to complex colonial histories. The lack of research on international civil claims for restitution and repatriation of ethnographic material in public and private collections means that any ethic of responsiveness in PrIL has remained hidden.

Respect for the human rights of peoples who were deprived of their historical record and culture has not been achieved, but it would be fair to say that human rights doctrine enjoys a firmer foothold than PrIL approaches do. PrIL fails to resolve many of the group-specific problems that can undermine the ability of groups to proceed with claims, both within their composite political unit and internationally (Last 2007: 123, 131, 133–134). Communities that have not transferred the authority to represent their interests to the political bodies of the state into which they are integrated, may assume an adverse position in relation to the state in question. This potential is reduced for Native Americans in the United States and the First Nations in Canada who are organised as institutions which have been granted authority that corresponds with this status (DMB *Care of Collections* 2021: 22).

Groups whose community interest requires protection may need to litigate their cultural rights in European courts. Claimants would be required to demonstrate injury or imminent injury to a cultural right; that it is likely, as opposed to speculative, that the injury is traceable to the challenged action of the defendant; and that a favourable court decision will redress the injury (Gilbert and Sena 2018: 207). Among the factors that undermine the potential of legal systems to resolve disputes and provide remedies are limited access to legal resources; the interpretative approach of local courts; lack of clarity in substantive areas of the law that may be pertinent to the outcome of cases; whether deprived owners can identify competent legal representatives; and whether any remedy is available. Because group interests are not considered to align with the interests of title holders, adjudicatory responses to title claims involving material and sacred cultural heritage rarely recognise the legal interest that can secure *locus standi* in civil proceedings when true owners institute restitutory actions against possessors for the immediate return of their property. Standing to sue is connected to people's access to and experience of their culture. The French court accorded standing to the non-profit organisation Association Survival International France in the Hopi Masks cases but denied it to the Hopi Masks, which the court classified in aesthetic terms as art objects (*Hopi Tribe v Néret-Minet and Estimations Ventes aux Enchères*, Tribunal de Grande Instance de Paris, Interim Order, 27 June 2014, No. RG 14/55733; Tribunal de Grande Instance de Paris, Interim Order, 06 December 2013, No. RG 13/59110). The courts in Hawaii denied standing to Mokapu remains under the NAGPRA and common law (*Na Iwi O Na Kupuna I Mokapu v Dalton* 894 F Supp 1397 D Haw 1995, 1406–1408). Redefining sacred materials primarily as art objects facilitates their commodification and promotes an analysis that looks to this commodification as merely another phase in their life cycles in a global capitalist market (Conaty 2015: 82).

Access to court can impede a claimant's progress. Other obstacles that may arise in a PrIL context are: a) securing competent legal representation; b) impediments to the exercise of jurisdiction on the merits of a case due to prescription, statutory limitations, decisions not to prosecute; c) gaps in information arising as in the 'Blue Book' example referred to earlier; d) obstacles that manifest during the court process in relation to standing; and e) obstacles external to the court process that may prevent the enforcement of a foreign judgment.

The facts of the Zhanggong Zushi Buddha Mummy case span China, Hong Kong, and the Netherlands. The normative conflict manifested at the level of the proceedings, which were instituted in China and the Netherlands, and at the level of classification and choice-of-law rules. Where cultural heritage is at stake, it is common for arguments to turn on private law commercial interests or PrIL, but human rights arguments may be roped in.

The Sanming Court in China, which was approached first but released its ruling after proceedings were instituted in parallel in Amsterdam, held that the statue in question was the same one that was stolen from Yangchun village in China (San Min Chu Zi 2020). The parties did not object to the facts as stated at trial. The date in the official transcript of the Sanming court stipulates that the theft took place on 14 December 1995. These facts were confirmed by the People's Higher Court (Min Min Final 2022: sub 'Trial court ruling'). It acknowledged the village committees as legitimate plaintiffs with standing to pursue their claim cross-border to demand the return of their stolen relic from the possessor (Min Min Final 2022: sub 'Trial court ruling'). The Amsterdam District Court denied the village committees the right to proceed with their action. The court effectively circumvented a determination as to whether the group interest required protection. It dismissed the village committees' claim and issued a cost order against the claimants (Min Min Final 2022: sub 'Trial court's fact findings' paras 15, 16). Confusingly, the defendant, private collector Oscar van Overeem, denied that the statue in question was the same one stolen from Yangchun during the Amsterdam proceedings.

This study analyses the PrIL method which the Chinese courts followed to achieve the restitution order in the normative conflicts that prevailed in the case.

1.5 Potential legal bases for claims

A clear positive law basis for return is not always available as there is no one-size-fits-all prohibition of depletion of cultural material during colonial rule in the international law of the 19th and 20th centuries. The quest to find an appropriate legal basis for the restitution of human remains and looted cultural heritage continues to bring scholars to investigate (a) critical moral standards; (b) conventions; (c) customary international law; (d) *jus cogens*, and (e) rights-based frameworks including a human rights model. The litigious potential of the safeguarding of intangible cultural heritage has not attracted systematic attention, but it is vital not to undermine it (Hance 2020b: 178). Art historians, anthropologists, and archaeologists recognise the added layer of meaning that sacred object possess, but legal systems only exceptionally distinguish such objects clearly. Sacred objects remain altogether undistinguished as a class from the greater category of cultural objects in French law and adjudication. This situation permits sales of historical materials with technically accurate provenance to proceed unhindered. Unless sacred objects are given a proper legal definition, the gap between the sacred and material worlds will remain (Hai 2013: 217).

1.5.1 Critical moral standards

Law cannot create universal moral rights. Law can only recognise, modulate, and turn moral rights into human rights in the strict sense when conditions for doing so are favourable (Besson 2011: 245). Human rights are critical moral standards that are inherently legal, and they alsohave political and ethical dimensions. The 'complex normative practice' of human rights combines all these elements (Besson 2011: 215, 217).

As international law, human rights require the consent of states. Numerous vaguely defined rights grant governments considerable discretion to ignore or prioritse groups of rights in the well-known and widely ratified human rights treaties (e.g., the Universal Declaration of Human Rights; International Covenant on Civil and Political Rights; International Covenant on Economic, Social and Cultural Rights; European Convention for the Protection of Human Rights and Fundamental Freedoms; International Convention on the Suppression and Punishment of the Crime of Apartheid of 1973; UN Declaration on the Rights of Indigenous Peoples or 'UNDRIP' A/RES/61/295, 13 Sep 2007). Enforcement mechanisms in international human rights instruments are generally weak (Chechi 2013: 185).

It is conceivable to consider cultural heritage claims in terms of human rights norms, for cultural rights are grounded in existing norms and principles within a wider human rights system (Byrne 2015: 8; see e.g., Article 1.1 and Article 15.1 of the International Covenant on Economic, Social and Cultural Rights, 16 December 1966, 993 UNTS 3; International Covenant on Civil and Political Rights, 16 December 1966, 999 UNTS 171; General Comment No. 21 on the Right of Everyone to Take Part in Cultural Life, adopted by the Committee on Economic, Social and Cultural Rights at the Forty-third Session, E/C.12/GC/21,

21 December 2009). Rights associated with cultural rights include freedom of expression, freedom of thought, conscience and religion, the right to education, economic rights, and the right to development (articles 18, 26–27 UDHR; articles 18–19 ICCPR, articles 9–10 ECHR; articles 1–2 Protocol 1; articles 13, 15 ICESCR; International Convention on the Suppression and Punishment of the Crime of Apartheid of 1973 1015 UNTS 243; and the UNDRIP). Peoples have a right to determine their own priorities and to reject external impositions. Cultural rights-claims and policies of multicultural accommodation are not all 'group rights' in any meaningful sense. Levy contends that they can be 'disaggregated and clustered' into component parts that include exemptions from generally applicable laws, assistance afforded by states to allow a minority to take part in the same activities as the majority, e.g., in respect of the recognition and enforcement of customary law, self-government, external restrictions on the activity of outsiders who might weaken a community, internal restrictions on what members of a community may do and still remain members, representation, and claims for symbolic recognition (Levy 2000: 127). Developing cultural rights through adjudication and scholarly analysis is among the least explored areas of human rights law (David 2020: xiv).

In Africa, Indigenous peoples' rights are perceived to be in their infancy due to the delayed adoption of the UNDRIP by a group of African states. The UNDRIP accommodates conceptions of ownership and repatriations based on the communal or spiritual value of objects (Stahn 2023: 49). The standards of behaviour embodied in it are UN standards that have moral force for every state in its relations with Indigenous peoples.Domestic law reform can be measured against these standards. While the UNDRIP's normative effect is indisputable, many African states remain reluctant to recognise the specific rights of Indigenous peoples and European authorities are quick to highlight the 'non-binding' status of the UNDRIP (Gilbert 2011: 246; Thielecke and Geißdorf 2021: 161, espousing that the UNDRIP does not prescribe return of cultural property in the 2021 DMB Guidelines on *Care of Human Remains in Museums and Collections*).

1.5.2 Conventions

The primary norms of property law have not been the subject of encompassing harmonisation. Because the distinctive features of individual European property law systems are not easily set aside for the sake of promoting European integration, the PrIL drive for harmonisation in the EU has not met with success in respect of property law. The quality of the transposition of a convention's standards and priorities into domestic law can mean the difference between success and failure for a claim. For example, the ambiguous status of treaties in domestic law can lead to a situation where the ratification of a convention produces a discrepancy between domestic and international law, creating ongoing uncertainty. The challenges relating to the time factor, highlighted earlier, have not been surmounted either.

1.5.3 Customary international law

Customary international law on returns evolved from—or in parallel to—the conventions on cultural property and heritage. To determine whether and when binding international obligations have emerged, there must be evidence of a customary, general state practice accepted as a legally binding obligation. Customary international law is notoriously difficult to identify (Liu 2016: 67). The 'Venus of Cyrene' case illustrates the principles of customary international law interacting to give rise to a legal obligation in international law to undertake return of cultural objects removed because of war and colonisation. Italy declared war against the Ottoman Empire in 1911. The colonial occupation by Italy lasted until 1943. Italian troops found a headless marble sculpture, later identified as a Roman copy of a Greek masterpiece of the goddess Venus, which was taken to Italy in 1915. In 1989, decades after Libyan independence (in 1951), the Libyan government requested that the Palazzo Massimo Museum in Rome return the Venus. The resulting case, which closed litigation on the matter, was the first reparation claim and the first formal apology since the end of the colonial era. Italy's legal obligation to return the 'Venus of Cyrene' to Libya was affirmed by the *Consiglio*, the Supreme Administrative Court of Italy, a body that ensures the legality of public administration in Italy (*Associazione Nazionale Italia Nostra Onlus v Ministero per i Beni e le Attività Culturali et al.*, Consiglio di Stato, No. 3154, 23 June 2008). The 'Venus' was returned to the Cyrene Sculpture Museum in Shahhat, Libya, where barely five years later, during the Arab Spring in 2013, it was looted. Nonetheless, the decision is a sound example of a general and autonomous customary principle that has crystallised as the corollary of the interplay between two principles of customary international law—the prohibition of the threat or use of force enshrined in article 2.4 of the UN Charter, and the right to self-determination of peoples in articles 1.2 and 55 of the UN Charter. The international instruments and soft law that shape the principle of self-determination interact with the prohibition of use of force, producing an autonomous customary principle that a legal obligation exists to restitute cultural heritage taken from colonies. The Italian government did not oppose the return in court. The historical wrongs committed during the occupation were not referred to in the Treaty of Friendship, Partnership and Cooperation which Italy concluded with the Great Socialist People's Arab Jamahiriya (Law No. 2 of 1377 FDP/2009 AD). Adjudicators must consult both the formal and informal sources of PublIL to decide on the merits of restitution claims.

Customary international law proscribes pillage during military expeditions and protects cultural heritage in armed conflict. However, while domestic legal systems have criminalised theft and robbery, neither the PCIJ nor the ICJ have adjudicated cases that attest to the unlawfulness of pillage as a general principle of law. Neither court has applied such principles directly in interstate cases. An objective moral consensus concerning the ownership of cultural property and heritage across cultures could become a legally binding norm to restitute cultural heritage taken from colonies, but the existence of such a norm has not been convincingly argued and this makes its meaning hard to gauge (Liu 2016: 68–69). Absent a clear conception of a duty to return colonial era loot to the deprived owner or community, an expectation that the ICJ will uphold the principle that cultural heritage wrongfully acquired should be returned, may be unrealistic. To take the Parthenon Marbles dispute to the ICJ might also be counter-productive when there has not been a case in either a Greek or English court. A legal precedent that could destroy Greece's hope of recovery would be too devastating. Lauterpacht cautions states to avoid international litigation as far as possible because of the high risk of uncertain and unpredictable results, and because, in the absence of a rule that the loser pays the winner's costs, proceedings will be costly (Lauterpacht 2009: 485–487).

In the 19th century, the 'sentiments and usages of civilised nations' qualified as international law (Wheaton 1866: para 15). The conviction that a practice has normative effect as a rule of positive law—*opinio juris*—had not yet crystallised as a separate requirement for the formation of customary international law before that (Zhang 2021: 1107). Over time, the importance ascribed to *opinio juris* increased. The 1945 Statute of the ICJ considers the statements and practice emanating from a state about the normativity of a rule of positive law (Article 38(1)(b); Liu 2016: 66). Instruments embodying such rules have accumulated steadily since 1860.

Commentators have considered the type of evidence that would support a conclusion that there is a state practice of returns confirming the existence of a legal duty to respect and restore ownership of cultural property removed from territories during periods of dependence (Siehr 1994: 156–157). International state practice is evidenced in the normative declarations of states; duties states have assumed under cultural property conventions that acknowledge the special nature of (certain) cultural property; statements made by international bodies and scholars; and international instruments and any other materials used to determine which rules of international law apply to a given situation. Determining exactly when a customary international law rule prohibiting pillage of cultural objects during armed conflicts came into existence can be challenging. There is authority for the argument that Germany's appropriations of sacred cultural objects from Cameroon after its 1899 annexation violates contemporary customary international law and lawful state conduct (Campfens 2019: 91, 95). Scholars remain divided on whether a customary law obligation exists with respect to returns. Without referring expressly to the 'sacred,' Titi asserts that the international legal framework for the protection of cultural property has evolved to the point where returning the Parthenon Marbles to Greece is required on several distinct legal grounds. A former colony could raise a restitution claim on the basis that the restoration of ownership in such cases is a general practice accepted as law or a binding authoritative rule. Alternatively, a restitution claim might be based on the removal being in breach of binding rules of customary international law (ILC 2001 Draft Articles on Responsibility of States for Internationally Wrongful Acts). These bases and standards are evolving towards a minimum harmonised standard for States party to international instruments and those participating in standard-setting to implement in domestic law.

Titi expresses doubt over whether museum activity contributes to state practice (Titi 2023: 265–266, 275, 304). Given that repatriation practice provides a good indicator of the recognition of cultural rights, and that ethical codes and policy guidelines supply information on this practice, it is fair to say that museum practice acts as an indicator of the extent to which recognition is given to cultural rights (Byrne 2015). Best practice and ethical guidelines for museums can contribute towards a reasonable outcome in so-called 'hard cases', for moral philosophy can support the weighing exercise needed in these cases. A 'hard case' may arise when legal principles conflict; *lex* (rules) and *jus* (principles) are at odds; values expressed in primary legal principles or rules clash but evaluation or judgment is still necessary; the facts of a case are contentious and necessitate incommensurate values represented by principles to be weighed up; the concepts at issue in a case are 'essentially contested concepts' (i.e., concepts that characteristically admit of substantive disagreements that cannot be settled to everyone's satisfaction); or clashing systems of knowledge claim application (Zeidler 2016: 90). The 'surplus' of legal principles beyond statutory regulation (e.g., legal precedent) could enable rational, just, equitable and suitable decisions (*ius*); an unjust law is no law at all (*lex iniustissima non est lex*) (Zeidler 2016: 24).

1.5.4 **Jus cogens**

Peremptory norms of general international law, or *jus cogens*, are defined as 'a norm accepted and recognised by the international community of States as a whole as a norm from which no derogation is permitted and which can be modified only by a subsequent norm of general international law having the same character' (Article 53 of the Vienna Convention on the Law of Treaties, 23 May 1969). A treaty is void if, at the time of its conclusion, it conflicts with a peremptory norm of general international law. Treaties that contravene any aspect of these qualifying standard-setting norms would be rendered void. Nullification extends to all lesser norms in national law, treaty law or customary international law that directly conflict with peremptory norms or that are otherwise inconsistent (O'Connell 2011: 97). States' attempts to derogate from them or dispense with them in ordinary interstate transactions are futile. A claim for reparation for injury by restitution, compensation or satisfaction may be mounted based on higher moral or ethical norms in the international legal community that constitute *jus cogens* (O'Connell 2011: 78, 85–86). These higher norms differ from the larger category of human rights in important respects. The following have been marked as *jus cogens* in case law: prohibitions of acts of aggression, genocide, protection from slavery, arbitrary killing or causing the disappearance of individuals, systemic acts of racial discrimination, Apartheid, and torture (O'Connell 2011: 97).

International criminal law is the body of public international law that establishes individual criminal responsibility for international crimes. The framework of international criminal law is not tailored to the enforcement of obligations arising from colonialism. Unlike war crimes, crimes against humanity may occur in situations without armed conflict and they do not require the special intent that is necessary for establishing genocide. Nonetheless, there is little scope to categorise colonialism as an 'international crime' in legal interpretation. The brutality committed by German colonial authorities against the Herero and Nama between 1904 and 1908 violated the 1864 Red Cross Convention on the Amelioration of the Condition of the Wounded in Armies in the Field, amounted to war crimes under the 1899 Hague Convention (II), and constituted the first 'genocide'. Imperial Germany acted in violation of its duties under international law which, in 1904, formed part of its domestic law, yet the Hague Convention applied only between signatory states; neither the Herero nor the Nama was a state party. As a result, these communities lack capacity to raise claims against Germany based on the convention. When a successor state refuses to restore dispersed cultural property removed by its predecessor, a normative gap arises. A lack of standing cannot render the actions of German forces lawful, but the payment of reparations would require modern-day Germany to admit that imperial Germany committed genocide.

While there is no case law confirming that colonialism violates *jus cogens* and amounts to a crime against humanity, the content of *jus cogens* has shifted over time with the addition of the non-applicability of statutes of limitations to crimes against humanity (*Almonacid-Arellano et al.* Judgment of 26 September 2006 IACHR Series C No. 154) and the right of access to justice (*La Cantuta v Peru*, Merits, Reparations and Costs, Judgment of 29 November 2006 IACHR Series C No. 162: para 160). There are no conclusive findings as to the *jus cogens* status of the right to self-determination. As matters stand, states remain duty-bound not to knowingly assist other states in the perpetuation of internationally wrongful acts, or risk being found complicit in breaching international law (Article 16). The supposition that the right of peoples to recover their appropriated cultural heritage, or that a recently developed peremptory norm could be applied to events in the distant past, will garner different responses however (e.g., Liu 2016: 60–61). The implications of the philosophical starting point of the discourse are seldom recognised or anticipated in scholarly commentary, and this keeps the contemporary debate about the nature and consequences of legal norms with elevated status in the shallows. A legal idealist and a positivist will disagree about the explanation for the existence of the *jus cogens* category.

A legal positivist might view the *jus cogens* regime as establishing a hierarchical relationship among rules. Idealists who agree that *jus cogens* norms are located at the top-end of a hierarchy of values might be more open to the suggestion that, by their very nature, these are ethical norms that constrain the will of states or define the limits of acceptable state behaviour in national law just as public policy does when it operates in national law (O'Connell 2011: 85). These norms derive from legal ideals that may undergo modification over time (Linderfalk 2020: 13–14, 95).

There will also be disagreement on the role of state consent in the creation and modification of *jus cogens* norms. The true *loci* of the consensus needs to be established, and one's viewpoint regarding the function of the jus cogens norms—whether to execute the will of states, or to constrain it—will affect one's conception of which norms qualify, the criteria by which they are differentiated from norms of general international law, and what their consequences are. The 1969 Vienna Convention denies the retrospective effect of *jus cogens*. When a new peremptory norm of general international law comes into existence under Article 64, it does not create a retrospective assumption of responsibility (Article 72 (2) (b)).

1.5.5 Rights-based frameworks

Cultural rights appear at first blush to constitute a ground on which a community could petition for entitlements while full recognition in international law is not yet guaranteed. Since the Second World War, efforts to promote peace through international cultural collaboration have emphasised group rights to dispersed cultural property as a distinctive part of the human rights regime (Jakubowski 2015: 138). Nonetheless, culture is not a 'bottom-line entitlement' and the right to culture is not an international norm. Whilst the right of a cultural community to be fully human or to have their cultural objects returned may be advocated for, advocacy does not create an enforceable right or even one that can always be successfully asserted. Cultural rights continue to be shaped by an 'evolving mix of practice, soft law, textual reinterpretation and political philosophy' (Muir Watt 2014: 369). Joel Paul, law professor and author, highlights the deception that was at work when European colonial powers offered Indigenous peoples 'culture' and Christianity in exchange for land and wealth (Paul 2003: 920). He argues that, when states seek to create cultural exceptions to international legal norms, they necessarily privilege the traditions, values, and practices of one subgroup over another within the same territory, with the likely result of empowering elites to impose their values over disenfranchised groups. Scholarship on the link between cultural rights and the protection of cultural property and heritage is under-developed (Byrne 2015: 4, 6; Logan 2007: 33). International cultural heritage law and international human rights law are distinct areas of international law as far as binding legal instruments are concerned. New perspectives and narratives are now starting to draw them together (e.g., Hance 2020a: 81ff). Additionally, assumptions that the jurisdictional framework of circulation is the only operational framework worth considering will prevent realistic conclusions being drawn at the interface between the protection of cultural heritage, and the imperialist and colonial legacy within which international cultural heritage law is embedded.

In domestic contexts, cultural rights may evolve to form integrated frameworks of rights to culture. Museum practice around repatriation claims is typically a space in which the right to culture can be realised. The right to culture must be petitioned for, and claimants depend on decisions of the political machinery (which includes museums) that confers rights (Matthews 2014: 130). Culture mandates may incorporate numerous aspects at state, social, and private levels, from the individual to peoples' collective right to their own cultural wealth. Their protection is achievable when infrastructure and sufficient resources exist to give a voice to the voiceless and meet commitments to donors and the public, but their recognition and protection are suppressed where robust non-discrimination models and public measures that protect and promote cultural identity are absent. The responsibilities and duties placed on distributors of knowledge that bridge nature and culture, sciences, and humanities, such as museums and educational institutions in the service of the entire society, presuppose the power and responsibility to help prevent social and cultural collapse (Janes 2022: 736). Institutions that engage with cultural rights and undertake education in this area are better placed to avert a mimetic crisis than those that promote collecting and research (Byrne 2015: 7, 27).

A principal point of orientation for the western world is private ownership and the control it offers. Libertarian property law is constructed on a rights-based property paradigm that foregrounds individual liberties. Located on a property rights spectrum, legal traditions reflect varied approaches to property shaped by context, ideology, and philosophy. Distinctive histories, cultures and 'family traits' affect what may be considered 'tangible' or 'intangible.' The spectrum runs from the full and exclusive control of private owners that entitles them to treat cultural property as chattels to the wholesale preclusion of private ownership of cultural objects. Broadly conceived, rights-based Euro-American property law frameworks resonate with two theories of private property. The first considers property a *pre social* notion, or a natural right expressing the rights of persons that existed prior to the state and law (e.g., the natural law theorist Hugo Grotius). The second theory considers property a *social* notion, or a positive right created instrumentally by community, state, or law to achieve other goals (e.g., utilitarians such as Jeremy Bentham, and legal sociologists such as Emile Durkheim (1885–1917) and Max Weber (1864–1920); Panesar 2000: 113). Based on the understanding that, even when objects of cultural significance belong to a private person, a collective interest based on the significance of the objects or collection prevails, the social theory imposes a duty of care on owners of cultural heritage resources to protect and preserve them in the public interest, limiting their ownership rights (Lixinski 2019a: 58ff). The common responsibility they engender does not equate to these resources being owned by everyone. Uncoupled from responsibilities, the existence of rights could become hard to explain, and so the relationship between rights and obligations requires analysis.

The relationship between facts, customs, and the function of property rights can be difficult to discern clearly in restitution claims. The term 'right' tends to be used generically and indiscriminately to denote any sort of legal advantage, rather than narrowly as the correlative of duty, conveying the same meaning as a 'claim' (Cook ed. 1923: 14, 71). The concept of 'right' has several meanings as is evidenced by the theory of property as a bundle of 'rights,' which includes claims (of non-interference), liberties (to use), powers (to transfer the property rights partly or fully), and immunities (to escape from another's legal power) (Van Hoecke 2015: 1). When exceptions to more general prohibitions may be claimed, 'privileges' are at work. The sum of rights, privileges, powers, and immunities which a legal person has in relation to tangible and intangible things may imply a concomitant duty in everyone else to stay off, not use, not exercise a privilege. However, one person's right does not invariably imply an absolute obligation for others. Certain privileges or liberties imply correlatives that would be more accurately described as 'no-rights' or 'no-privileges' (Cook ed. 1923: 36–50). More precise usage of the term 'right' would benefit the development of law and the solution of legal problems. This would require differentiation between the sub-concepts of 'right' and its correlatives and opposites.

Contemporary legal thought simply separates public and private property and does not recognise cultural property and heritage as a separate de jure category, unlike the Roman legal tradition that recognised the separate categorisation of cultural heritage within cultural property. In western conceptions cultural property is inclusive of cultural heritage and things kept in museum collections. Limitations on private and public ownership are important in the modern western conception. Euro-American property law frameworks are based on rights, whereas libertarian property law foregrounds individual liberties, limiting state activity to protective and guarantor functions. An example of the latter is the view that a state can justify the imposition of narrow protections against force, fraud, and theft, among other things but anything more extensive would violate people's rights (Nozick 1974: 149, 162). Limitations on private ownership of cultural heritage resources are necessary when ownership undermines the cultural rights that serve a group's self-determination, while limitations on public ownership are needed when access or use favours select sectors of society.

At the European law level, the basic understanding is that common property belongs to all and must be protected and managed in the general interest (Bailey 2013: 107ff). The cultural property of Indigenous communities is fully articulated, however, at the domestic tribal law level. They find it difficult to regain control of their heritage without utilising the mechanisms of western property law. The dilemma is that property is a right that excludes, rather than incorporates, marginalised groups and Indigenous communities from heritage governance (Lixinski 2019a: 64). Citizens of a state or members of a community of villagers may have group claims to control their heritage, but the property law framework may lend ontological primacy to the claimant or dispossessed owner while failing to acknowledge identifiable group interests in property and heritage, such as those based on religion or history, political boundaries, language, or ethnicity. Communities brought together by spiritual tradition are challenged by property law in a similar way; they must contend with legal frameworks that compromise the safeguarding and exercise of their religious rights at state, group, and individual levels.

Objects that are under legal protection to safeguard the interests of future generations embody social good. They are likely to possess qualities that justify the imposition of limits on the rights of private owners in a western paradigm. In repatriation claims generated by historical and personal injustice, persons may plead rights in respect of things, such as ownership rights (Matthews 2014: 121, 129). Anthropologists have warned against object-beings being 'caught up' in repatriation when rights-based frameworks are used as a basis. In the case of sacred objects or stones and object-beings, their intangible qualities render the exclusive private property rights that exist in high art and other collection items inappropriate (Zeidler 2016: 13, 54, 87). Asserting rights over object-beings as 'things' in ownership claims may offend the cultural and religious beliefs of communities that use them in ceremonies. Even if the physical material is not fully representative of the associated ritual or ceremonial practice, its intangible qualities do not replace its tangible dimension. A rights-framework may also suppress the potential of communities to act in accordance with an Indigenous cultural understanding that no person exists without, or before, their culture. However, eschewing the conceptions of property in restitution claims can be to the detriment of claimants because success often hinges on them. Property law is a valuable starting point in international heritage law to reconceptualise heritage as an integral part of property and of culture (Lixinski 2019a: 61). In the interest of universality, heritage discourses at the level of international law push the mechanisms of property law into the background, but this supposedly more universal discourse may end up serving the needs of an expert-driven conservation paradigm which fails to support Indigenous populations who prioritise the life and use of 'sacred' material over conservation. Consequently, Indigenous communities find it challenging to comply with conditions accompanying repatriation of cultural material. Abandoning 'property' from restitution discourses does not always benefit marginalised communities or promote their participation in decision-making in heritage management, for pushing the mechanisms of property law into the background may block them from assessing which heritage is worth safeguarding (Lixinski 2019a: 50, 57, 64). Therefore, 'property' remains an important yardstick connecting the values of international heritage discourse to the needs of people on the ground. Rather than skirting around conceptions of property, its foundations should be revisited as they relate to heritage in certain contexts (Lixinski 2019a: 27, 64). There is also a general need to recover the narratives about the role of heritage vis-à-vis property and of property (Lixinski 2019b: 585).

Lixinski's proposals are not specifically tailored to the restitution debate. They consider primary legal norms. If cultural heritage denoted simply what a nation's laws qualified as 'owned' or what legally required export approval, a rights framework might be satisfactory, yet many repatriation claims demonstrate there is more to cultural heritage than legal questions about property rights. An added complication is how easily issues of cultural heritage are easily co-opted to fit larger narratives in complex colonial histories. Issues of repatriation have much in common with legal concepts in personal injury law. The question as to with whom culture heritage 'belongs' makes traditional concepts of property law seem remote at best (Shapiro 1998: 99).

There is scholarly support for switching to a human rights framework in restitution and repatriation (e.g., Campfens 2021: 3). A human rights law model enjoys strong support based on the hope that the method will, directly or indirectly, provide standards in cases that concern communal (often sacred) cultural objects. The human rights model turns the focus to: (i) a continuing cultural link (also: cultural affiliation) and not only on a loss in the past; (ii) on sub-state actors as independent right holders (indigenous peoples and communities); and (iii) on differentiated rights of access, control, or return that depend on the identity value at stake (Campfens 2021: 233). The western property framework and 'modern museum-as-lender' perspective may expect a collection item to be returned to a museum. To realise cultural rights, however, assurances must be given that Indigenous protocols will be observed. Sharing culturally sensitive information or putting sacred material on display might transgress the cultural protocols of and disrespect the communities to which they belong.

Ethical codes, policy guidelines, and recommendations that support restitution and repatriation indicate that cultural rights are recognised but the realisation of cultural rights may depend on communities' access to the cultural institutions that hold their ceremonial objects and to interact with or re-incorporate them in ceremonial use. Heritage can confirm and communicate identity. It contributes to self-understanding forming one's identity and connecting with the past. Access to cultural objects, historic sites, memorials, museums, preservation efforts, and other forms of cultural heritage supports the development of a sense of self, reminding individuals and communities where they come from and the culture of which they are a part. Missing or misrepresented heritage is bound to leave the collective memory worse off. However, the reasons behind claims indicate that more than identity is at stake. Claims may be brought to complete the historical record; transmit culture to future generations; reverse the legacy of imperialism; decide on the preservation of the item and its surviving context; or optimise gains that can be achieved only once fragmentation no longer drains the material of their meaning (Soirila 2022: 13 ff; Audi 2007: 145). Furthermore, cultural rights cannot secure every person's unrestricted access to their heritage. Their application may also be limited by socio-economic conditions. Regular visits by all the members of a community are not a realistic option if the holding institution is overseas. Geographical distance makes the development of reciprocal trust between the community and the cultural institution harder. When empathy and trust are lacking repatriation is unlikely to be the first choice of the institution concerned.

Changing from a property framework into a human rights framework emphasises the primacy of the human in relation to the object and creates space to argue that specific sacred practices as forms of spiritual expression deserve protection as part of cultural and property rights. For instance, the western notion of the right to freedom of religion or belief might enable recognition of spiritual ties to natural resources and could facilitate recognition of the importance of 'sacred natural sites' (e.g., Gilbert 2018: 138; Lixinski 2019b: 603). The freedom to espouse a religion and profess one's faith depends heavily upon human rights and upholding equal rights to defined commitments (Fagan 2017: 228). Moral progress invites and welcomes diverse perspectives that can help rebuild the social and legal frameworks that Eurocentrism has denatured. In liberal democracies the structure of conversations about restitution is shaped in part by conceptions of individual responsibility. The moral aspirations and claims of the law are discernible in the results which long overdue conversations about rightful ownership have begun to yield. Aligning provenance research with human rights approaches and cultural diversity would further support moral progress, although it is possible that groups that prioritise the cultural life of their sacred material over conservation may be met with hostility (Lixinski 2019a: 54–57).

The primary legal norms of property law may or may not offer what the group requires. A western social perspective ascribes greater value to an individual's connection to a thing than a group. In non-democratic societies and states that permit or propagate intolerance of religion or faith, freedom of religion arguments that are designed to safeguard the religious heritage of faith traditions may not be readily accommodated, nor would they provide the necessary basis for a restitution claim. International cultural heritage law resonates with the social work that religion does, but its relationship with religion and human rights is complex (Lixinski 2024: 437ff). To assume that stolen objects of spiritual or religious importance always enjoy protection in their place of origin may not be realistic if the freedom of faith traditions is being controlled there. If what these faith traditions display or what links they are allowed to build with other faith communities is centrally controlled, state support for return may remain subject to uncertainty.

Traditional practices are increasingly often invoked against the regulations of public institutions claimed to encroach upon religious rights and freedoms or property rights. As 'heritage holders,' Indigenous peoples and religious groups are subject to the inevitable tensions arising between the culture of cultural groups and the national identity promoted by the state that sets and controls the cultural and legal framework within which these holders can act and defend their traditions. Tensions between local and national communities can make it challenging for communities, groups, tribes recognised by the state, and associations to establish their standing in courts. The framework for public support and the heritagisation procedures which states set out to define their national identity turn the safeguarding of intangible cultural heritage into a 'conflictual space' (Hance 2020b: 171, 176–177).

Sacred objects, ceremonial objects, rituals, and human remains are lifelines for many people, but the hesitation to acknowledge any normative effect of the UNDRIP, and the failure to consider the mitigating provisions in the conventional framework that permit special agreements and arrangements, narrow the scope for an integrative definition of sacred objects. Inadequate interpretations and selective referencing create the impression that respect for the rights of Indigenous peoples is discretionary and depends on cordiality. It would be accurate to think that a human rights approach at state, group, and individual levels could support the restitution of artefactual, enshrined human remains such as those used in Buddhist rituals, as well as raise the legitimacy of group ownership of ceremonial and ritual material and their associated intangible resources (Human Rights Council Report 2020: para 8). However, human rights frameworks are merely a way of talking about social justice; they do not equate to social justice and thus are subject to methodological limitations. Numerous practical challenges are encountered in the enforcement of rights based on religion or language.

Switching to a human rights framework may accelerate the evolution of international cultural property law, but without a clear demarcation of the type of cultural material to be prioritised, it distorts the operation of property law. A human rights approach to cultural heritage also brings with it the theoretical complication of not indicating why, or how, the sacred may direct the evolution of restitution norms.

One of the novel contributions made by this study is to start mapping what can be learnt from the policy, law, provenance, and ethical implications of the rulings that emanated from litigation in the Parthenon Sculptures dispute, the Buddha Mummy case, and cases in which the human remains of Nama and Herero peoples were in issue, and to highlight a more suitable legal basis for claims. The protection of cultural diversity relies on much more than the 'consensual dynamic of this field' as expressed in the 2003 UNESCO Convention alone (Hance 2020b: 178). Collecting practices impacted on cultural preservation and the intangible cultural heritage of a source culture (Byrne 2015: 19–20, 33–34). Repatriation can contribute to cultural preservation (Simpson 2009: 128–129). However, museums face formidable but universal challenges when their collections contain unethically collected material. The definition of intangible cultural heritage in Article 2 of the 2003 UNESCO Convention does not refer to the need to prove that a link exists between the alleged intangible cultural heritage and a geographical zone or between the territory and the intangible heritage; and that local traditions have been practised in an uninterrupted manner over extended periods of time, and yet these aspects have turned out to be significant for successful litigation (Hance 2020b: 171). It is also necessary to consider the evidentiary standards of domestic law which may undermine claims to intangible cultural heritage.

1.6 Ideas about justice

In the 17th and 18th centuries, law and ethics were in a symbiotic relationship that did not require clear demarcation of scope (Glenn 2011: 249). The consciousness of what constitutes 'injustice' today is different; it demands closer inspection of the role of the law as a gatekeeper, one that permits certain conduct but sanctions other behaviour. Removal and loss of control of cultural heritage deserve careful analysis under both normative systems—law and morality—at the point of interaction. Morality cannot be equated and assimilated to law. It cannot be 'legislated' through formal criteria and procedures that are set up to 'stand in' for the individual conscience. Nonetheless, it is connected to law in the sense that both normative systems respond to the demands of practical reason. However, the instant answers that positivist conceptions of law can provide will not address matters of weight and substance in 'hard cases' as the ethics of law ('practical reason') and moral philosophy do (Zeidler 2016: 48).

Law forms part of the power structure of society, but it is more than just an expression of power relations in developed capitalist economies (Deakin et al 2017: 189). It functions as an institutionalised form of normativity made of historical processes and a system of knowledge infused with moral aspirations. National laws that require repatriation of human remains and sacred (ceremonial) items to Indigenous peoples, such as the NAGPRA, may be said to have moral aspirations that are visible in the rights and obligations encapsulated in legal norms (Delacroix 2006: 144; Human Rights Council Report 2020: paras 19, 20). At times it may seem that the effects of law depend on the power and prestige of the actors involved, but in liberal democracies, law should not depend on outside forces and their power. Compliance with legal norms is not simply a matter of acting on command in the way a computer would. Opinions about the normative dimension of a given rule, whether public or private, affect compliance with that rule.

The normativity of law is embedded in its concern with social behaviour, which includes the behaviour of 'role occupants' in legislation. Some rules address every member of society, e.g., 'thou shalt not steal.' Other rules address a defined class of persons, e.g., directors of companies. Yet others address the social and professional behaviour of state officials. Habermas emphasises that the law is a 'system of action.' The enacted law depends on 'justification' as well as the 'institution of the law.' It is a system that supplements autonomous morality in ways that make effective action possible (Habermas 1996: 106, 114).

The idea of law as 'a binding custom or practice of a community' and 'the whole body of such customs, practices, or rules' is indispensable to the organisation of social life and limiting social conflicts. Although facts and norms are not in the same categories of thinking, they are correlative, and internal tension arises between them in law (Habermas 1996). The origin of law's normativity is frequently ascribed to the factual character of positive law, for it is possible to consider law as social fact. However, reasonable decision-making involves more than social fact. Those whose cultural heritage had been targeted for appropriation may have encountered only a very 'rough justice' and have had to lower their expectations about restitution for their losses. Integrating law with its underlying ethic that takes into consideration the moral aspirations of the law for purposes of restitution can help serve as a reminder of past wrongs and balance the scales of justice.

Restitution is connected to justice on the 'wheel of restoration' which Wouter Veraart, professor of legal philosophy, uses to explain different ways of dealing with past injustice. There are three spokes on the wheel, each with different priorities (Veraart 2015: 211). Restitution of cultural objects and heritage sits part-way to peace between the points of 'order' and 'reconciliation' in the process of restoration. It represents a way of remembering injustice and committing to correcting it. Returning cultural objects visibly and publicly, encourages us to remember. The glimpses of justice that come into view draw attention to the past, spurring us to undo some of the harm when it is no longer possible to make up for the suffering of those affected. Thus, it restores past wrongs as far as humanly possible. Remembering also helps diaspora communities link their past with their present and future. Recalling what was happening in source communities when their sacred material was taken may revive the memory of the associated rituals and ceremonies. This cannot be achieved by information drawn solely from and about those who supplied material to museums. Justice is within reach when the memory of the injustice has been restored, but suppressing the past will make real peace impossible to achieve. While return to the *status quo ex ante* may be achieved by returning sculptures and fragments to reconstruct a temple, return cannot undo or change the past efforts of those who set out to decimate a culture (contra Winkelmann 2020: 40). That said, seeking to settle every score in historical events that determined the fate of cultural property will sabotage peace efforts (Zeidler 2016: 186–187). The best opportunities to re-evaluate norms, rules, rights, obligations, and the role of law concerning restitution arise between the extremes of suppression and fixation.

There are many forms of justice—restorative, climate, economic, social, and more. Aspirations of social justice may conflict with democratic values that legitimate governmental outcomes by process and not by moral content. Claims for return brought by those dispossessed through colonisation will not share the same ideas about justice as the current possessors of their cultural material. The justice evoked in restitution and repatriation claims involving museum collections, could be distributive (who gets what); procedural (what we ought to be doing to treat claims fairly); corrective (directed at material restitution as a form of compensation for harms done to people in an earlier period, demonstrating retrospective effect); or rectificatory (how to repair harm done; for instance, reversal of an act of theft by returning property, ideally alongside the payment of compensation to counterbalance losses and emotional damages inflicted, accompanied by an apology and steps to prevent future similar injustices). Judges, like historians, partake in restorative justice when assisting with the rebuilding of social and institutional frameworks that allow life to resume without conflict.

The call to speak openly of restitution is a call to 'speak of justice' (Sarr and Savoy Report 2018: 29). Museums and archives have been called upon to undertake repatriation as part of a wide redistribution of cultural goods in the name of distributive justice (Matthes 2017: 950). Restorative justice goes beyond museum inventories. A result of negotiation on an equal footing, it affects curations, inter-museum relations, and even relations between an individual museum and a state, as the 2006 agreement reached between Italy and the Metropolitan Museum of Art illustrates in the context of illicit trafficking of culture. The Met transferred title of several looted antiquities to Italy in exchange for long-term loans of similar objects.

Justice as redistribution and representation is not synonymous with reparative justice. Reparative justice expects legal systems to take on a new role because restitution is insufficient to repair the loss of knowledge or the social and spiritual disturbances resulting from the disappearance or dispossession of human remains, sacred artefacts, and items associated with unique ancestral know-how (Labadie 2021: para 28). Other damages will have arisen from material deprivation for which causation, unlawfulness, and fault requirements will be set. Even the most advanced legal systems are vexed by the new problems of responsibility in the unfamiliar territory of historic wrongs that have grievously impacted the core legal interests of peoples, their survival and flourishing.

Descendants of people who lost their lives in colonial genocide have implored the courts to apply international law to determine whether they are owed general compensation as reparations (Sarkin 2008). Under international law, 'reparation' encompasses restitution and compensation, and may consist of satisfaction; rehabilitation; cessation and guarantees of non-repetition (Commentary, Report of the International Law Commission Seventy-first session, 29 April–7 June and 8 July–9 August 2019, 108 para 20). Reparations such as those foreseen in the 1919 Versailles Treaty were designed to wipe out the consequences of the unlawful act and re-establish what would have existed in all probability had the unlawful act never taken place. Restitution of cultural objects does not take the form of monetary compensation that may be claimed as part of reparations, but it could be a way of negotiating historical injustices in claims for the return of state and private property looted during armed conflict, taken illegally from a party entitled to it, and of making up for the damage which one state inflicted on another by plundering property. Settlements are more likely if reparative justice arguments are ventilated and there is political pressure to find solutions that go beyond what civil remedies may achieve (Moran 2019: 461, 472). Seeking reparations differs from justice as 'recognition' of the right to be heard in democratic dispensations.

The extreme inequality in human and institutional development in the colonies restricted the access of local communities to economic opportunities. It makes justice appear distant. Yet the indiscriminate pursuit of justice evident in modern war poses its own challenges and warns that a balance must be found. The philosopher and economist Amartya Sen's capability theory focuses on advancing justice by means of expanding human capability (Sen 2009: vii–ix). A refusal to be informed by the experiential knowledge which cultural communities hold concerning their own sacred cultural material, cannot expand human capability and development in Sen's terms, as it fosters mummified thinking that permits the status quo to continue unhindered. Whenever social justice is defined as capability, education lies front and centre, as education nurtures and conditions capabilities. Sophia Labadi advances this argument in the field of heritage and museum studies. She indicates that honing debating skills and critical thinking makes the expansion of social justice possible (Labadi 2017: 7). Cultural activities and practices, education, and knowledge about the past that surpasses the primal force determining one's feelings of safety, security and belonging all have the potential to support the expansion of human capability. These factors may foster a new relational ethic that strengthens the role of relational justice in restitution decisions and repatriation policy.

1.6.1 Primary legal norms

Adjudicators and policymakers must take responsibility for the institution of the law and its application (Van Roermund 2013: 272). The concept of restitution in PublIL encompasses property law and property transfer, but it does not provide a satisfactory explanation of the role of primary legal norms of property in the broad structure of law.

Primary legal norms are the material legal norms that govern the behaviour of individuals and co-ordinate their rights. The earliest foundations of primary legal rules regarding liability originate from Babylonian and Assyrian sources, ancient Greek philosophical texts, and general maxims of Roman law through which philosophers influenced the development of responsibility (Winiger 2018: 10–13; 29 ff). The idea of granting everyone rights and respecting their property was reflected in the maxim 'live honestly, hurt no one, give everyone his due' (Justinian *Institutiones* 1.1.3, 30 December 533 (text reproduced in Thomas 1975: 3); Winiger 2018: 67–68). Roman law acknowledged broad principles that required offenders who inflicted material losses on victims to replace what was destroyed with identical items. 'Restitutio in integrum' was a remedy Roman magistrates could proclaim when coercion or deceit was in evidence, to restore a thing and the victim to their original state, either by replacing the thing destroyed, or by paying money to the owner at the highest market value to indemnify them and to restore the imbalance created by the damage, loss, suffering or injury. This remedy seldom features in modern liability law, yet modern law still acknowledges restoration to the original condition or state as the highest guiding principle when illegally acquired property is returned (Zeidler 2016: 26).

The modern law of liability and compensation are encapsulated in primary legal norms in tort and delict. In a dispute within a single political unit, different primary legal norms can be expected to apply in the domestic law categories of claims for the payment of compensation and for the return of property. Typically, the nature of the dispute would be characterised based on, e.g., whether the claim is for compensation or return of the object; what the decision-maker considers to be appropriate and proportionate in the circumstances; and whether the material legal norms governing the behaviour of individuals in relation to property can be proved. In contemporary private law, 'restitution in kind' may take the form of monetary payment. There is the possibility that a perpetrator might return their own cultural property as an equivalent for things that had been destroyed, which would qualify as a type of 'substitute restitution' (Zeidler 2016: 28). General maxims, principles, and determinations continue to inform modern primary legal rules on liability, e.g., the principle that awards of damages should return injured parties to the positions they were in before suffering loss. The legal consequences of damage are expressed in terms of monetary compensation to help victims deal with pecuniary difficulties or provide comfort in the face of long-term hardships. When the damage is irremediable, complete restoration cannot be achieved. Guidance may then be found in the principle of restoration (Winiger 2018: 69).

De-accession policies that exclude moral considerations separate law and morals. The 'cultural relational principles of justice' which Stahn proposes in respect of primary legal norms includes a review of national legal frameworks that accommodate inalienability principles, constrain de-accession, and promote the unbridled use of capital power (Stahn 2023: 514, 533ff). Procedural justice is as important as justice in decision-making.

Perspectives on justice and the norms that aspire towards it are distorted by 'looping' law and ethics arguments. The dispute concerning the Parthenon Sculptures divides into a legal and a moral argument. Whereas the UK government has focused on the strictures of the UK law Greece adopts a moral argument that the Ottoman authorisation was granted by an occupier whose permission to access the Acropolis was meaningless in any ethical sense. Focusing on either the legal or the ethical discourse has fostered a stale circularity on the restitution of the Parthenon Sculptures that suppresses meaning to maintain the status quo. Moreover, every legal argument yields a counter-argument. Whatever one side argues, the other side can turn it around to its advantage (Soirila 2022: 7). Legal argument also proceeds in 'sound-bites' that follow a certain sequence and 'nesting' pattern. The rules discussed are rendered meaningless through the indeterminacy of the language. Absent settled law that resolves gaps, ambiguities, and conflicts, stereotyped argument-bites are deployed in a circular pattern (Audi 2007: 131). The general effect of argument circularity is not difficult to predict. Moreover, argument circularity prevents the complexity of the factual pattern from being grasped. It masks the ethical stance of the decision-maker (Kennedy 1991: 106). Counter-bites assume stereotypical form as a denial or exception to the principle under discussion or when instantly turned over (Muir Watt 2014: 359). Economic and social inequality concerns are precluded from surfacing and novel ideas are stifled (Kennedy 1991: 359; Muir Watt 2014: 358, 363). The dialogue becomes intractable instead of gaining ground.

The letter of primary English law is the fall-back position if meaningful change in the restitution discourse is to be prevented. The power of the governing bodies of national museums in the UK that receive central government funding is circumscribed when it comes to de-accessioning objects which are kept in their collections. They are obliged to protect, conserve, and make available and accessible their collections to the public in perpetuity. The wider national legislative framework that constrains the actions taken by these museums consists of five Acts of Parliament, i.e., the British Museum Act 1963; the Public Libraries and Museums Act 1964; the National Heritage Act 1980 and 1983; and the Museums and Galleries Act 1992. When Sir Hans Sloane's bequest was codified into law in 1753, the Board of Trustees of the British Museum became legally bound to protect the collection by virtue of common-law fiduciary duty principles and British law of trusts and estates (Godwin 2020: 158–159). The British Museum Act of 1963 prohibits the de-accessioning and disposal of museum items in almost all instances, with only narrow exceptions, such as where the object is deemed unfit to be retained in the collections and no longer useful to the educational or scientific mission of the museum (Section 5). Under the de-accession provision in s 5(1)(c) of the 1963 Act, the Trustees may consider disposal if the object is unfit to be retained in the collections of the Museum and can be disposed of without detriment to the interests of students,

> provided that where an object has become vested in the Trustees by virtue of a gift or bequest the powers conferred by this subsection shall not be exercisable as respects that object in a manner inconsistent with any condition attached to the gift or bequest.

The administrative procedure in French law has a similar thrust, but French law permits disposal only in respect of objects that cannot be linked to an acquisition process or a gift or bequest, whereas the British Museum Act of 1963 draws attention to the conditions attached to a gift or bequest and links disposal to the transfer of ownership of collection items. Disposal on grounds of being 'unfit to be retained' is made subject to multiple conditions and provisos that preclude conditions set in gifts and bequests from being overridden (British Museum *Policy on Deaccession of Objects from the Collection* 2018). The policy includes the exception in relation to objects 'unfit to be retained the collection' and can be disposed of 'without detriment to the interests of the public or scholars' (para 3.3).

The decision to return the Parthenon Sculptures rests mainly on the British government and its willingness to pass a law enabling their return to Greece. Bills have a first, second and third reading in the House of Commons before they can move on to the House of Lords in the British Parliament. Most bills are government-sponsored but the Parthenon Sculptures (Return to Greece) Bill was raised as a private member's bill in 2016 to amend the British Museum Act 1963. Promulgating legislation demands parliamentary time and requires a political consensus. If the British government wanted to repatriate a collection item, it could legislate to allow de-accessioning and disposal. It would be easy enough to rescind the 1816 Act authorising the purchase of the Elgin collection, including the Parthenon Sculptures, and make an exception to or change the British Museum Act 1963 if the political will existed. The Parthenon Sculptures are a governmental responsibility, and the Amendment Bill of 2016 was designed to put an end to skirting a decision but the 2016 initiative was not promoted by the group holding political power at the time. Lack of support from the mainstream in the House of Commons meant that it never reached the second reading stage in 2017. On 2 March 2020, a fresh debate was introduced on the stalemate caused by the legislation protective of the British Museum and the ownership of the Museum Trustees in English law (Hansard HC Deb. vol. 672, cols. 722, 728). A short Parliamentary debate on the question of what assessment has been made of 'proposals to loan the Elgin Marbles to Greece' was inconclusive (Hansard HL Deb. vol. 834, cols. 1992–2006, 14 December 2023). The focus returned to loans at the behest of the Board of Trustees, and latterly to the small marble foot fragment emerging from the folds of a gown known as the 'Fagan fragment'. The Regional Archaeological Museum in Palermo, Sicily, returned the fragment in January 2022 and it was exhibited as a 'long-term deposit', but whether this is a museum loan or a restitution is unclear.

An acute disconnect between law and ethics arises when museums use the legal position to resist moral pressure to restitute cultural material. In 2020 the national museum sector in the UK came under ministerial pressure to act in ways which the government considered 'impartial.' It recalled the period in the late 1970s and 1980s when European museums were actively encouraged to resist moral pressure and to employ the law to do so. A push for 'impartiality' against the backdrop of a pervasive and ever-present belief in cultural superiority, one which promotes stereotypical depictions of other cultures, further disincentivises museums from accounting for historical injustice. Few British Museum professionals are actively campaigning for law reform or vocalising their support for removal of the legal barrier to restitution. Ideas of cultural superiority have now started to contaminate discourses of technological advancement (Stahn 2023: 42). Strategic changes to the legislative framework could respond to technical or ethical demands. Test cases may shift the paradigm or change the direction of the discourse, but there must be a willingness to move beyond 'mutually beneficial solutions' to address the issue of ownership and location. When objects cannot be studied and viewed due to their sacred character, there is no reason whatsoever for institutions to keep them.

Physical conflict puts pressure on legal and moral norms. Their disintegration is an inevitable accompaniment of genocidal conflicts. While conversion, theft, looting, forced sale, or genocide are not normally considered to be part of a discussion of claims under civil law, it is much clearer today that different modes of transfer come within the scope of civil law. Restitution is one of the ways in which property may be transferred, even if one prefers to talk about 'transfer,' but civil law cannot escape the policy implications of transfers that occur through plunder and theft. The juridical framework of exception cannot be discounted from a public policy exception perspective.

Primary legal norms include special laws promulgated to create exceptions to their general circulation. Special laws creating exceptions to the general rule offer an important example of primary legal norms in the field. In Belgium, for example, based on the premise that there is no international, European, or internal legal obligation in force that imparts a duty on the Belgian State to return a property 'acquired' during Belgian colonial rule, the federal government launched a pioneering initiative in the form of positive, hard law—Bill of 3 July 2022 Recognizing the Alienability of Goods Linked to the Belgian State's Colonial Past and Determining a Legal Framework for Their Restitution and Return, Le Moniteur Belge 28 September 2022, No. 2022042012—hereinafter 'Belgian Bill 2022'). This regulatory intervention creates an exception to the general rule that public property linked to the Belgian State's colonial past is inalienable to address the social problem of unlawful behaviours that never conferred legal title. It makes a substantial contribution as the first general legislative framework for the restitution of objects acquired during the political and administrative domination of the state of origin to be promulgated by a former colonial power in Europe. Its point of application starts from 1885, when the Congo Act was signed, to the date of the independence of the State of origin (Article 3.2). It requires guarantees to be issued that the returned objects will be properly cared for. Return procedures are to be set out in bilateral agreements (De Clippele and Demarsin 2022: 277ff).

Bilateral agreements specifically tailored to human remains, sacred items and intangible cultural heritage, are to be encouraged. They play an important stabilising role in relations between states (De Clippele and Demarsin 2021). Apart from easing cross-border tensions and facilitating dispute resolution, the results obtained through the thrice-renewed memorandum of understanding that prevents the trafficking of Chinese artefacts into the United States shows they help to curb the illicit cultural trafficking of cultural objects (Sutton 2024). Namibia concluded a bilateral agreement with South Africa for the return of archive material, and thereafter agreed to cooperate with Germany for the return of the human skulls. When the contractants make their own law and both sides have control over the stipulations contained in a bilateral agreement, the ambiguity of imperial and unwritten local law can be removed. The contractants act in accordance with what they consider to be their 'duty' and assume responsibility when agreeing the terms of restitution. Normative uncertainty will however prevail until the agreement is concluded. Meanwhile, France has continued to pursue a case-by-case approach since the Sarr and Savoy Report 2018 rather than attempting to accelerate returns by bilateral agreements (Stahn 2023: 515). While a general restitution framework could speed up restitutions, it could also create tension between different conceptions of justice.

A new article, L. 124-1, in the *Code du Patrimoine* prepares the way for the judge to arrange restitution to the original owner. It leaves the criteria to be formulated by the judiciary on a case-by-case basis instead of mandating an administrative official or panel to issue recommendations about the moral considerations at play.

Disappointingly few legal exceptions exist in the form of ready-made laws authorising restitution as the Belgian Bill does. When restitutory aims are not expressed in positive law, the law and ethics of competing claims must be reconciled with the law and ethics of international law before restitution or repatriation can be achieved in transnational disputes. Without such a special law, restitution and repatriation can be overlooked because it is not set as a clear aim of general domestic law. The proposed Belgian framework remains incomplete, however. Indigenous peoples exhibited in human zoos are not included, human remains have not been covered, and participation by local communities is not recognised (Stahn 2023: 515). A law was tabled in 2023 to regulate the restitution of human remains and to make the ban on the trade of human remains explicit. It is expected to be put to a vote after the national elections in June 2024. Whether this initiative will strengthen the regulatory environment in Belgium depends on the scope of excluded material.

This study foregrounds ways to avoid unjust results and give greater scope to international standards or rules that co-ordinate the application of primary legal norms, even when there are no special primary legal norms or pertinent treaties that qualify for application. This dimension can be referred to under the rubric 'juridical framework of exception to the circulation of cultural goods.' It includes international humanitarian law of armed conflicts and international criminal law (Manacorda 2011: 25). The first international law principles and rules applicable to cultural heritage were entwined with the development of international humanitarian law in relation to the right to resort to war as well as limitations that accompanied adoption of the Covenant of the League of Nations, human rights, and international criminal law (known as *jus ad bellum*, literally 'right to war') (Hobbs 2014: 289). The rules and limitations were contained in both the *jus ad bellum*, which defined the limitation of the right to resort to war, and the *jus in bello* relating to just means, just cause, and fair treatment in rules of warfare. Specific armed conflicts were in the purview of multilateral negotiations when the time came. The Law of Geneva focuses on the humanitarian law aspect of the victims of armed conflicts as contained in the four Geneva Conventions of 1949 and their Additional Protocols. Justifications for exceptions are found in domestic legal systems, EU secondary law, and conventions that contain rules regarding offences relating to cultural property and heritage.

1.6.2 Secondary legal norms

Regardless of the form the law takes, valid legal title may provide the scope to advance a claim based on the gaps and ambiguity created by imperial law and international power relations during the colonial era (Goldmann 2021). Secondary legal norms may coordinate the application of primary legal norms in a way that confirms the validity of title.

Rules governing jurisdiction, choice-of-law, and recognition and enforcement of foreign judgments have indisputable policy implications. The public policy exception of PrIL may find application when a fundamental principle of justice would be violated in an egregious manner if the foreign law identified to apply under PrIL rules were to be given application in a litigated case concerning unethical collection of cultural objects in the colonial era. The public policy exception mechanism 'ejects' a foreign law indicated by the normal functioning of PrIL choice-of-law rules when 'its content leads to an outcome that is judged to be undesirable in the light of current societal values' (Muir Watt 2014: 373). The exception also finds application when foreign judgments are not recognised in the forum based on considerations of justice. It is submitted that, together with the public policy exception, the principle of comity belongs to the juridical framework of exception. Comity enables adjudicators to decide on legal personality of entities and the right to be subject to litigation under the law of formation. In Commonwealth countries, the principle of comity has resulted in a much wider recognition of entities as subjects of litigation (Garnett 2012: para 5.08).

As agitation for the return of imperial artefacts is growing across local, ethnic, national, and continental levels, 'social' legitimacy is an issue of growing importance for PrIL. The answers to the burning questions concerning the achievement of justice in human relations cannot go 'unquestioned' any longer. Juxtaposing distributive justice and relational justice defined by deontological arguments is a recent feature of scholarly studies on PrIL (e.g., Banu 2018: 302–303). To date, PrIL studies have not focused on questions involving distributive justice and relational justice in cultural heritage law.

An expansive scholarly literature focuses on the notion of 'conflicts justice', which ensures that the same set of facts in transnational cases is given consistent legal treatment. Conflicts justice is unconcerned with advancing justice or reducing or identifying redressable injustices. PrIL frequently fails to rise to the challenges of justice, and many PrIL scholars are disinterested in cultivating the toolkit needed for repairing the historical injustices of colonial looting. It is submitted that considerations of material justice cannot be ignored when the geographic localisation of transnational cases results in an 'evidently arbitrary' result that fails to promote international coordination or systemic coherence across the field (Glenn 2011: 263). The pursuit of material justice relativises national borders despite the differences in legal traditions, mechanisms, and approaches. 'Substantive justice' may be achieved with the purposive interpretation of private law, whereas conflicts justice points to systemic coherence that avoids the unevenness and inefficiency which legal diversity can precipitate in PrIL (Mills 2009: 17). It must be conceded though that conflicts justice is closely modelled on 'legal determinacy' because it promotes predictability or 'international legal harmony' (Glenn 2011: 264; Muir Watt 2014: 358).

Those interested in gauging the fitness of PrIL for the future have highlighted the historical and personal injustices resulting from limited perspectives and inadequate methods (e.g., Muir Watt 2014: 367). Probing the link between legal norms and provenance research can broaden our vision.

1.6.3 The link between legal norms and provenance research

In restitution claims the relationship between provenance research and law are often ambiguous. One of the perennial difficulties is to determine whether the state ought to bring the claim and if so, how to ensure that any resulting benefit is passed to those who were deprived of their cultural heritage. It is no simple matter to decide with whom objects belong when the communities who produced them are gone or transformed, or when different communities in the country of origin launch competing claims. The links between provenance research and subtle normative clashes are not always apprehended as fully as they deserve to be.

The 'value theory of property' holds that rights of ownership are transferred from owner to owner in a 'chain of title,' which appears to capture one of the dimensions of provenance. The chain maintains the value of stable ownership 'by ensuring that loss of possession ... will not, of itself, endanger the ownership right' (Bell and Parchomovsky 2005: 595). This hypothesis permits an owner to enjoy the status and benefits of ownership without having to be afraid about involuntary loss of the asset and over-investing in its protection for this reason. However, zero-sum ownership disagreements such as the dispute over the Parthenon Marbles will not be resolved through pieces of information about creators, owners, or transfers in a chain of transactions. The value theory does not map onto contexts of injustice from the colonial era in which sacred cultural property and heritage were extracted from the powerless. Theories on the economic justification of private property may reveal how the chain of ownership began or why ownership of the thing was recognised in the first place, which the law does not, but the communal obligations of sacred heritage will not necessarily have prominent western economic justifications. While it is fundamentally unjust to benefit from the fruit of exploitation and oppression, courts seldom apply this maxim as it was applied in *In re Flamenbaum* (2013 N.Y. Slip Op. 7510).

More generally, cultural property and heritage are situated on an in-between, which poses challenges for many theoretical property frameworks. The rights of the private owner will be subject to limits, whereas the rights of the state may be realised through the public interest in the protection and restitution of cultural property and heritage. Mechanical application of the primary legal rules of property could threaten the security of acquisitions and transactions. The operation of legal precepts ill-equipped to meet the exigencies of special circumstances and property would preclude individualised, tailor-made results.

The colonial masters rewrote history to put themselves in the best light, made the laws to safeguard their interests, and handpicked what to use as proof of ownership when they removed cultural material. Not only were Indigenous communities robbed of their sacred cultural material, but they are also made to produce documented records of ownership and mode of acquisition as evidence in repatriation claims that never existed in their cultures or that were skewed in favour of the colonisers. The collecting practices of the colonial era were not concerned with the objections their practices invited. What is considered 'stolen' today was simply 'collecting' in the colonial age. Before restitution of collection items to erstwhile colonised peoples became more common, the term 'restitution' simply referred to inventories of lost property or ad hoc returns of single objects from larger collections without any acknowledgement that the objects were wrong to take and wrong to keep. Use of the term has shifted into greater alignment with its legal meaning, which acknowledges that an object was removed unjustly and without consent. Systematic and proactive provenance research into the life story of an object helps establish the truth, which justice demands (Stahn 2023: 436). Provenance interacts with and depends on interpretations of law and questions of applicable law and ethics. Reliance on ethical principles alone discounts the complexity of legal relations and historical legal concepts (Stahn 2023: 52).

The bad fruits of colonial conquest may warp the requirement to perform provenance research and the results it yields. A cultural group may even be discouraged from pursuing a claim for return of sacred and funerary material if proof is required to verify its religious significance to the community rather than a utilitarian purpose. Progressive policies do not require such proof (National Policy (South Africa) on the Repatriation and Restitution of Human Remains and Heritage Objects of 2021: para 14.3.1). Methods of handling the human body that are shaped by spiritual beliefs may conflict with the view that human remains may be used to advance scientific knowledge for the good of society, and reluctance to share traditionally restricted knowledge is expected (Curtis 2014: 95). History is often easier to understand from the point of view of power, given that power determines interpretation (Flanagan 2016: 142). Without conversations about the legal history involved in the development of the law and the priorities for provenance and restitution, insight into the dynamics of sustained injustice tied to history will remain limited, and contemporary policies may continue to insist that claimant groups submit evidence that human remains and their treatment have a particular cultural or spiritual significance to their community.

Provenance research as well as choice-of-law method require adjustment in contexts of unethically acquired collections. Regarding provenance, it is fair to say that provenance research is not just an empirical enquiry into gaps or dubious entries in the chain of title that could be indicative of defective title, or that aims to detect successive illegal transfers. Critical inquiry and a critical reading of sources are called for so that alternative epistemologies may be accommodated. Regarding legal method, it is evident that law alone cannot explain or improve behaviour, but to ignore the role of law and legal institutions would waste the opportunity to build a just society. Criminals make immoral decisions to avoid accountability; wrongdoers take advantage of normative uncertainty to dodge responsibility for funnelling stolen cultural objects into the hands of those whose bad faith cannot be proved (Mimran 1994: 63). The return of select objects in peace treaties and rules regarding war and wartime booty have not seen an even application, as restitutions tended to be reserved for European states and the legal framework remains highly fragmented. A vast body of international soft law and transnational private regulation raise expectations that 'justice' will be done in support of return claims by former owners, but in civil law countries especially, cases frequently result in the inadmissibility and denial of claims, and claimants who rely on regular legal channels have no guarantee of success (Campfens 2021: 2, 218).

Restitution and repatriation claims frequently turn on fundamental determinations about property rights and ownership that are seen as ensuring the common good, for example, that profits received without justification and at another's expense are restored (McBride and Steel 2018: 113). Reforms and new legal constructions are part of the demand for action based on the simple principle that cultural property and heritage stolen or looted from source communities must be returned to them. No society should benefit from violence perpetrated against another society's culture. This guiding principle is a valuable point of orientation for civil claims in a transnational context but how this is to be achieved where intangible cultural heritage is concerned, remains uncertain.

1.6.4 Filling the gaps: new norms, past circumstances

The scope of judicial lawmaking in private and public law is co-determined by statutory interpretation, which may be described as the judge's primary function. The legislature cannot foresee every instance that may come within the purview of a legal rule, and the judiciary provides authoritative interpretations of statutory rules and other norms and principles. From time to time, unduly restrictive interpretations result from flawed judicial reasoning. Even when exhaustive research has been conducted into the mode of acquisition and the purpose and function of collection items, narrow and over-cautious interpretations of statutory restrictions may preclude return.

In liberal democracies, statutory interpretation is a way of lawmaking. Constitutional law guides both lawmaking and adjudication. It is a general rule of legal construction in most modern legal systems that legislation and legislative changes apply prospectively. Under English law, for example, unless a contrary intention appears, an enactment is presumed not to be intended to have retrospective effect (*Walker v Innospec Limited and others* [2017] UKSC 47). 'Old' laws apply to issues or events that occurred before the law was changed, whereas 'new' legislation applies prospectively to circumstances arising after its promulgation unless the statute in question is clearly intended to have retrospective effect. If this legislative intent is clear the statute will be construed accordingly. National bills of rights may have an important function in directing statutory interpretation in criminal cases but even in criminal cases legislation may be given retrospective effect where such a legislative intention is obvious. For example, the War Crimes Act 1991 allowed proceedings to be brought against anyone holding British citizenship who had committed a war crime in Germany or German-occupied territory during the Second World War, even if they were not a British citizen at that time.

Retrospectivity is succinctly defined as the application of new norms to past circumstances (Gruber 2019: 95). Non-retrospectivity is intended as a legal safeguard recognised at the national level (often included in constitutional texts) and international level (e.g., in the Universal Declaration of Human Rights, or in the Vienna Convention on the Law of Treaties). When the ICJ interpreted the notion of 'sacred trust' in the League Convention, it took account of legal developments that occurred after the facts it had to adjudicate. Contemporary ideas about self-determination in 1971 informed its ruling (*The Legal Consequences for States of the Continued Presence of South Africa in Namibia (South West Africa) Notwithstanding Security Council Resolution 276 (1970)* Advisory Opinion [1971] ICJ 16 paras 52–53). The same approach can be seen in the sovereignty dispute between the UK and Mauritius over the Chagos Archipelago in 2019 (*The Legal Consequences of the Separation of the Chagos Archipelago from Mauritius in 1965* Advisory Opinion [2019] ICJ GL No. 169). The subsequent development of legal principles and norms enables the continued existence of rights created under the law in force at the time.

Non-retrospectivity is guaranteed in national and international criminal justice. The rule against non-retrospectivity in criminal law points to the 'general principles of law recognised in civilised nations' which include 'principles of legality' requiring that there can be no crime without a criminal law, there can be no penalty without law, and neither the crime nor the penalty can be made retrospective. It is unjust to punish a man for an act which had not been a crime when it was committed (Smead 1936: 779). The liability of the accused can be evaluated only with reference to what they thought they were doing at the time (Olick 2007: vii, 138). The Inter-American Court of Human Rights has recognised that exceptional circumstances may conceivably dictate that the aversion against retrospectivity must make way for accountability. Defences based on statutes of limitations and prescription have been among measures ruled inadmissible because they eliminate responsibility or are intended to prevent the investigation and punishment of those responsible for serious human rights violations (*Barrios Altos* Judgment of 14 March 2001 IACHR Series C No. 75). In international law, the principle of non-retroactivity has never been understood as absolute.

Germany was unwilling to punish the war crimes committed in its own name during the First World War. The non-retrospectivity rule was acknowledged before the adoption of Article 38.1.c. of the 1945 Statute of the ICJ. In 1945, Germany entered a plea of non-retrospectivity. The prohibition of *ex post facto* laws, known as *nullum crimen sine lege, nulla poena sine lege* was contested during the Nuremberg trials. The Nuremberg trials were conducted in accordance with rules and procedures set out in the Charter for the International Military Tribunal at Nuremberg (Nuremberg Charter), to bring legal accountability for grievous and profound state-sanctioned wrongs (Moran 2019: 424). The International Military Tribunal of Nuremberg (IMT) couched *nullum crimen* not as a principle of law, but of justice, and thus amenable to be overridden by a higher-order principle of justice (6 Federal Rules Decisions 69 1946 108).

The refusal of the IMT to convict those accused of aggression as a matter of law was a legal and historical turning point (Bush 2002: 2328). As the first demonstration of complementary international criminal jurisdiction, it revealed the roots of criminal law in the international legal order which could provide solutions for violations, abuses, and losses if incorporated into international human rights and humanitarian law (Kress 2006: 15, 20, 21). Today, *nullum crimen sine lege* counts among the fundamental guarantees in criminal justice, but it deserves to be noted that, even where human rights considerations significantly strengthen the argument for non-retroactivity, historical exceptions exist in international criminal law.

The Convention on the Non-Applicability of Statutory Limitations to War Crimes and Crimes Against Humanity (adopted by the UN General Assembly on 26 November 1968; entry into force 11 November 1970), defines the juridical framework of exception in respect of time limitations. War crimes as defined in the Nuremberg Charter of 8 August 1945 and confirmed by resolutions 3 (I) of 13 February 1946 and 95 (I) of 11 December 1946 of the UN General Assembly, are not subject to any statutory limitation, irrespective of the date of commission. The same goes for the 'grave breaches' enumerated in the Geneva Conventions of 12 August 1949 for the protection of victims of international armed conflicts. Furthermore, no statutory limitation applies to crimes against humanity committed in times of war or peace as defined in the Nuremberg Charter; eviction by armed attack or occupation and inhuman acts resulting from apartheid, and the crime of genocide as defined in the 1948 Genocide Convention, even if such acts do not constitute violations of domestic law in the countries in which they were committed (Council of Europe, European Court of Human Rights, *Guide on Article 7* 2019: paras 16, 17).

Neither the 1970 UNESCO nor the 1995 UNIDROIT Conventions codified provisions with cut-off dates that legitimise earlier illicit transactions that occurred before entry into force. They do not seek to prevent states from pursuing remedies outside of the conventional framework for the restitution or return of cultural objects stolen or illegally exported before they took effect (cf Article 10(3) and Recital 6 of the 1995 UNIDROIT Convention). The 1970 UNESCO Convention recognises that certain practices and behaviours impoverish a country of origin's cultural heritage, and States Party are encouraged to offer redress when protected cultural objects have been exported or transferred in contravention of a country of origin's law. The application of the 1970 UNESCO Convention is non-retrospective, however. This much is 'assumed from customary international law, Article 28 of the 1969 Vienna Convention on the Law of Treaties and *travaux préparatoires* of the 1970 UNESCO Convention itself' (Vrdoljak 2008: 207). Article 7 expressly limits the application of the convention to theft or illegal export and import after 24 April 1972, when it entered into force. Article 15 urges states to conclude special agreements (UNESCO, 'Operational Guidelines for the Implementation of the Convention on the Means of Prohibiting and Preventing the Illicit Import, Export and Transfer of Ownership of Cultural Property of May 2015' UNESCO, Paris, 1970: paras 101–103). The effect of these provisions is that state action based on the 1970 UNESCO Convention will follow the instrument's entry into force; initiatives taken by states to protect their cultural treasures before entry into force will stand. For states joining later, entry into force is three months after the deposit of the instrument of ratification, acceptance, or accession. Article 22 of the 1970 UNESCO Convention accounts for the complex power distribution that marked the colonial era, but subsequent and current state practice is limited. As a dormant provision it highlights the inherent contradictions of the convention and contributes to the creation of 'black holes' in its implementation (Lixinski 2024: 415, 426). Despite its adoption in the wake of numerous newly independent states achieving their independence, the 1970 UNESCO Convention remains silent on cultural objects removed from territories under colonial domination and now kept in collections in the West. How to provide redress for past wrongs is a question that is yet to be solved. As a legal problem, it 'calls into question the principle of non-retroactivity of international treaty norms' and the habit of turning a 'blind eye' to the injustices of the past (Francioni 2024: 70–71).

The argument that retrospective application of new regulations will effect changes in legal rights that may be difficult to manage is frequently aired, e.g. that cultural objects may change ownership several times over the course of their history, and any retrospective change to the legal basis of prior ownership would require a reversal of every prior transaction and contract (Thielecke and Geißdorf 2021: 158–159). The context in which Thielecke and Geißdorf make their point refers only to primary domestic legal norms in German law. The observation does not seem to take account of the interface between domestic law and international law, and between the 'private' and 'public' in international law, and does not acknowledge that changes brought about by the developing interpretation of the sources of international law must be taken into account.

Specifically in international cultural heritage law, it has been argued that retrospective application of the 1970 UNESCO Convention would have had profound implications for the rights of property holders in different states, giving rise to constitutional and human rights which could not be implemented and honoured. Retrospectivity would have discouraged several States from signing up as potential parties (Forrest 2010: 40–41). Francioni (2024: 71) indicates, however, that the guidelines issued by the highest authorities of former colonial powers, such as the speech delivered by President Macron and the 2018 Sarr and Savoy Report, may be indicative of a broad international consensus concerning restitution that could fill the gap left by Article 2 of the 1970 UNESCO Convention. The non-retrospectivity of the 1995 UNIDROIT Convention expressed in the preamble and in Article 10 is counter-balanced by a declaration that the Convention does not legitimise illegal transactions concluded before it entered into force in the sixth recital to the Convention. Negotiation and other non-contentious procedures may be used to meet the claims of former colonies (Chechi 2024: 509–510).

The 1970 UNESCO Convention and the 1995 UNIDROIT Convention can be seen to balance the interests of the states exploited during the colonial era and those responsible for removing cultural objects before the Conventions took effect—former colonial powers whose art markets would be less prosperous if these Conventions applied retrospectively. The balancing act codified in the conventions does not encourage the dismantling of the colonial past. The conventions define cultural heritage for their own purposes, and structure the regimes with variable degrees of normative content. The issues these cultural heritage conventions seek to address reflect a unique political climate. Being products of their time, a principled approach is lacking across the conventional regime (Forrest 2010: 405).

Both the African and the Asian regional conferences held in preparation of the UN 2001 World Conference against Racism mooted the possibility of achieving the retrospective application of certain international rules of law in the context of slavery and colonialism, but no firm decision was reached. Adjudicators may modify the intertemporal principle, but it would be important to effect substantive reform and avoid cosmetic justice (Gruber 2019: 109).

1.6.5 Filling the policy gaps: the museum sector

As the demand for repatriation and restitution from the Global South has increased in the past few decades, filling remaining policy gaps in the museum sector is becoming more urgent. Several Western European and American states have recently adopted new policies, criteria, and procedures on restitution and repatriation. New guidelines for conversations and action confirm the idea that erstwhile colonial powers can take responsibility for the removal of cultural material and reconceptualise the importance of the ethics of collecting. The restitution of several objects to Senegal and Benin in the wake of the publication of the Sarr and Savoy Report 2018 offers a prominent example. Ideas about civilisation and enlightenment may form part of the package of new policies and initiatives issued by industrialised states that maintain similarly hegemonic positions of power, wealth, and influence on the global stage.

Proposals to share and circulate looted and trafficked objects resemble a specific form of legal doublespeak. In the countries situated in the Global North, museums have responded by having recourse to such concepts (Effiboley 2020: 78):

> The rhetoric behind these concepts is … that the museum is in the service of every nation … and the fact that an object is in place A or B is not what matters unless it serves the whole humanity. The weak point in this argument is that the concepts of circulation and sharing create a kind of double standard … non-European cultural objects and artworks need to be circulated and shared among the whole humanity … [b]ut no provision is made for the circulation of European artworks in Africa or … in the Global South.

Opportunities for doublespeak expand when law and ethics augments are deliberately separated out. Personal prejudice against minorities can be concealed as political expediency or the desire to protect institutional reputation. If the Ottomans' failure to take positive steps to halt the removal of the Parthenon Sculptures 'ratifies' their removal, the circularity of the argument may lend normative thrust to mimesis. The normative significance of mimetic theory will continue to prosper in restitution discourses if integrated law and ethics approaches are not actively incentivised. Britain has clung to an all-encompassing worldview of peoples and their cultures and their encyclopaedic museums are marketed as 'a global resource for the citizens of the world' (MacGregor and Williams 2005: 57ff re the British

Museum). Arguments about which social order can provide the best level of care and conservation for objects, and engaging in comparisons between institutions while insider thefts weaken their position, merely add fuel to the fire of the ownership debate, prompting new claims and demands for return (e.g., Ware 2024). The mere presence of a national policy does not necessarily render the normative environment for restitution adequate. For instance, the colonial overhang of conditional loans remains lurking in the shadows and papers over some of the real issues. Critical scrutiny is necessary in respect of cultural partnerships in the form of long-term loans of artefacts to source nations that take issue with the ownership of those artefacts. With programmes of conservation, curatorial exchange, knowledge-sharing, and partnership established around them, the holding party may too readily assume that both parties will benefit equally. For instance, the spiritual significance and authenticity of medicine bundles cannot be maintained when conservation standards inhibit their decay and regeneration. Another example is the National Policy (South Africa) on the Repatriation and Restitution of Human Remains and Heritage Objects of 2021, which attempts to clarify criteria and procedures while the primary heritage legislation, the National Heritage Resources Act of 1999, omits detail on the restitution of sacred ceremonial objects (Ingelson and Owosuyi 2022: 217ff).

1.6.6 'Common rules of adjudication'

Chechi identifies 'common rules of adjudication' to be applied when ordinary legal norms of property fail to ensure a satisfactory resolution. He extracted these special culture-sensitive rules from legally binding norms, such as the general principles of international law that evolved from the laws of war and humanitarian law; general domestic law or treaty norms and standards in force; or norms and obligations that are nascent and whose formation may be supported by soft law, internal guidelines, and technical standards. Chechi predicts that cross-fertilisation in international cultural heritage disputes will assist adjudicators in transforming the common rules of adjudication into an autonomous, composite body of rules—'transnational cultural heritage law.' This new *lex specialis* or *lex culturalis* 'excludes the mechanical application of the norms enacted for business transactions involving ordinary goods' (Chechi 2014: 246). The obligation to protect cultural objects in the event of armed conflict, the prohibition on the exportation of works of art from occupied territories, and the duty to return cultural objects taken by enemy forces correspond to the general principles of international law. Other 'common rules' form part of the special protection regime for cultural heritage that is designed to spare cultural heritage from the direct and indirect effects of armed conflict. Chechi acknowledges that the 'common rules' he proposes do not constitute state practice for purposes of the formation of customary international law. States observe the principles only with considerable delay and reticence, and regularly withhold consent to any obligation to restitute material removed during colonial occupation. State practice at the diplomatic, legislative, judicial, contractual, and administrative levels does not comport with the existence of an obligation to return cultural objects wrongfully removed in peacetime either (Chechi 2014: 271ff). Instead of being intended to function as legal bases for claims, the 'common rules of adjudication' are intended to fill the policy gap in legal regimes that do not recognise the special nature of art and cultural objects, to bolster the legal protection they can provide.

Included among Chechi's 'common rules of adjudication' is the rule that adjudicators must allow restitution claims to be heard on their merits by reining in the problems caused by the non-retrospectivity of the 1970 UNESCO Convention and the 1995 UNIDROIT Convention and hold time limitations inapplicable (Chechi 2014: 285–292). The proposal, which favours multi-level cooperation over legal defences such as the non-retroactivity of criminal law and of cultural heritage treaties, is based on the reasoning that, because culture-sensitive decisions will contribute to the formation, application, and dissemination of common rules in this area, cultural priorities need to be introduced into the decision-making process and weight must be assigned to them through a process of cross-fertilisation. The tailored application of the law in disputes involving cultural heritage which the proposed 'common rules of adjudication' encourage in cultural heritage disputes, is intended to provide guidance to adjudicators and policymakers when serious ethical, historical, and political problems hamper progress. Consultation, consensus-building, and cooperation are preferred over legalistic and adversarial approaches which encourage recourse to the law of ownership (Chechi 2014: 300–302).

1.6.7 **Balancing mechanisms in the law**

Judicial interpretation is not a closed system. German law does not have special provisions for what was taken from colonial contexts but contemporary German state liability law recognises a claim to eliminate the unlawful consequences of state action that interfered with an individual's rights, regardless of whether the initial state action was lawful or not. The *Folgenbeseitigungsanspruch* is unlike claims for damages and compensation, for it does not involve money (BVerwG NJW 2001, 1878, 1882). The past injustice is hard to prove, but the claim focuses on the unlawful situation that may be attributable to the state actor and that may be continuing in the present, based on current interpretation of constitutional rights. The legal bases of this claim originate from fundamental rights and the German *Rechtsstaatprinzip*, or the principle of the rule of law (BVerwGE 69, 366, 370). One of the requirements for the action is that time limitations should not be invoked in cases involving human remains and cultural or spiritual objects in museum collections, and ideally the local law of the deprived cultural community must be recognised and consulted.

Historians detect and classify relations between terms and concepts, but legal interpretation classifies and requires that the relationship between facts, norms, concepts, or aims, including who has authority to decide legal disputes, be determined. The relationship between different claims is determined by balancing mechanisms in the law. Influential philosophers Robert Nozick and Tony Honoré famously locked horns on the relationship between obligation and just title in the 1980s. Nozick theorised that the distribution of property is 'just' if brought about by free exchange among consenting adults from a fair starting position, and he maintained that this holds true even if subsequent inequalities emerged from the process. Nozick considers goods justly distributed if the person who acquires a thing and the persons who subsequently acquire from them are entitled to possess it. The state has no right to redistribute benefits to secure a more equal spread (Nozick 1974: 151ff). His premise resembles the idea of a chain of title. Honoré asserted that Nozick's theory of just title to property is incomplete, selective, and rests on an untenable assumption. Its rules for tracing just title 'require only that the principles of acquisition and transfer should themselves be just' to conclude that the distribution of goods is just. Nozick made assumptions about acquisitions and transfers. For instance, consensual transfers are just in a free society; or that the interest acquired in consensual transfers consists in a western view of property ownership based on Roman law (Honoré 1987: 215, 217ff). Honoré pointed out that Nozick's theory does not cover aspects of compulsory acquisition. It neglects rules that permit public authorities to expropriate private property but precludes opportunists or thieves from doing so, as well as rules pertinent to lapse of title, i.e., the rules on limitation of actions and prescription based on the idea that someone else may acquire property from a negligent owner. Honoré labelled the latter a 'sort of private expropriation' (Honoré 1987: 217–219). The western system of property law reflects the liberal concept of ownership as a permanent, exclusive, and transmissible interest in property, which cannot be readily justified from a moral perspective. Honoré emphasised that while the system of entitlements may be justifiable on economic grounds, it may not be on moral grounds. If it cannot be justified, state intervention is necessary to correct the imbalance and ensure that justice is done. Honoré disapproves of selective theorems that reproduce aspects of western property law favourable to private owners but exclude aspects that favour claims of the community which balance the former.

Repatriation of 'sacred' cultural material is 'other-regarding.' The moral authority of repatriation practices derives from being other-centred and oriented to restore capacity to those for whom the material denotes sacrifice. Claimants' moral authority in restitution cases is oftentimes all the power they have. Efforts to hold western societies accountable for their duty of care for cultural heritage by balancing concern for human rights with human responsibility are frustrated by conflicting interpretations of the definitions of rights. Agreement on compromises and trade-offs needed between different rights is lacking. Reluctance to acknowledge the inequalities in the bargaining power of the parties to the treaties that were concluded, or the content of the laws and customs of the source community at the time of the removal, will create scope for misreading the past (Vrdoljak 2008: 28). Groups that seek to subjugate other groups treat human rights selectively and appropriate their emancipatory discourses (Perugini and Gordon 2015).

Too much free-floating discretion can threaten the equilibrium of society (Zeidler 2016: 176). What ought to be subject to rule and what should be left to discretion is one of the most fundamental problems in jurisprudence. Fortunately, no difference of opinion arises on the need for adjudicators to exercise discretion in borderline areas between 'legal/extra-legal.' Adjudicators are concerned with the legal effect of facts, but non-legal disciplines treat the legal interpretation of facts differently (Möllers 2019). Within the space the law leaves for interpretation, discretion, or obtaining special permissions, adjudicators may have a margin of discretion to invite a paradigm in legal meaning (such as the 'common rules of adjudication' in Chechi's model) to settle a matter (Langbroek et al 2017: 6).

In processes of reappraising historical injustices during colonialism for reparations, the good will of all the parties involved matters greatly (Theurer 2023: 1163). Contrastingly, restitution differs from acts of generosity and good will in colonial contexts (Salvioli *2021 Report on Transitional Justice Measures* para 60; Stahn 2023: 436). Goldmann typifies it as an educational choice, for voluntary restitutions may increase the risk of succumbing to self-aggrandisement (Goldmann 2021). New restitution policies or procedural adjustments to prevent injustices should avoid self-congratulatory smugness for voluntary acts of magnanimity, which could create scope for competition and self-importance. If historic injustice is a mere moral responsibility resting on previous generations, subsequent generations cannot be expected to make rectifications, leaving mimetics with a free hand.

1.6.8 Legitimacy of the law in restitution claims

Treaty instruments and cultural heritage law introduced specific language to distinguish colonial takings from contemporary forms of looting or illicit trafficking of cultural objects. In settler societies, such as Canada, the United States, Australia, and New Zealand, legal frameworks have been created for return claims of Indigenous communities. However, 'objects taken in extractive colonial contexts have mostly been returned as an act of comity, rather than out of a sense of legal obligation in order not to set precedents and avoid the formation of a customary rule' (Stahn 2023: 32–33). This creates the flawed impression that PublIL law has nothing to say about the legality or conditions of takings in the colonial period or contemporary practices of return. A more accurate assessment becomes possible when the contradictions at play in categorisations of 'legal,' 'illegal,' and 'immoral' are openly acknowledged. Multiple shades of illegality are at work as Stahn indicates, and the frames of reference for assessing 'legality' are diverse and complex. Legal positivism serves only the Eurocentric conception of law and order but in all fairness the law cannot and indeed it does not, obviate all possibility of contradictory conclusions (Bollée 2019: 343). It cannot capture the nuances of the removals and the contestations accompanying them.

'Legitimacy' is an all-encompassing term that expresses *de facto* legitimacy, which is the sociological fact that people within a community regard their law as morally binding.*De jure* legitimacy refers to law that is morally binding by virtue of its status as law in the normative sense.Content legitimacy concerns the content of the law and, specifically, whether this content reflects correct value judgments (Tasioulas 2020: 468). To maintain legitimacy, laws and adjudicatory decisions must: a) take account of both history and morality; b) be consistent with the treatment of past similar cases; and c) align with the existing legal system within the 'horizon of a present future' (Habermas 1996: 198).

Regarding a), moral responsibility requires consideration of the 'legitimacy' of the law. A legal order can be legitimate only if it does not contradict basic moral principles. A principled morality can inform other spheres of action more effectively if it remains internally coupled to law (Habermas 1996: 106, 118). Both law and ethics are 'normative phenomena,' but humans alone can be the addressees of moral norms whereas legal norms may also address legal persons. Legal and moral rules appear side by side and precise distinctions may be hard to make (Zeidler 2016: 20–21). Moral and legal questions refer to the same problems but do so in different ways. Habermas postulates that legal and moral rules became 'simultaneously differentiated from traditional ethical life.' Legal norms took shape to offset deficits arising with the collapse of traditional ethical life and have since appeared as 'two different but mutually complementary kinds of action norms' (Habermas 1996: 105, 113). 'Norms' evoke standardisation in a particular field. They can be found in technical standards and in other places where the sphere of the law is not active. Coercion is not a prerequisite for a 'norm' since both social and ethical norms operate without coercion (De Benedetto 2021: 6–7). The enforceability of domestic law counts among its characteristics, but legislative initiatives that become overly intrusive or merely symbolic in their functioning will have their authority and legitimacy challenged in due course. The law also contains secondary rules that serve the production of primary rules thatguide behaviour.

As regards b), primary and secondary legal norms act together to stabilise behavioural expectations and regulate behaviour, but primary legal norms make it easier to see the legal meaning of the moral contents and the weight ascribed to the range of variation in these norms (Habermas 1996: 106, 117, 204). Even when laws do not expressly reference moral norms, they affect the interpretation and application of legal norms, the modification of which is frequently justified by moral judgments. The coherence of positive law with the legal ideal is a matter of degree and is rarely perfect (Linderfalk 2020: 59). The legal norms governing the validity of the acquisition of ownership assume relevance when a decision must be made on the substance of a restitution claim involving a collection item acquired in a colonial context. When 'content' legitimacy comes into play, it is easier to acknowledge the discordance between restitutions made to Western European States for cultural heritage removed as rules of war were being violated, and the lack of restitution to formerly colonised peoples when crimes were committed against their heritage. Holding institutions may allow the imperial laws of the time to frame the argument when they maintain that cultural objects were legitimately obtained in accordance with the laws that applied at the time of acquisition.

As for c), 'presentism' is the interpretation of historical events through the lens of present-day concerns and values. In the discourse on the law and ethics of colonial histories, it is discernible in the condemnation of past behaviours. The 'colonial present' reverts the criteria and standards for human behaviour back to the hierarchical mindset of the colonial era. The 'colonial present' nourishes unreflective, retrospective assumptions about colonial law, its implementation, and the opinions held about it. Un-historical perspectives that foster misinterpretations of historical data or the mishandling of primary source materials must be avoided, but the presentism argument should not be used to avoid engagement with the issue of restitution, however. Repatriation claims do not simply apply today's moral norms and standards to the distant past. Nor should the norms of yesteryear that allow 'might' to triumph over 'right' be regarded as the definitive standard. Such norms have always been heterogenous and contested (Joy 2020: 24). Moreover, thorough historical research must cast light on the 'legal grey zones' in which colonial takings occurred, for 'lawful'/'unlawful' cannot provide a definitive categorisation. 'Entangled legalities' call for moral judgment (Stahn 2023: 337, 339, 344). Adjudicators and policymakers must ascertain when diverse, local legal orders were drowned out by European assertions of power. In-depth legal historical research into a greater variety of source material is the only way to determine when exactly European international law substituted other rules and standards and the distinction between 'civilised' and 'uncivilised' disappeared (Theurer 2023: 1160–1161, 1167). The methods employed to obtain knowledge about what may be considered 'real,' and for resolving disputes arising from conflicting norms, can be expected to shift along with one's understanding of the origins, functions, and objectives of the law (Muir Watt 2016: 391). Paradigm shifts in our way of understanding the world are most fully reflected where legal thought takes form. This occurs in the realm of theory, wherewhat is worth studying and which pathways deserve to be surveyed, can be identified.

1.6.9 Reversing the burden of proof and adapting common law rules of evidence

Germany's festering resentment after the Second World War complicated restitution efforts. The restitution programme launched by the Allies to reverse the effects of destruction and plunder of cultural property during armed conflict was intended for conflicts fought between states. The concept of 'force' was accorded a generalised meaning that took account of discriminatory measures towards ethnic and national groups. The programme acknowledged that restitution of cultural objects to their source communities is vital to ensure the continuation of the contribution of all peoples to the cultural heritage of mankind, and to reverse and ameliorate discriminatory and genocidal policies. The 1954 Hague Convention for the Protection of Cultural Property in the Event of Armed Conflict codified the duty to preserve the cultural property of the enemy. A later revision awarded the dispossessed owner the right to recover 'any cultural property [that] has changed hands during an occupation' from 'the person in whose possession it is found.' A rebuttable presumption of illegality transferred the *onus probandi* (burden of proving) that the sale was regular, valid and compliant with export prohibitions, to the possessor. Usually, if the *onus probandi* rests on the claimant, the holding institution is in a stronger position simply because the claimant bears the burden of proving the basis for ordering return. If the burden is not discharged, the object or collection remains with the possessor (Zeidler 2016: 198). The Hague Convention also acknowledged the common law principle whereby a person with no legal title to an object cannot transfer title, and if objective good faith could be proved, then restitution had to be made subject to payment of just compensation. The right to retain war booty is effectively derogated and excluded as a principle of international law. In practice, however, the retention of war booty is widespread (Zeidler 2016: 158).

The position in Germany developed remarkably fast during the last decade. It used to be up to individual museums to plan and implement any provenance research they deemed necessary, but the German Museums Association (Deutscher Museumsbund or 'DMB') produced several sets of guidelines for the care of human remains and for collections from colonial contexts, with the clear intention to reveal its colonial past. The DMB *Care of Collections Guidelines* provide international and non-European perspectives on three interrelated types of cases differentiated by the colonial context (DMB 2021: 30). Establishing that the removal occurred in a colonial context is not intended to be an automatic indication that the provenance must be classified as problematical or that return is indicated, but signals that sensitivity and scrutiny are needed (DMB *Care of Collections* 2021: 13).

Recognition of aboriginal title in Canada implied the adaptation of Common Law rules of evidence to give due weight to practices, customs and traditions and their relationship with the land. Oral histories are permitted in litigation of aboriginal property rights (Hance 2020b: 173).

The 2018 Sarr and Savoy Report proposes presumptions. A process is set up to identify the category/ies to be repatriated fully, as a matter of priority, which concerns items taken through colonial violence (war booty or 'spoils' of war); war booty given to a museum through a private collector; objects that were either stolen or bought far below market prices; gifts from private collectors deriving from 'exploratory' missions and scientific 'raids'; and objects 'taken by force or presumed to be acquired through inequitable conditions' by administrators, scientific expeditions before 1960 and others (Sarr and Savoy 2018: 49–10). Where these identifications are made, the returns are not subject to provenance research in France or through the art market, and the burden of proof that items were obtained without coercion or force rests on the holding institution or possessor. Full returns are to be made unless current possessors can affirm, by evidence, rightful acquisition including consent. The report singles out four Francophone African countries—Benin, Senegal, Cameroon, Mali—while Algeria and Egypt are left aside (Sarr and Savoy 2018: 3 n4). The new models emanating from Belgium and Austria will make room for provenance research to inform decisions about de-accession and return, but others will continue to operate based on presumptions. Combinations of these may follow. The language of putting the claimant in the same position they would have been in had no wrong been committed, becomes severely strained in reparative justice claims. The demand to acknowledge the wrong then becomes more pressing (Moran 2019: 463). Determining the interpretation of legal rules and norms and their value for policymaking implicitly requires permitting our conceptions of right and wrong to challenge our assumptions.

In light of the above, the evidentiary standard which civil courts apply to determine not only the interpretation of letter issued in July 1801 but also the legality of the actions taken, does not align well with the fact of Ottoman occupation at the time of the removal of the Parthenon Sculptures. Arguably, the British Museum must affirm its rightful acquisition with the consent of the Athenians.

History has no definitive outcome. Ambiguous loss may mean that closure cannot be achieved, and the 'justice' we anticipate never attained. Asking better questions about the legal frameworks of former colonial powers and the treaties instigated by them remains a worthy pursuit nonetheless.

1.7 Aims of this study

A central tenet of the method adopted in this study, which is located at the intersection of law, ethics, history, and anthropology, lies in restoring the capacity of the material to challenge fragmented, hierarchical thinking. It proposes a methodology that defines 'sacred' stolen, looted, and pillaged cultural material in private and public collections, for definitions are lacking and the legal understanding of how to qualify such objects tends to be absent or superficial. This is part of the preparation needed to dissect the most troubling hurdles encountered by those who claim restitution or repatriation through legal pathways and norms, which is the focus of a follow-up study (*Restoring the Law of Restitution: Complex Colonial Contexts*).

Embedded dichotomies and classifications have proved troublesome. For instance, in the dichotomy between science and the sacred, the supposed 'superiority' of science protects the juridical framework for circulating 'sacred' cultural material. One example of this is the manifest despoliation of Chinese culture in travelling exhibitions and scientific research conducted notwithstanding the 'sacred' character of material, the knowledge they bear, and what meaning they hold for the source community. The way in which 'rapacious foreigners' are despoiling Chinese culture is not altogether dissimilar from the diminishment of the culture of Athens by Lusieri, Hunt and Elgin (Hooper and Pflaker 2017).

In western institutions the study of human remains is classified with the natural sciences, while human beliefs are classified as 'material culture' within the humanities and social sciences (Curtis 2014: 85, 90). To this day ethics guidelines for the curation of human remains differ substantially from those relating to material culture associated with human beliefs. For instance, mummies enter museum collections as objects of curiosity despite widespread awareness that Egyptians, for example, prefer to leave mummies in their tombs (Woodhead 2002: 337). Curatorial requests for the removal of material hidden within artefactual human remains disregard the duty to treat human remains with dignity and respect, but this is seldom acknowledged. The structure of reality is a field in which humanness also finds expression in replicable patterns that manifest in material culture, which scientific processes can keep track of. The intangible heritage value at the core of claims to sacred material is not yet reflected in the rudimentary legal tools available across the categories of Nazi-looted art, stolen and illegally exported antiquities, and colonial takings (Campfens 2021: 3).

Fragmentation at the material level infiltrates associated systems of knowledge. It finds expression in language that relies on cemented dichotomies. Conceptual fragmentation in restitution claims for sacred heritage affects museum, conservation, and legal professionals. It thrives at the level of specialisms focused on 'private'/'public' or 'law'/'ethics' and is apparent at the level of the structure and method of international law, both PublIL and PrIL. It befuddles restitution claims, not least because formalist legal argument based on legal positivist notions of 'law' facilitates non-compliance with moral standards and puts pressure on 'justice.' Mummified assumptions about normativity and 'normative pluralism' complicate the interplay between historical events and legal mechanisms that rely on a time factor.

Artificial classifications in relation to human remains deriving from genocide such as the Nama and Herero genocide in German SWA, artefactual human remains embedded in statues such as Zhanggong Zushi's self-mummified remains, and fragments of sacred monuments and sanctuaries that speak of sacrifice, create classificatory tensions that affect adjudicatory outcomes, policy, and policy positions. These transnational cases call for deeper reflection on the demarcation between procedure and substance that plagues disputes over sacred cultural material. Restitution claims involving complex sacred material prompt a rethink of the absurd distinctions drawn between looting, plunder, and theft. New thinking is needed in respect of the method for collisions between primary and/or secondary legal norms in local law and colonial law, and the intangible 'sacred' dimension of cultural heritage in its relationship to the tangible, corporeal.

Ad hoc procedures can be carved out to fit the exigencies of a restitution claim, but considerable scope remains for the reconstruction of the legal basis of restitution claims for sacred cultural material and human remains. Instead of debating the intellectual property rights dimension of cultural heritage, it is necessary to shed light on the emerging field of repatriation of intangible cultural heritage. The field embraces the normative regulation of digitisation of cultural heritage, jurisdiction, legal standards, intellectual property protection, attribution, the permission to copy, and many other rights in materials that are being returned. New possibilities for digitisation to make available and protect cultural material bring legal challenges that are acutely under-researched. This study argues that claims for the repatriation of tangible material must acknowledge the intangible dimensions of sacred heritage, but the intangible dimensions must acknowledge the tangible. To deepen community and promote integration, the law of restitution must be 'restored' to a fully functioning state. An integrated normative framework must be constructed around 'sacred' intangible cultural heritage and the ethic of PrIL, since a successful claim depends on adjudicators' firm grasp on normativity at the PrIL frontier of global justice, where different legal norms vie for application in the same interspatial plane, be it external or internal.

Reparative justice cases marked by violent looting and theft during the colonial era have the normative leverage needed in restitution claims to suspend the application of ordinary commercial rules, shift PrIL categories, and justify non-application of procedural protections and non-application of prescription and statutes of limitation. The success of restitutionary claims to sacred heritage looted and trafficked during the colonial era depends on an understanding of the 'sacred' to encompass tangible and intangible and to cut across social sciences and humanities. To accomplish a perspective that mediates clashes between law and history and values, questions must be asked about secondary legal norms that aspire to 'global justice.' How do these norms link to other legal disciplines, and to provenance research on human remains and other sacred material? How do PrIL's common principles affect claims for sacred heritage in transnational disputes? What implications does the 'sacred' have for the taxonomies of private and public law?

1.8 Outline

All claims to cultural property and heritage give expression to the conflict between private and public/common good, but Britain's historic refusal to return the Parthenon Sculptures to Athens cast a 'dominant, stifling shadow over cultural property argument' (Audi 2007: 141). As a paradigmatic cultural property case that has not resulted in restitution, it makes all claims to cultural property appear idle (Audi 2007: 145). The dispute is comprehensively documented and demonstrates many angles of the legal, ethical, curatorial, and political discourses in restitution (Zeidler 2016: 7, 19–52).

The introductory chapter considered the manifestations of mimetic human desire in respect of cultural material that had been plundered, looted, or coercively taken—whether by duress or manipulation—in the colonial era. Sarr and Savoy refer to the urgency of having to establish 'new cultural relations based on a newly reflected upon ethical relation' (Sarr and Savoy Report 2018: 29). Scattered plunderings yielded multiple mutable meanings for what had been taken. Is there any core stability in the definition of plundered 'things' that could assist the law better to support and develop new cultural relations? This study suggests that a broad-based theory that applies across the humanities and social sciences is the first necessary step that needs to be taken before more consistent and widespread legal reform could take place.

Chapter 2 commences with a clarification of the dimensions of Girard's 'mimetic theory' and its definition of the 'sacred.' To incorporate knowledge that can identify the 'sacred' from outside of its own tradition, museology, art history, applied ethics, and law require a vantage point much wider in scope than just its own. The mimetic tendencies present in lawmaking and implementation are highlighted in Chapter 2; they affect the application of secondary legal norms that control the application of the legal systems in former colonial territories, which Chapter 3 introduces.

Bibliography

Alexandrowicz, Charles Henry. 1973. *The European-African Confrontation: A Study in Treaty-Making* Leiden: A.W. Sijthoff.

Amin, George Forji. 2023. *International Law and the History of Resource Extraction in Africa: Capital Accumulation and Underdevelopment, 1450–1918* London: Routledge.

Anghie, Antony. 1999. 'Finding the Peripheries: Sovereignty and Colonialism in Nineteenth Century International Law' *Harvard International Law Journal* 40(1): 1–80.

Audi, Alan. 2007. 'A Semiotics of Cultural Property Argument' *International Journal of Cultural Property* 14(2): 131–167.

Bachmann, Klaus. 2018. *Genocidal Empires: German Colonialism in Africa and the Third Reich* Frankfurt/Main: Peter Lang.

Bailey, Saki. 2013. 'The Architecture of Commons Legal Institutions for Future Generations' in Saki Bailey, Gilda Farrell & Ugo Mattei (eds.) *Protecting Future Generations Through Commons–Trends in Social Cohesion, No 26* Strasbourg: Council of Europe Publishing 107–139.

Banu, Roxana. 2013. 'Assuming Regulatory Authority for Transnational Torts: An Interstate Affair? A Historical Perspective on the Canadian Private International Law Tort Rules' *Windsor Yearbook on Access to Justice* 31(1): 197–211.

Banu, Roxana. 2018. *Nineteenth Century Perspectives on Private International Law* Oxford: OUP.

Banu, Roxana. 2022. 'Teaching by Historicising Private International Law' *International Journal of Law in Context* 18(4): 383-392.

Bell, Abraham & Gideon Parchomovsky. 2005. 'A Theory of Property' *Cornell Law Review* 9: 531–616.

Berman, Nathaniel. 2019. 'Drama Through Law: The Versailles Treaty and the Casting of the Modern International Stage' in Michel Erpelding, Burkhard Hess & Helene Ruiz Fabri (eds.), *Peace Through Law: The Versailles Treaty and Dispute Settlement After World War 1* Baden-Baden, Germany: Nomos Verlagsgesellschaft 31-64.

Besson, Samantha. 2011. 'Human Rights: Ethical, Political ... or Legal: First Steps in a Legal Theory of Human Rights' in Donald E. Childress III (ed.) *The Role of Ethics in International Law* Cambridge: CUP 211–245.

Bhandar, Brenna. 2018. *Colonial Lives of Property: Law, Land, and Racial Regimes of Ownership* Durham: Duke University Press.

Biskup, Thomas & Martin Kohlrausch. 2016. 'Germany' in Nigel Dalziel & John MacKenzie (eds.) *The Encyclopedia of Empire* Hoboken, NJ: John Wiley & Son Ltd 1–16.

Bix, Brian H. 2011. 'Radbruch's Formula and Conceptual Analysis' *American Journal of Jurisprudence* 56: 45–57.

Bollée, Sylvain. 2019. 'Thoughts on the Dallah Case: The Hypothesis of the Indeterminacy of the Legal System' in Horatia Muir Watt, Lucia Bíziková, Agatha Brandão de Oliveira & Diego P. Fernández Arroyo (eds.) *Global Private International Law: Adjudication without Frontiers* Cheltenham: Edward Elgar Publishing 342–349.

Bosman, Hendrik. 2011. 'A Nama 'Exodus'? A Postcolonial Reading of the Diaries of Hendrik Witbooi' *Scriptura* 108: 329–341.

Botha, Christo. 2007. 'Internal Colonisation and an Oppressed Minority? The Dynamics of Relations between Germans and Afrikaners against the Background of Constructing a Colonial State in Namibia, 1884–1990' *Journal of Namibian Studies* 2: 7–50.

British Museum. 2018. *Policy on Deaccession of Objects from the Collection* <https://www.britishmuseum.org/sites/default/files/2019-10/De-accession_Policy_Nov2018.pdf>.

Brown, Alison K. 2014. *First Nations, Museums, Narrations: Stories of the 1929 Franklin Motor Expedition to the Canadian Prairies* Vancouver: UBC Press.

Bruijn Eric, Amelie Alterauge, Stephanie Zesch, Ben Heggelman, Sylvia Mitschke, Francesca Coletti, Wilfried Rosendahl, Albert Zink & Vincent van Vilsteren. 2015. 'Die Mumie in Inneren–eine übermodellierte Mumie eines buddhistichen Mőnchs' in Alfried Wiexzorek, Michael Tellenbach & Wilfried Rosendahl (eds.) *Mumien: Der Traum vom ewigen Leben* (Reiss-Engelhorn-Museen: 2. teilweise überarbeitete Auflage) Darmstadt: gGmbH und WBG 337–342.

Bush, Jonathan A. 2002. '"The Supreme...Crime" and Its Origins: The Lost Legislative History of the Crime of Aggressive War' *Columbia Law Review* 102(8): 2324-2424.

Byrne, James G. 2015. *Factors Determining the Repatriation of Cultural Heritage from Museums; the Place of Cultural Rights in British Museums Practice* Master Thesis, SOAS University of London.

Campfens, Evelien. 2019. 'The Bangwa Queen: Artifact or Heritage?' *International Journal of Cultural Property* 26(1): 75–110.

Campfens, Evelien. 2021. *Cross-Border Title Claims to Cultural Objects: Property or Heritage?* PhD Thesis, Leiden University (Meijers-reeks Eleven).

Campfens, Evelien. 2024. 'Private International Law and Cultural Heritage' in Lucas Lixinski & Lucie K. Morisset (eds.) *The Routledge Handbook of Heritage and the Law* London: Routledge 145–156.

Cash Cash, Phillip E. 2001. 'Medicine Bundles: An Indigenous Approach to Curation' in Tamara Bray (ed.) *The Future of the Past: Archaeologists, Native Americans and Repatriation* London: Routledge 139–148.

Chamberlain, Russel. 1983. *Loot! The Heritage of Plunder* London: Thames & Hudson.

Champagne, Duane. 2012. 'Indigenous Self-government, Cultural Heritage and International Trade: A Sociological Perspective' in Christopher B. Graber, Karolina Kuprecht & Jessica C Lai (eds.) *International Trade in Indigenous Cultural Heritage: Legal and Policy Issues* Cheltenham: Edward Elgar Publishing 31–58.

Chechi, Alessandro. 2013. 'Plurality and Coordination of Dispute Settlement Methods in the Field of Cultural Heritage' in Francesco Francioni & James Gordley (eds.) *Enforcing International Cultural Heritage Law* Oxford: OUP 177–205.

Chechi, Alessandro. 2014. *The Settlement of International Heritage Disputes* Oxford: OUP.

Chechi, Alessandro. 2024. 'The Preamble to the 1995 UNIDROIT Convention' in Ana Filipa Vrdoljak, Andrzej Jakubowski & Alessandro Chechi (eds.) *The 1970 UNESCO and 1995 UNIDROIT Conventions on Stolen or Illegally Transferred Cultural Property: A Commentary* Oxford: OUP 499–513.

Clegg, Margaret. 2020. *Human Remains: Curation, Reburial and Repatriation* Cambridge: CUP.

Conaty, Gerald T. 2008. 'The Effects of Repatriation on the Relationship Between the Glenbow Museum and the Blackfoot People' *Museum Management and Curatorship* 23(3): 245–259.

Coody Cooper, Karen. 2008. *Spirited Encounters: American Indians Protest Museum Policies and Practices* Lanham, Maryland: AltaMira Press.

Cook, Walter W. 1941. '"Characterization" in the Conflict of Laws' *Yale Law Journal* 51(2): 191–212.

Crennan, Susan M. 'Review: Asian Art Provenance Project' National Gallery of Australia, Canberra, July 2021 <https://nga.gov.au/media/dd/documents/NGAIndependentReview_SCrennan.612fde9.pdf>

Cummings, Catherine. 2017. 'Queen Victoria's Samoan Bonnet' in Paul Basu (ed.) *The Inbetweenness of Things: Materializing Mediation and Movement Between Worlds* London: Bloomsbury Academic 191–208.

Curtis, Neil. 2014. '"A Welcome and Important Part of their Role": The Impact of Repatriation on Museums in Scotland' in Louise Tythacott & Kostas Arvanitis (eds.) *Museums and Restitution: New Practices, New Approaches* Burlington: Ashgate 85–104.

David, Valeska. 2020. *Cultural Difference and Economic Disadvantage in Regional Human Rights Courts: An Integrated View* Cambridge: Intersentia.

De Benedetto, Maria. 2021. *Corruption from a Regulatory Perspective* Oxford: Hart Publishing.

De Clippele, Marie-Sophie & Bert Demarsin. 2021. 'Rights, Wrongs and Remedies – Working Towards Colonial Heritage Repatriation Legislation for Belgium Paper Presented at 'Imperial Artefacts: History, Law and the Looting of Cultural Property', Conference organised by the University of Leiden, 27–28 January 2021.

De Clippele, Marie-Sophie & Bert Demarsin. 2022. 'Pioneering Belgium: Parliamentary Legislation on the Restitution of Colonial Collections: Country Report: Belgium' *Santander Art and Culture Law Review* 8(2): 277–294.

De Lathuy, Philippe. 2018. *The Parthenon Marbles: A Landmark Case for the Future of the Repatriation Movement* LLM Thesis by Research, University of Ghent.

Deakin, Simon, David Gindis, Geoffrey M. Hodgson, Kainan Huang & Katharina Pistor. 2017. 'Legal Institutionalism: Capitalism and the Constitutive Role of Law' *Journal of Comparative Economics* 45(1): 188–200.

Declaration of the Second Russia-Africa Summit. 28 July 2023. <https://summitafrica.ru/en/about-summit/declaration-2023/>.

Dedering, Tilman. 1999. 'The Prophet's "War Against Whites": Shepherd Stuurman in Namibia and South Africa, 1904–7' *The Journal of African History* 40: 1–19.

Dedering, Tilman. 2000. 'The Ferreira Raid of 1906: Boers, Britons and Germans in Southern Africa in the Aftermath of the South African War' *Journal of Southern African Studies* 26(1): 43–60.

Delacroix, Sylvie. 2006. *Legal Norms and Normativity: An Essay in Genealogy* Oxford: Hart Publishing.

Dudley, Sandra H. 2018. 'The Buzz of Displacement: Liminality Among Burmese Court Objects in Oxford, London and Yangon' in Paul Basu (ed.) *The Inbetweenness of Things: Materializing Mediation and Movement between Worlds* New York: Bloomsbury Academic 38–56.

Eaton, Natasha. 2018. 'Colonial Iconoclash: Mimetic Rivalry, Collecting and Idolatry Between India and Britain' in Benedicte Savoy, Charlotte Guichard & Christine Howald (eds.) *Acquiring Cultures: Histories of World Art on Western Markets* Berlin: De Gruyter 31–46.

Effiboley, Emery Patrick. 2020. 'Reflections on the Issue of Repatriation of Looted and Illegally Acquired African Cultural Objects in Western Museums' *Contemporary Journal of African Studies* 7(1): 67–83.

Fagan, Andrew. 2017. *Human Rights and Cultural Diversity: Core Issues and Cases* Edinburgh: Edinburgh University Press.

Fagbayibo, Babatunde. 2021. 'Studying the Past in the Present Tense: International Law in the Benin Empire' *Politikon* 48(3): 468–485.

Fanon, Franz. 1964. 'Racism and Culture' in *Toward the African Revolution: Political Essays* (tr. Haakon Chevalier) New York: Grove Press 31–44.

Fanon, Frantz. 1986. *Black Skin, White Masks* (tr. Charles Lam Markmann 1952) London: Pluto Press.

Fitzmaurice, Andrew. 2017. 'Skepticism of the Civilizing Mission in International Law' in Martti Koskenniemi, Walter Rech & Manuel Jiménez Fonseca (eds.) *International Law and Empire: Historical Explorations* Oxford: OUP 359–382.

Flanagan, Owen. 2016. *The Geography of Morals: Varieties of Moral Possibility* Oxford Scholarship Online.

Flint, John E. 1974. *Cecil Rhodes* Boston: Little Brown 248–252.

Förster, Larissa. 2020. 'The Face of Genocide' in Cressida Fforde, Timothy McKeown & Honor Keeler (eds.) *The Routledge Companion to Indigenous Repatriation* London: Routledge 101–127.

Forrest, Craig. 2010. *International Law and the Protection of Cultural Heritage* London: Routledge.
Francioni, Francesco. 2024. 'Article 2 of the 1970 UNESCO Convention: Purposes' in Ana Filipa Vrdoljak, Andrzej Jakubowski & Alessandro Chechi (eds.) *The 1970 UNESCO and 1995 UNIDROIT Conventions on Stolen or Illegally Transferred Cultural Property: A Commentary* Oxford: OUP 66–77.
Garnett, Richard. 2012. *Substance and Procedure in Private International Law* Oxford: OUP.
German Museums Association (DMB). 2021. *Guidelines for German Museums: Care of Collections from Colonial Contexts* 3rd ed, April 2021 <https://www.museumsbund.de/wp-content/uploads/2021/03/mb-leitfaden-en-web.pdf>.
Gilbert, Jérémie. 2011. 'Indigenous Peoples' Human Rights in Africa: The Pragmatic Revolution of the African Commission on Human and Peoples' Rights' *International & Comparative Law Quarterly* 60(1): 245–270.
Gilbert, Jérémie. 2018. *Natural Resources and Human Rights: An Appraisal* Oxford Scholarship Online.
Gilbert, Jérémie & Kanyinke Sena. 2018. 'Litigating Indigenous Peoples' Cultural Rights: Comparative Analysis of Kenya and Uganda' *African Studies* 77(2): 204–222.
Girard, René. 2010. *Battling to the End: Conversations with Benoit Chantre (Studies in Violence, Mimesis, and Culture)* (tr Mary Baker 2007) East Lansing: Michigan State University Press.
Glenn, H. Patrick. 2011. 'The Ethic of International Law' in Donald E. Childress III (ed.) *The Role of Ethics in International Law* Cambridge: CUP 246–270.
Godelier, Maurice. 1996. *The Enigma of the Gift* (tr. Nora Scott) Chicagoe: University of Chicago Press.
Godwin, Hannah R. 2020. 'Legal Complications of Repatriation at the British Museum' *Washington International Law Journal* 30(1): 144–170.
Goldmann, Matthias. 2021. 'Imperial Law's Ambiguity: A Postcolonial Approach to Restitution and Reparation Claims', Keynote Presented at 'Imperial Artefacts: History, Law and the Looting of Cultural Property', Conference organised by the University of Leiden, 27–28 January 2021.
Goldmann, Matthias. 2024. 'The Ambiguity of Colonial International Law: Three Approaches to the Namibian Genocide' *Leiden Journal of International Law* 37: 580–607.
Gould, Cecil. 1965. *Trophy of Conquest: The Musée Napoléon and the Creation of the Louvre* London: Faber and Faber.
Greaves, Ida. 1954. 'The Character of British Colonial Trade' *Journal of Political Economy* 62(1): 1–11.
Greenfield, Jeanette. 2007. *The Return of Cultural Treasures* 3rd ed. Cambridge: CUP.
Greenhalgh, Michael. 2019. *Plundered Empire: Acquiring Antiquities from Ottoman Lands* Leiden: Brill.
Grimme, Gesa. 2020. 'Systemizing (sic) Provenance Research on Objects from Colonial Contexts' in Philipp Schorch (ed.) Special Issue on Sensitive Heritage: Ethnographic Museums, Provenance Research, and the Potentialities of Restitutions, *Museum and Society* 18(1) 52–65.
Gruber, Manuel. 2019. 'Time for a Reappraisal? The Intertemporal Principle of International Law Examined' *Australian International Law Journal* 26: 91-109.
Habermas, Jürgen. 1996. *Norms and Facts* Cambridge, MA: The MIT Press.
Hai, Mariam. 2013. 'Selling the Sacred: An Examination of Sacred Objects in Legal Contexts' *DePaul Journal of Art, Technology & Intellectual Property Law* 24(1): 193–217.
Hance, Clea. 2020a. 'The Interaction Between Intangible Cultural Heritage and Human Rights' in Marie Cornu, Anita Vaivade, Lily Martinet & Clea Hance (eds.) *Intangible Cultural Heritage under National and International Law: Going Beyond the 2003 UNESCO Convention* Cheltenham: Edward Elgar Publishing 81–96.

Hance, Clea. 2020b. 'The Judicialization of the Tension between the Cultural Identity of States and Intangible Cultural Heritage' in Marie Cornu, Anita Vaivade, Lily Martinet & Clea Hance (eds.) *Intangible Cultural Heritage under National and International Law: Going Beyond the 2003 UNESCO Convention* Cheltenham: Edward Elgar Publishing 171–178.

Hansard HC Deb. vol 672, col. 722, 2 March 2020.

Hansard HL Deb. vol 834, cols. 1992-2006, 14 December 2023.

Harari, Yuval Noah. 2011. *Sapiens: A Brief History of Humankind* London: Vintage.

Harju, Kaisa. 2019. 'A Joint Effort: Owambo Agency in the Karl Emil Liljeblad Collection' in Marjo Kaartinen, Leila Koivunen & Napandulwe Shiweda (eds.) *Intertwined Histories* University of Turku: Spin Press 76–84.

Hartman, Geoffrey H. 1997. *The Fateful Question* New York: Columbia University Press.

Herman, Alexander. 2023. *The Parthenon Marbles Dispute: Heritage, Law, Politics* Oxford: Hart Publishing.

Hitchens, Christopher. 1997. *The Elgin Marbles: Should They be Returned to Greece?* (with essays by Robert Browning & Graham Binns) London: Verso.

Hobbs, Patricia. 2014. 'The Interaction Between Domestic Law and International Humanitarian Law at the Extraordinary Chambers in the Courts of Cambodia' in Derek Jinks, Jackson N. Maogoto & Solon Solomon (eds.) *Applying International Humanitarian Law in Judicial and Quasi-Judicial Bodies* The Hague: TMC Asser Press 289–314.

Hobbes, Thomas. 1651. *Leviathan* Minneapolis: First Avenue editions.

Hohfeld, Wesley Newcomb; Cook, Walter Wheeler ed. 1923. *Fundamental Conceptions as Applied Legal Reasoning and other Essays* New Haven: Yale University Press.

Honoré, Tony M. 1987. *Making Law Bind: Essays Legal and Philosophical* Oxford: Clarendon Press.

Hooper, John & Ted Plafker. 2017. 'The Body in the Buddha' *The Economist*, 4 May.

Hubert, Jane. 1992. 'Dry Bones or Living Ancestors? Conflicting Perceptions of Life, Death and the Universe' *International Journal of Cultural Property* 1(1): 105–128.

Human Rights Council Report. 2020. *Expert Mechanism on the Rights of Indigenous Peoples, Repatriation of Ceremonial Objects, Human Remains and the Intangible Cultural Heritage under the United Nations Declaration on the Rights of Indigenous Peoples* A/HRC/45/35 21 July.

Ingelson, Allan & Ifeoma Owosuyi. 2022. 'Reviewing the Experience with the Repatriation of Sacred Ceremonial Objects: A Comparative Legal Analysis of Canada and South Africa' *International Journal of Cultural Property* 29(3): 217–241.

International Law Commission. 2001. Draft Articles on Responsibility of States for Internationally Wrongful Acts, with Commentaries, 53rd session, United Nations 2008.

International Law Commission. 2019. Commentary on Report, 71st Session, 29 April–7 June and 8 July–9 August 2019, Geneva.

Jagielska-Burduk, Alicja & Derek Fincham. 2024. 'Article 3 of the 1995 UNIDROIT Convention: Claims for Restitution of Stolen Cultural Objects' in Ana Filipa Vrdoljak, Andrzej Jakubowski & Alessandro Chechi (eds.) *The 1970 UNESCO and 1995 UNIDROIT Conventions on Stolen or Illegally Transferred Cultural Property: A Commentary* Oxford: OUP 545–560.

Jakubowski, Andrzej. 2015. *State Succession in Cultural Property* Oxford: OUP.

Janes, Robert R. 2022. 'The Value of Museums in Averting Social Collapse' *Curator: The Museum Journal* 64(4): 729–745.

Jayme, Erik. 2005. 'Globalization in Art Law: Clash of Interests and International Tendencies' *Vanderbilt Journal of Transnational Law* 38(4): 927–945.

Jenkins, Tiffany. 2011. *Contesting Human Remains in Museum Collections: The Crisis of Cultural Authority* London: Routledge.

Joy, Charlotte. 2020. *Heritage Justice* Cambridge: CUP.

Kaczorowska, Alina. 2010. *Public International Law* 4th ed. London: Routledge.
Kakaounaki, Marianna. 2024. 'A Greek Archaeologist's Dig into the Elgin Archive' *Kathimerini* 2 April.
Kennedy, Duncan. 1991. 'A Semiotics of Legal Argument' *Syracuse Law Review* 42(1): 75–116.
Kennedy, Duncan. 1997. 'New Approaches to Comparative Law: Comparativism and International Governance' *Utah Law Review* 545–593.
Kennedy, Duncan. 2010. 'Savigny's Family/Patrimony Distinction and its Place in the Global Genealogy of Classical Legal Thought' *The American Journal of Comparative Law* 58(4): 811–841.
Koot, Stasja & Robert K. Hitchcock. 2019. 'In the Way: Perpetuating Land Dispossession of the Indigenous Hai//om and the Collective Action Lawsuit for Etosha National Park and Mangeti West, Namibia' *Nomadic Peoples* 23: 55–77.
Koskenniemi, Martti. 2017. 'Introduction: International Law and Empire–Aspects and Approaches' in Martti Koskenniemi, Walter Rech & Manuel Jiménez Fonseca (eds.) *International Law and Empire: Historical Explorations* Oxford: OUP 1–18.
Kowalski, Wojciech W. 2002. 'Restitution of Works of Art Pursuant to Private and Public Law' *Recueil des Cours* 288 (2001): 13–244.
Kreps, Christina F. 2003. *Liberating Culture: Cross-Cultural Perspectives on Museums, Curation, and Heritage Preservation* London: Routledge.
Kress, Claus. 2006. 'Versailles-Nuremberg-The Hague: Germany and International Criminal Law' *The International Lawyer* 40(1): 15–39.
Labadi, Sophia. 2017. *Museums, Immigrants and Social Justice* London: Routledge.
Labadie, Camille. 2021. 'Decolonizing Collections: A Legal Perspective on the Restitution of Cultural Artifacts' *ICOFOM Study Series* 49(2): 132–146.
Lagardien, Ismael. 2022. *Too White to be Coloured, Too Coloured to be Black: On the Search for Home and Meaning* Cape Town: Melinda Ferguson Books.
Lamprecht, Sterling P. 1940. 'Hobbes and Hobbism' *The American Political Science Review* 34(1): 31–53.
Langbroek, Philip, Kees van den Bos, Marc Simon Thomas, Michael Milo & Wibo van Rossum. 2017. 'Editorial: Methodology of Legal Research: Challenges and Opportunities' *Utrecht Law Review Special Issue* 13(3): 1–8.
Last, Kathryn V. 2007. 'Cultural Pluralism and the Return of Cultural Heritage' in Stephen Tierney (ed.) *Accommodating Cultural Diversity* Burlington: Ashgate 123–143.
Lauterpacht, Sir Elihu. 2009. 'Principles of Procedure in International Litigation' *Recueil des Cours* 345(2009): 387–530.
Levy, Jacob T. 2000. The Multiculturalism of Fear online ed, Oxford Academic, 1 Nov. 2003.
Linderfalk, Ulf. 2020. *Understanding Jus Cogens in International Law and International Legal Discourse* Cheltenham: Edward Elgar Publishing.
Little, Janet P. (ed and tr). 2003. *Simone Weil on Colonialism: An Ethic of the Other* Lanham, Maryland: Rowman & Littlefield Inc.
Liu, Zuozhen. 2016. *The Case for Repatriating China's Cultural Objects* Singapore: Springer.
Liu, Zuozhen. 2017. 'Will the God Win?: The Case of the Buddhist Mummy' *International Journal of Cultural Property* 24(2): 221–238.
Lixinski, Lucas. 2018. 'Across Public/Private International Legal Divide in the Governance of Global Public Goods' *Denver Journal of International Law & Policy* 47(1): 1–28.
Lixinski, Lucas. 2019a. *International Heritage Law for Communities: Exclusion and Re-Imagination* Oxford Scholarship Online.
Lixinski, Lucas. 2019b. 'A Third Way of Thinking About Cultural Property' *Brooklyn Journal of International Law* 4(2): 563–612.
Lixinski, Lucas. 2024. 'Religious Heritage and the Law' in Lucas Lixinski & Lucie K. Morisset (eds.) *The Routledge Handbook of Heritage and the Law* London: Routledge 473–488.

Logan, William S. 2007. 'Closing Pandora's Box: Human Rights Conundrums in Cultural Heritage Protection' in Helaine Silverman & D. Fairchild Ruggles (eds.) *Cultural Heritage and Human Rights* New York: Springer 33–52.

Lubina, Katja. 2009. *Contested Cultural Property: The Return of Nazi Spoliated Art and Human Remains from Public Collections* PhD Thesis, University of Maastricht.

Lyon, William Blakemore. 2015. *The South West Africa Company and Anglo-German Relations, 1892–1914* MPhil Thesis, Sidney Sussex College.

MacGregor, Neil & Jonathan Williams. 2005. 'The Encyclopaedic Museum: Enlightenment Ideals, Contemporary Realities' *Public Archaeology* 4(1): 57–59.

Maine, Sir Henry. 1861. *Ancient Law* London: JM Dent & Sons Ltd.

Manacorda, Stefano. 2011. 'Criminal Law Protection of Cultural Heritage: An International Perspective' in Stefano Manacorda & Duncan Chappell (eds.) *Crime in the Art and Antiquities World: Illegal Trafficking in Cultural Property* Springer 17–48.

Matthes, Erich Hatala. 2017. 'Repatriation and the Radical Redistribution of Art' *Ergo: An Open Access Journal of Philosophy* 4: 931–953.

Matthews, Maureen. 2014. 'Repatriating Agency: Animacy, Personhood and Agency in the Repatriation of Ojibwe Artefacts' in Louise Tythacott & Kostas Arvanitis (eds.) *Museums and Restitution: New Practices, New Approaches* Burlington: Ashgate 121–137.

McBride, Nicholas J. & Sandy Steele. 2018. *Great Debates in Jurisprudence,* 2nd ed. Great Britain: Palgrave.

McLachlan, Campbell. 2009. Lis Pendens in International Litigation Leiden. Martinus Nijhoff Publishers.

Michaels, Ralf. 2019. 'Private International Law as an Ethic of Responsivity' in Verónica Ruiz Abou-Nigm & Maria Blanca Noodt Taquela (eds.) *Diversity and Integration in Private International Law* Edinburgh: Edinburgh University Press 11–27.

Miles, Margaret M. 2002. 'Cicero's Prosecution of Gaius Verres: A Roman View of the Ethics of Acquisition of Art' *International Journal of Cultural Property* 11(1): 28–49.

Miles, Margaret M. 2011. 'Still in the Aftermath of Waterloo: A Brief History of Decisions about Restitution' in Peter Stone (ed.) *Cultural Heritage, Ethics, and the Military* Suffolk: The Boydell Press 29–42.

Mills, Alex. 2009. *The Confluence of Public and Private International Law* Cambridge: CUP.

Mimran, Jean-Michelle. 1994. 'L'Office Central pour la Répression du Vol d'œuvres et Objets d'art' *Revue Internationale de Police Criminelle* 60–64.

Möllers, Thomas M. J. 2019. *Legal Methods: How to Work with Legal Arguments* (tr Gill Mertens) Munich: Beck.

Moran, Mayo. 2019. 'The Problem of the Past: How Historic Wrongs Became Legal Problems' *University of Toronto Law Journal* 69(4): 421–472.

Muir Watt, Horatia. 2014. 'Future Directions?' in Horatia Muir Watt & Diego P. Fernández Arroyo (eds.) *Private International Law and Global Governance* Oxford: OUP 343–382.

Muir Watt, Horatia. 2016. 'Jurisprudence without Confines: Private International Law as Global Legal Pluralism' *Cambridge Journal of International and Comparative Law* 5(3): 388–403.

National Gallery of Australia, Provenance Assessment Guidelines, July 2021 <https://nga.gov.au/art-artists/provenance/>.

National Policy (South Africa) on the Repatriation and Restitution of Human Remains and Heritage Objects 2021 <https://www.westerncape.gov.za/assets/departments/cultural-affairs-sport/draft_national_policy_on_the_repatriation_and_restitution_of_human_remains_and_heritage_objects.pdf>.

Négri, Vincent. 2020. 'Receiving in Domestic Law Concepts Born by the 2003 Convention: Focus on the Notion of Community' in Marie Cornu, Anita Vaivade, Lily Martinet & Clea Hance (eds.) *Intangible Cultural Heritage under National and International Law: Going Beyond the 2003 UNESCO Convention* Cheltenham: Edward Elgar Publishing 44–53.

Neidhardt, Alberto Horst. 2018. *The Transformation of European Private International Law A Genealogy of the Family Anomaly* PhD Thesis, European University Institute.
Newland, Bryan. 2022. *Federal Indian Boarding School Initiative Investigative Report* Washington, DC: Office of the Assistant-Secretary for Indian Affairs, US Department of the Interior.
Nozick, Robert. 1974. *Anarchy, State, and Utopia* Oxford: Blackwell Publishing.
O'Connell, Mary E. 2011. '*Jus Cogens*: International Law's Higher Ethical Norms' in Donald Earl Childress III (ed.) *The Role of Ethics in International Law* Cambridge: CUP 78–98.
Oh, Si-Jin. 2018. 'Historical Injustice in East Asia: A Case for Interspatial Law' *Pacific Focus* 33(3): 414–433.
Olick, Jeffrey K. 2007. *The Politics of Regret* London: Routledge.
Panesar, Sukhinder. 2000. 'Theories of Private Property in Modern Property Law' *The Denning Law Journal* 15: 113–138.
Parsons, Neil & Alinah Kelo Segobye. 2009. 'From Banyoles to Botswana: The Return of a Bushman to Africa' in Lyndel V. Prott (ed.) *Witnesses to History: A Compendium of Documents and Writings on the Return of Cultural Objects* Paris: Unesco Publications 391–398.
Paul, Joel R. 2003. '*Resisting Culture*' *Leiden Journal of International Law* 16: 915–927.
Perugini, Nicola & Neve Gordon. 2015. *The Human Right to Dominate* Oxford: OUP.
Prott, Lyndel V (ed.). 2009. 'Note on Terminology' *Witnesses to History: A Compendium of Documents and Writings on the Return of Cultural Objects* Paris: Unesco Publications xxi–xxiv.
Radbruch, Gustav. 1946. 'Statutory Lawlessness and Supra-Statutory Law' (tr. Bonnie Litschewski Paulson & Stanley L. Paulson) *Oxford Journal of Legal Studies* 2006(26): 1–11.
Report from the Select Committee of the House of Commons on the Earl of Elgin's Collection of Sculptured Marbles, 1816 London: W. Bulmer and Co.
Robertson, Geoffrey. 2019. *Who Owns History?: Elgin's Loot and the Case for Returning Plundered Treasure* Hull: Biteback Publishing Ltd.
Roodt, Christa. 2018. 'Engaging with Foreign Export Controls and Declarations of State Ownership of Antiquities' in Lucia Di Costanzo (ed.) *The Ownership of Cultural Heritage: Public-Private Partnership* (Series Studi Sul Sistema Giuridico Internazionale, Collana diretta da Giancarlo Guarino) Napoli: Satura Editrice 177–220.
Roodt, Christa. 2024. 'Article 4 of the 1995 UNIDROIT Convention: Possessor's Rights and Claims for Restitution of Cultural Objects' in Ana Filipa Vrdoljak, Andrzej Jakubowski & Alessandro Chechi (eds.) *The 1970 UNESCO and 1995 UNIDROIT Conventions on Stolen or Illegally Transferred Cultural Property: A Commentary* Oxford: OUP 561–578.
Rosén, Frederik. *NATO and Cultural Property: Embracing New Challenges in the Era of Identity Wars, Report on Best Practices for Cultural Property Protection in NATO-led Military Operations 2014–2017* (NATO SPS project G4866) 2017.
Rudenstine, David. 2002. 'Lord Elgin and the Ottomans: The Question of Permission' *Cardozo Law Review* 23(2): 449–472.
Ruiz Abou-Nigm, Verónica. 2019. 'Bridging and Balancing: Diversity and Integration in Private International Law', in Verónica Ruiz Abou-Nigm & Maria Blanca Noodt Taquela (eds.) *Diversity and Integration in Private International Law* Edinburgh: Edinburgh University Press 362–388.
Sarkin, Jeremy. 2008. *Colonial Genocide and Reparations Claims in the 21st Century: The Socio-Legal Context of Claims under International Law by the Herero against Germany for Genocide in Namibia, 1904–1908* Westport, CT: Greenwood Publishing Group.
Sarr, Felwine & Bénédicte Savoy. 2018. *The Restitution of African Cultural Heritage: Toward a New Relational Ethics* (November 2018) <https://www.about-africa.de/images/sonstiges/2018/sarr_savoy_en.pdf>

Sandholtz, Wayne. 2008. 'Dynamics of International Norm Change: Rules against Wartime Plunder' *European Journal of International Relations* 14(1): 101–131.
Schlag, Pierre. 1988. 'Cannibal Moves: An Essay on the Metamorphoses of the Legal Distinction' *Stanford Law Review* 40(1): 929–972.
Schuerch, Res. 2017. 'Legal Colonialism by European States' in *The International Criminal Court at the Mercy of Powerful States: An Assessment of the Neo-Colonialism Claim Made by African Stakeholders* Berlin: Springer 43–58.
Sen, Amartya. 2009. *The Idea of Justice* London: Allen Lane.
Shapiro, Daniel. 1998. 'Repatriation: A Modest Proposal' *New York University Journal of International Law and Politics* 31(1): 95–108.
Shelton, Dinah (ed.). 2000. *Commitment and Compliance: The Role of Non-binding Norms in the International Legal System* Oxford: OUP.
Siehr, Kurt. 1994. 'International Art Trade and the Law' *Collected Courses of the Hague Academy of International Law* 243 (1993): 25–288.
Silvester, Jeremy & Jan-Bart Gewald. 2003. *Words Cannot Be Found: German Colonial Rule in Namibia: An Annotated Reprint of the 1918 Blue Book* Leiden: Brill.
Silvester, Jeremy & Napandulwe Shiweda. 2020. 'The Return of the Sacred Stones of the Ovambo Kingdoms: Restitution and the Revision of the Past' Special Issue on Sensitive Heritage: Ethnographic Museums, Provenance Research, and the Potentialities of Restitutions (Philipp Schorch ed.) *Museum and Society* 18(1): 30–39.
Simpson, Moira G. 1996. *Making Representations: Museums in the Post-Colonial Era* London: Routledge.
Simpson, Moira. 2009. 'Museums and Restorative Justice: Heritage, Repatriation and Cultural Education' *Museum International* 61(1–2): 121–129.
Smead, Elmer E. 1936. 'The Rule Against Retroactive Legislation: A Basic Principle of Jurisprudence' *Minnesota Law Review* 20(7): 775-797.
Smith, Arthur Hamilton. 1916. 'Lord Elgin and His Collection' *The Journal of Hellenic Studies* 36: 163–372.
Soirila, Pauno. 2022. 'Indeterminacy in the Cultural Property Restitution Debate' *International Journal for Cultural Policy* 28(1): 1–16.
Spitra, Sebastian M. 2020. 'Civilisation, Protection, Restitution: A Critical History of International Cultural Heritage Law in the 19th and 20th century' *Journal of the History of International Law* 22(2–3): 329–354.
Spitra, Sebastian M. 2021. 'The Administration of Culture in International Law Since the 19th Century: A New Historical Narrative' *University of Vienna Law Review* 5(1): 121–158.
Stahn, Carsten. 2023. *Confronting Colonial Objects: Histories, Legalities, and Access to Culture* Oxford: OUP.
Stark, Rachel Rose, Jen McCormack & Stephan Cornell. 2011. *Native Nations and US Borders: Challenges to Indigenous Culture, Citizenship, and Security* Tucson: Udall Center for Studies in Public Policy, The University of Arizona.
Steinmetz, George & Julia Hell. 2006. 'The Visual Archive of Colonialism: Germany and Namibia' *Public Culture* 18(1): 147–184.
Stockdale, Eric. 2023. *Law and Order in Georgian Bedfordshire* Martlesham: Boydell & Brewer.
Stoecker, Holger & Andreas Winkelmann. 2018. 'Skulls and Skeletons from Namibia in Berlin: Results of the Charite Human Remains Project' *Human Remains and Violence: An Interdisciplinary Journal* 4(2): 5–26.
Struycken, A.V.M. 2009. 'Co-ordination and Co-operation in Respectful Disagreement: General Course on Private International Law' *Recueil des Cours* 311(2004): 8–551.
Sutton, Benjamin. 2024. 'US Authorities Return 38 Antiquities to China' *The Art Newspaper*, 19 April.
Taşdelen, Alper. 2016. *The Return of Cultural Artefacts. Hard and Soft Law Approaches* Berlin: Springer.

Tasioulas, John. 2020. 'Sumption on Law, Democracy, and Human Rights' *King's Law Journal* 31(3): 467–479.
Theurer, Karina. 2023. 'Minimum Legal Standards in Reparation Processes for Colonial Crimes: The Case of Namibia and Germany' *German Law Journal* 24(7): 1146–1168.
Thielecke, Carola & Michael Geißdorf. 2021. 'Collections from Colonial Contexts: Legal Aspects' DMB *Guidelines for Care of Collections* Berlin: German Museums Association 153–164.
Thomas, Joseph Anthony Charles. 1975. *The Institutes of Justinian: Text, Translation and Commentary* Amsterdam: North-Holland Publishing Company.
Titi, Catherine. 2023. *The Parthenon Marbles and International Law* Switzerland: Springer.
Treaty 7 Elders & Tribal Council. 1996. *The True Spirit and Original Intent of Treaty 7* Montreal: McGill-Queen's University Press.
Trope, Jack F. 2013. 'The Case for NAGPRA' in Sangita Chari & Jaine M. N. Lavallee (eds.) *Accomplishing NAGPRA: Perspectives on the Intent, Impact, and Future of the Native American Graves Protection and Repatriation Act* Corvallis: Oregon State University Press 19–54.
UN General Assembly. 2020. *Report of the Expert Mechanism on the Rights of Indigenous Peoples, Repatriation of Ceremonial Objects, Human Remains and the Intangible Cultural Heritage under the United Nations Declaration on the Rights of Indigenous Peoples* UN Doc. A/HRC/45/35 21 July 2020.
UN General Assembly. 2021. *Report on Transitional Justice Measures and Addressing the Legacy of Gross Violations of Human Rights and International Humanitarian Law Committed in Colonial Contexts* by Fabián Salvioli, Special Rapporteur on the Promotion of Truth, Justice, Reparation and Guarantees of Non-Recurrence UN Doc. A/76/180 19 July 2021.
US Department of State. 1999. *Washington Conference Principles on Nazi-Confiscated Art,* Released in connection with The Washington Conference on Holocaust Era Assets, Washington, DC, 3 December 1998.
US Department of State. 2024. *Best Practices for the Washington Conference Principles on Nazi-Confiscated Art*, Washington, DC, 5 March 2024.
Van Hoecke, Mark. 2015. 'Methodology of Comparative Legal Research' *Law and Method* 1–35.
Van Niekerk, Gardiol J. 2007. 'The Case of the Hottentot Venus: An Exercise in Legal History' *Fundamina* 13(2): 146–174.
Van Roermund, Bert. 2013. *Legal Thought and Philosophy* Cheltenham: Edward Elgar Publishing.
Van Woudenberg, Nout. 2016. 'Adherence to the 1995 UNIDROIT Convention: Wider Than One Would Think at First Sight' *Uniform Law Review* 21(1): 120–128.
Veraart, Wouter. 2015. 'Between Justice and Legal Closure: Looted Art Claims and the Passage of Time' in Evelien Campfens (ed.) *'Fair and Just Solutions?' Alternatives to Litigation in Nazi-Looted Art Disputes: Status Quo and New Developments* The Hague: Eleven International Publishing 211–221.
Vigneron, Sophie. 2020. 'The Repatriation of Human Remains in France: 20 Years of (Mal) practice' *Santander Art and Culture Law Review* 6(2): 313–339.
Virdee, Satnam, Mhairi Taylor & Cassie Masterton. 2021. *Understanding Racism, Transforming University Cultures and Action Plan Report issued by the University of Glasgow*, 17 February.
Von Bülow, Bernard. Letter dated 24 November 1904 to the Emperor, German Federal Archives, Berlin, Reichskolonialamt Vol 2089, R1001/Bl. 8.
Von Trotha, Lothar. Letter dated 2 October 1904 to the Ovaherero, German Federal Archives, Berlin, Reichskolonialamt Vol 2089, 7r.
Von Schlieffen, Alfred. Letter dated 23 November 1904 to German Imperial Chancellor Count von Bülow, German Federal Archives, Berlin, Reichskolonialamt Vol 2089, 4r.

Voudouri, Daphne. 2008. 'Greek Legislation Concerning the International Movement of Antiquities and its Ideological and Political Dimensions' in Dimitris Damaskos & Dimitris Plantzos (eds.) *A Singular Antiquity: Archaeology and Hellenic Identity in Twentieth Century Greece, 3rd Supplement* Athens: Mouseio Benaki 125–139.

Vrdoljak, Ana F. 2008. *International Law, Museums and the Return of Cultural Objects* Cambridge: CUP.

Vrettos, Theodore. 1997. *The Elgin Affair: The True Story of the Greatest Theft in History* New York: Arcade Publishing.

wa Thiong'o, Ngũgĩ. 1986. *Decolonising the Mind: The Politics of Language in African Literature* Nairobi: EAEP.

Ware, Joe. 2024. 'UK Government Should Intervene to Prevent Museum Thefts, Says Expert after Reports of Missing Objects Across the Country' *The Art Newspaper* 12 April.

Waldron, Jeremy. 1988. *The Right to Private Property* Oxford: OUP.

Waschefort, Gus. 2016. 'Africa and International Humanitarian Law: The More Things Change, The More They Stay the Same' *International Review of the Red Cross* 98(2): 593–624.

Westerman, Frank. 2004. *El Negro en Ik* Herengracht: Atlas.

Weststeijn, Arthur. 2017. 'Provincializing Grotius: International Law and Empire in the Seventeeth-Century Malay Mirror' in Martti Koskenniemi, Walter Rech & Manuel Jiménez Fonseca (eds.) *International Law and Empire: Historical Explorations* Oxford OUP 21–38.

Wheaton, Henry. 1866. *Elements of International Law* (Eighth edition, edited, with notes by Richard Henry Dana, Jr.) London: Sampson Low, Son & Co.

White, Liz, Stuart Campbell & Suzie Thomas. 2019. 'Introduction' in Stuart Campbell, Liz White & Suzie Thomas (eds.) *Competing Values in Archaeological Heritage* Switzerland: Springer 1–6.

Williams, Andrew J. 2014. *France, Britain and the United States in the Twentieth Century 1900–1940: A Reappraisal* London: Palgrave Macmillan.

Winiger, Benedict. 2018. *Responsibility, Restoration, Fault* Cambridge: Intersentia.

Winkelmann, Andreas. 2020. 'Repatriations of Human Remains from Germany – 1911–2019' Special Issue on Sensitive Heritage: Ethnographic Museums, Provenance Research, and the Potentialities of Restitutions (in Philipp Schorch ed.) *Museum and Society* 18(1): 40–51.

Wood, Philip. 2016. *The Fall of the Priests and the Rise of the Lawyers* London: Bloomsbury Publishing.

Woodhead, Charlotte C. 2002. 'A Debate Which Crosses All Borders – The Repatriation of Human Remains: More than Just a Legal Question' *Art Antiquity & Law* 7(4): 317–347.

Zeidler, Kamil. 2016. *Restitution of Cultural Property: Hard Case, Theory of Argumentation, Philosophy of Law* Gdańsk: Gdańsk University Press.

Zhang, Yue. 2021. 'The Right to Restitution of Cultural Property Removed as Spoils of War during Nineteenth-Century International Warfare' *University of Pennsylvania Journal of International Law* 42(4): 1097–1156.

Zimmerer, Jürgen. 2021. 'European Colonialism: Political, Economic, and Cultural Aspects of Early Globalisation' in DMB *Guidelines on Care of Collections* Berlin: German Museums Association 94–104.

2 Mimetic desire and restitution

2.1 Introduction

In physics, mimetism is the force of attraction known as gravity. It holds planets, stars, and galaxies together in space, and simultaneously keeps them apart, preserving the autonomy of all bodies in space. Without it, motion would hurl them against each other, fusing them. Similarly, human mimetic desire and its movement assure that the social fabric coheres while keeping human beings apart to allow them to achieve autonomy and live as individuals (Oughourlian 1991: 11). The fundamental identity of humans and human society is found in imitative behaviour that also carries the seed of rivalry. The imitative predisposition of humans fosters envy and a desire to have more than others. Colonial mimicry manifests as the narcissistic demands of colonial powers for land and the cultural property and heritage of Indigenous communities living within their national territory (Byrne 2015: 5).

Imitative admiration of a model becomes a desire to exceed it. The theory that each person desires, craves, and mimics the others' increasing desire in a 'duel between twins,' offers a convincing explanation for why parties to a restitution dispute refuse to engage in fair play. It acknowledges that individuals, groups, cultures, businesses, and states engage in imitative behaviours to possess what others have. Emulating European symbols of power was prompted by the colonial encounter (Goldmann 2024: 595). For example, the consolidation of territorial control by Maharero proceeded under a seal that identified him as 'King of Hereroland' in 1884. Museum-making in Africa between 1860 and 1910 also followed imitativepatterns. Many of these newly established museums would go to great lengths to obtain sufficient empirical data in the shape of ethnographic objects about which they could make scientific statements. Some would continue to collect human remains even when source communities communicated their wish for these remains to be returned and buried. The European thinking reflected in colonial museums established by the colonial powers suppressed the development of home-grown methods based on African languages and customs to support African heritage (Deliss 2021: 15ff).

As soon as states start to compete with communities in their territories for cultural heritage, inadequate representation for those communities is almost assured (Lixinski 2019b: 607). The recent challenge to the 2021 draft Joint Declaration with Germany filed in the Namibian High Court in 2023 avers that the level of

DOI: 10.4324/9781003565314-2

participation of affected communities renders them invisible (*Bernadus Swartbooi MP et al. v Speaker of the National Assembly et al.* HC-MD-CIV-MOT-REV-2023/00023, Founding Affidavit (20 January 2023) para 336). Between 2007 and 2011 the Namibian government embraced the role of mediator between the German government and affected communities and wanted to facilitate reconciliation, but by 2015, when the interstate negotiations began, it had changed its position to align with that of Germany. The Namibian and German governments switched to holding their negotiations in secret that year. The Namibian executive's legal reasoning, that German colonial rule did not violate legal norms, prompted accusations of complicity in the replication of colonial racism and white saviourism (Theurer 2023: 1151). The behaviours on the part of the formerly colonised that replicate the coloniser—the racist distinction between 'civilised and uncivilised' nations and the state-centred approach adhered to in the draft Agreement—may be seen as violating the participation rights of affected communities under international customary law (Theurer 2023: 1149, 1164, 1166). Since the prohibition against race discrimination is a core principle of international law, mirroring and replicating the racist distinction in legal reasoning is counter-productive.

Scholars have elucidated the dynamics of mimetic competition in the relations between France, Britain, and the United States (e.g., Williams 2014: 96–97). The only other dynamic studied so far is the competition between East and West since the adoption of the Antiquities Law of 1874 by the Ottomans. The Law was supposed to signal the end to large-scale looting in Greece as well as the Ottoman Empire (Greenhalgh 2019: 547–548). Human desire manifested in plundering cultural heritage from Ottoman lands and the international competition among Western nations and museums in the 19th century (Greenhalgh 2019: 518ff, 538ff, 552). Ottoman officials attempted to prevent clandestine digging and smuggling by foreign expeditions. Their earliest efforts were imitations of Greece's strategy of 1834 to regulate the movement of antiquities uncovered by archaeological excavation and vesting ownership (Act on Scientific and Technological Collections, on the Discovery and Conservation of Antiquities and the Use Thereof of 16/28 June 1834 s 61; Greenhalgh 2019: 518ff; 552). Western institutions resisted the Ottomans' expanding state control over antiquities primarily because the control invoked visions of returning loot to its source. Notwithstanding the promulgation of the Antiquities Law of 1874, it remains unknown how much went undeclared (Greenhalgh 2019: 547–548). The West dismissed the Ottomans' initiatives as insults to civilisation to which 'all antiquities belonged.' Western counter-offensives insisted that finds belonged to all humanity and not to the country where they were found (Greenhalgh 2019: 552–555). The development of nationalist ideas in the East threatened Western interests and contradicted the Western notion of 'world heritage.'

To date there has not been any study focused on the mimetic dynamics in restitution and the implications for normativity. Scholars have made observations about the element of competition, but the normative effects of mimesis have not received attention. The first three chapters of Stahn's recently published monograph feature the competition that raged among colonial powers for influence and prestige while subsequent chapters move away from this focus (2023: 89, 126–135). A recent study on new directions for cross-border claims to cultural objects takes sacred cultural material on board as a baseline and touches the sacred attributes of pillaged material (Campfens 2021: 3, 106–107). Campfens argues that states in possession of sacred material have a duty under international law to return those objects (Campfens 2019: 91, 95). The study adopts the NAGPRA definition of the 'sacred'. It does not link the 'sacred' to mimetic human behaviour and neither does it theorise the 'sacred' (e.g., Campfens 2021: 3ff, 138). Referencing 'holiest relics' and 'talismans,' Shapiro highlights 'the intimate connections between a people and their artifacts and intangibles.' While these connections epitomise the sacred, his general point is about repatriation of cultural property in a broader sense. Only when describing the difficulty of asserting control over intangible property does he refer expressly to the 'sacred' (Shapiro 1998: 97–98).

Influential social scientific theories and major ideologies are prone to either overestimating or under-estimating the agency of individuals. Girard's anthropological 'discoveries', however, make a realistic assessment of individual agency that have had considerable impact across the social sciences and in debates on political values, forms of state, and artistic styles representing these ideals, such as classical Greek sculpture. To date, neither the discovery that mimetic rivalry repeats incessantly and cyclically, nor the discovery that the sacrifice of a surrogate scapegoat contains this rivalry have been applied to the restitution of sacred items from museum collections and no sustained attempt has been made to apply the competition element in relation to the sacred as Girard theorises it. This study does not stop at foreshadowing novel manifestations of mimetic competition, but instead, uses Girard's theory as a general explanatory principle of human culture in both anthropological 'discoveries'. The elaborate and sweeping anthropology of religion in Girard's 'mimetic theory' is the basis for what communities hold sacred and how they manage their relationships with it. He completed the wide-ranging historical analysis of these dimensions before he died in 2015. The object of human desire (mimesis) must be taken from whomever holds it, and the desire intensifies when the thing that is coveted cannot be replicated or shared (Girard 2013: 5). It may become so intense as to drive people to the extremes of violence but the 'sacred' provides a space where all members of society, including the vulnerable and dependent, are protected from injury and find sanctuary, and allows a culture to survive, grow, and become better integrated (Cayley ed. 2019: 16). Because of the strong tendency to turn everyone into a potential adversary, a mechanism is needed to establish areas of non-violence in a culture. Girard's conception of the scapegoat is the mechanism that makes social co-existence possible because it displaces violence in the community. His conception not the popular notion of mere arbitrary, irrational cruelty and victimisation. Instead, the scapegoat gathers discontent and turmoil unto itself and is sacrificed (Girard 1972: 144). To achieve peaceful co-existence, it *must* be enacted. It is inescapable. Girard also connected the scapegoating mechanism to human communities' sense of collective identity that develops when they unite around the ritual sacrifice of targeting an innocent outsider victim and projecting false accusations and condemnation on them. Highlighting the normative effects of mimetic competition and promoting the adoption of a more universal understanding of the sacred as a strategy best suited to countering these effects differ markedly from theories and methods used in other scholarly analyses in the field. While the literature on cultural removal during the era of expanding empire and collecting mania in complex colonial contexts frequently refers to the Parthenon Sculptures and the Zhanggong Zushi Buddha statue disputes, no study analyses the nature and implications of these restitution claims alongside each other.

'Sacred' heritage is considered part of realities that are essential to the life and security of societies. As a realm 'at the core of existence,' it supports their survival and has a transformative impact on society. Taking away this heritage threatens their security at the deepest level, which is where the self is constructed. The 'sacred' is equivalent to being human (Godelier 2002: 30). Girard maintained that the inability of social and human sciences to arrive at a unified point, and their skirting around the questions that would procure a unifying model, keeps them in a state of perpetual infancy that hiders progress (Kirwan 2009: 20). Following this line of thought further into the nascent field of restitution and repatriation of intangible dimensions of sacred cultural heritage, the methodology in this study is uniquely suited to fill the gap in scholarly literature. The broader question is that of countering the normative thrust of mimetics in 'decolonisation' efforts and the implications for the restitution of cultural property and heritage.

Casting its lens across the social sciences and humanities, this studyaims to find ways to improve the normative environment, restore the law for the restitution of sacred cultural material, and to formulate a more comprehensive theory on restitution and repatriation claims. In the process, constructive observations can be made about private and business practices based on due diligence standards where 'sacred' material in collections are concerned. Stahn's proposed Principle 13 states that due diligence structures and human rights duties are needed on the part of businesses (Stahn 2023: 534). He suggests that buyers be required to prove due diligence in market transactions to protect against cultural trafficking or that recognition that certain entangled objects are extra commercium must be widened, which confirms that work is needed in this area.

For PrIL scholars and adjudicators, Girard's theory provides a perspective on many foundational questions of their discipline, including which rules to apply to determine how an object gets or loses its sacred character. Should courts apply the internal rules of the various religious societies such as canon law, the private law rules of a religious denomination, or the rules of civil law? It would soon be evident to the court that has to decide, that different Indigenous laws or African customary rules may compete with the general law of the country in question. The theory can be related not only to the process of identifying the appropriate law in cases that have colonialism as a backdrop, but also to the inter-connective dimension at which common PrIL rules such as comity and the public policy exception operate. This chapter takes the first step, that of linking Girard's theory on mimetics and the 'sacred' with the restitution question on colonial-era removal. This will prepare the ground for the application of the theory to PrIL's secondary legal norms in subsequent work.

2.2 Behavioural mirroring as driver in conflict

The image of the twins at war relays how peoples' hostilities 'mirror and magnify' each other. Mirroring led Girard to consider the impulse to violence endemic to human society and human identity (Cayley ed. 2019: 25). Underlying mimetic forces shape the twin-like similarities in the conflict between Israel and Palestine, for instance. This 'new war' is aptly described as an arch-conflict that fixates on the slightest differences, escalates them to extremes, and projects its mimetic core onto global politics while the contenders lack the sacrificial and legal devices to inhibit and contain the reciprocal enmity (Farneti 2013: 190, 198). As the resemblance between rivals grows, admiration turns into envy. Resentments build, hostilities accelerate, and eventually the drive to usurp the other's authority takes over. Violence erupts at the point when lesser wants are overtaken by the desire to dominate the rival. Land, territory, resources, and life may be taken once rhetorical violence switches to the phenomenal (Girard 2010: 39–40; 43–44). Ideologies that perpetuate ideas that the world cannot exist without repression are destructive forces without equal.

Western international law endorsed the institutions and beliefs of Christian priests and missionaries. Missionaries introduced translations of Wheaton's legal texts to China and Japan, for instance. As they took hold, non-western international theories and normative orders lost vital ground and status (Oh 2018: 422–423, 426, 431). By the early 20th century Christian ideas had gained currency among Africans across southern Africa. The dissemination of these ideas through networks has not yet been uncovered by scholars, but it has been established that African resistance politics fed off the evangelising of missionaries and priests. Large-scale conversions to Christianity occurred among the surviving Herero and Nama prisoners in SWA, instilling fear in white settlers that Christian ideas and the proliferation of independent Christian movements would foster an indigenous vision of social and political independence and spur an insurrection. Hendrik Witbooi, Chief of the Nama, belonged to the Oorlam Nama tribe but received a formal Christian education from a Rhenish missionary whose teaching inspired him to establish an independent Christian church (Dedering 1999: 1, 15–16).

In contemporary continental theory 'alterity' is worthy of hospitality, whereas 'aliens' are unwelcome invaders. Kearney distinguishes 'aliens' from 'others' in this way. The 'aliens' are those scapegoated by xenophobic, racist, or anti-Semitic practices (Kearney 2003: 67). In Girard's theorem, most societies achieved coherence through a strategy of sacrificing scapegoats. They are based on the ritual sacrifice of a maligned other or outsider. 'The immolation of the "other" on the altar of the "alien"' furnishes communities with a binding identity (Kearney 2003: 26). In times of chaos and corruption the need for expiation grew and the range of 'eligible aliens' would expand accordingly. The persecutory strategies of genocidal xenophobia, racism and the Holocaust are examples of the purging rituals needed for purification (Kearney 2003: 33, 37).

The Ghent Altarpiece is an example of the painful mimetics triggered by the restitution terms in the 1919 Versailles Treaty. Commissioned in the 1420s to be a functional object of contemplation and prayer in the St Bavo Cathedral chapel, it was also the first work of art to be reintegrated into a nation's historical and artistic heritage by treaty. The wings open to reveal saints, pilgrims, prophets, knights, and philosophers coming forward to worship the sacrificial Lamb of God, a symbol of Christ's crucifixion. The travails and trajectories of the individually painted panels highlight the potential of sacred cultural property and heritage to invite and accelerate mimesis. Sacred Christian art in the western tradition that serve as objects of contemplation slow down the mimetic drive, but if coveted, it will be vulnerable to iconoclasm, confiscation, seizure, looting, theft, fraud. At different points in history, several panels were stolen, confiscated, and restituted (1794–1816); pawned, traded, and displayed (1816–1918); burned, looted, and returned (1822–1914); and once again burned, copied, and seized (1822–1914). One of the two panels stolen from St Bavo in 1934 remains missing to this day. Napoleon's all-purpose pillaging unit confiscated the central panels in 1792, during the French Occupation of the Southern Netherlands (Flanders) (Gould 1965: 109). France wanted to retain the panels when the Duke of Wellington's army defeated Napoleon at Waterloo but the Count of Provence (Louis XVIII) returned them to Belgium, and in 1816 they went back to St Bavo's in Ghent. German forces removed the central panels from the Cathedral during the First World War. The 1919 Versailles Treaty imposed the return of 6 panels to Belgium. Germany interpreted Article 247.2 as a directive to restitute art as part of war reparations and to return cultural objects to remedy the cultural losses Germany inflicted in Louvain. The Nazis resented this and, in 1942, Hitler ordered German troops to seize the Altarpiece panels in an apparent effort to avenge the injustice inflicted by Article 247. The panels were taken to Neuschwanstein Castle and later stashed in a salt mine in Altaussee. The practice of returning art to settle war reparations was later outlawed. The First Protocol to the 1954 Hague Convention stipulates that cultural property imported during armed conflict cannot be retained as war reparations (Article 3). The Second Protocol to the 1954 Hague Convention reiterates that cultural property shall never be retained as war reparations (Article I.3).

Almost all the panels of the Ghent altarpiece survived the overwhelming intensity of human mimetic desire to possess. They were not destroyed by the protracted conflicts over war reparations in the interwar and post-war years. The turbulent history of the altarpiece opens new avenues for research on the Hague Conventions and Protocols, alerting us to the potential to control society's drive to aggression and counter the normative effects of mimesis. Rivalries can be prevented from escalating. Cultivating awareness of the underlying drive to 'get even' interrupts the inevitability of 'doubling' or 'reciprocity,' which makes life impossible as long as there is no sacrifice that can transmute the impulse to violence (Girard 2010: 57, 60–61). Without this awareness, vengefulness is interminable and repetitive as neither side recognises that they are the aggressor.

2.3 Masking mimesis, cloaking, and reversal

The disinclination of humans to acknowledge their participation in mechanisms of mimesis is correlated to the crisis of violence, for when each contender believes they were wronged first, no one assumes responsibility for war. The actors in a mimetic struggle justify the deaths and suffering as sacrificial violence. They will fabricate fictitious causal stories about their behaviour that employ stereotypes and distorted truths. These stories blind them to their propensity for mimetic violence. Acutely aware of others' ignorance to their propensity for mimetism, they never acknowledge that all cultures partake in mimetic competition. Yet the only real difference between the so-called 'ancient' and 'advanced' societies is the extent to which their sacrificial mythology is masked when persecutory impulses prevail. Ancient cultures did not mask their participation in the mechanics of mimetics. For instance, the custom of human and animal sacrifice in Great Benin has not been denied (Roth 1903: 51–53; 69–71). 'Advanced' cultures, on the other hand, mask the sacrificial stereotypes and their need for the persecution mechanism (Girard 1982: 52; Kearney 1995: 3). The scapegoat conceals the genesis of sacrificial stereotypes in historical persecutions.

Anthropologists devised a 'hierarchy' for religions based on their propensity for mimetic violence—an arbitrary standard of level of 'civilisation.' The London Missionary Society Museum's collection of idol images dating from between 1791 and 1900 were differentiated as follows: those who fetishised nature were the heathens in Africa; those who participated in mimesis in the crude form of human sacrifice in the early post-European contact period were the heathens of Polynesia; Buddhists belonged to the 'highest heathen religion' of Asia (Eaton 2018: 44).

In the early 19th century, imitation among European colonial powers saw mimetic military rivalry between the British and the French. Napoleon appropriated art from Italy to recreate Paris as the new Rome (Stahn 2023: 23). The cultural programme of colonialism reaffirms the mimetic interpretation of the history of the Parthenon Marbles. Correspondence between Elgin and Lusieri shows that the original plan was to 'preserve' Athens' ancient temples and treasures on paper and canvas, for the British public to see. The intention to remove the sculptures from the Parthenon was not fully formed at the outset (Elgin to Lusieri, 10 July 1801; after Smith 1916: 191–192). In time, mimetic desire for the adornments in the upper reaches of the Parthenon turned the plan into pillage. The Parthenon Sculptures were taken after the desire became all-consuming. The Greeks lacked the necessary resolve to launch resistance, and the Athenians—an oppressed collectivity torn between their desire to claim exclusive rights to their antiquities and the need to please the Great Powers on whom they were dependent—were unable to put it to an end. Personal ambition left the Parthenon stripped and damaged, yet Lord Elgin blamed the Ottoman government's reluctance to accede to his requests on their religious intolerance and hostility towards Christians (*Report from the Select Committee of the House of Commons on the Earl of Elgin's Collection of Sculptured Marbles* (*HC Report*) 1816: 39).

The provenance of, and discourse on the Parthenon Frieze, which the celebrated ancient Greek sculptor Phidias was employed to design to recall the complete history of Athens, demonstrate the potential to cloak and reverse mimetics, and for sacrifice to transform it. The sacred, dispersed pieces of this powerful symbol of injustice attracted mimetic behaviours that have been masked. The masking extends to the very meaning of what the frieze depicts.

The classicist art historian Joan Breton Connelly argues that the Parthenon and its parts can be understood only if the larger question as to who the Athenians were is at the forefront (Connelly 2014: 158–159). Myth, landscape, memory, and the sacred were inseparable in the ancient Athenian consciousness (Connelly 2014: 4–6). The most comprehensive revelation at our disposal today is reflected in the horsemen, charioteers, divinities, and animals on the Panathenaic Frieze—square carved plaques of Pentelic marble that convey the genealogical history of Athens. The mythological programme includes the birth of Athena; the Athenian heroes in battle; and the primeval contest between Athena and Poseidon for divine patronage of Athens and dominion over Attica (Connelly 2014: 96, 160–161). Central to the location of the 2,450-year-old Parthenon Temple and its meaning is a competition to the death. It stands on the very spot where the mythical struggle between Athena and Poseidon took place—on the proverbial 'sacred' ground.

Enough of the Parthenon Frieze remains intact to permit conclusions about its meaning. Established orthodoxy on the composition above the main door of the temple has it that a Panathenaic procession is moving towards the Acropolis to commemorate the birthday of the goddess Athena and to present her with a new robe in the shrine in the Erechtheion. The theory that the depiction concerns the sacred is dismissed as a less popular alternative (Beard 2002: 132–135). Connelly's incisive scholarly reading casts the accepted dogma of the popular theory aside. Her interpretation considers the dogma a projection of western standards of civilisation onto the Parthenon. At the heart of the foundation myth of Athens is Erechtheus, the semi-offspring of Athena born of Gaia which all Athenians claimed to be descended from. Athena raises Erechtheus to be king, and with his wife Queen Praxithea, the couple consents to sacrifice their daughter to rescue Athens from ruin. This was the Delphic oracle's advice to Erechtheus when his rival, Poseidon's son, challenged his claim to the throne. Conneły's reading aligns with the evidence as it stands today and comports with the convention of Greek religious art to draw on images from mythology (Connelly 2014: 154–177). The human sacrifice motif coheres with many myths of Greek antiquity that depict the rites of human sacrifice, murder, cannibalism, and rape.

Connelly achieves a compelling conclusion concerning the final scene on the sculpted frieze through a combination of evidence uncovered since the 1960s and the foundation and genealogical succession myths of the time (Connelly 2014: x, xxii–xxii). The evidence referred to concerns a 3rd-century-BC Egyptian mummy excavated in 1901 and taken to Paris. More than 60 years passed before the layers of glued papyrus separated. The slow separation allowed the inscriptions on the papyrus wrapped around the mummy to remain intact. A researcher recognised the lines as belonging to the 'Erechtheus,' a lost play by Euripides that captures the central foundation myth of the royal family of Athens (Connelly 2014: 138). This evidence brought the central foundation myth of Athens into focus. It confirms that the procession depicted on the Parthenon frieze commemorates the victory sacrifice following the battle of Erechtheus and Eumolpos (Connelly 2014: 151). The east frieze with the 'Central Scene' depicts the dressing scene where the family adorns the Maiden, or 'Parthenos.' The scene is understated, yet there is no mistaking the solemnity of the moment in the Athenian myth. Erechtheus hands his youngest daughter the funerary shroud to prepare her for sacrifice, to save Athens from invasion. Euripides's play ends with Athena's speech demanding construction of the Parthenon ('of the Maidens') and the Erechtheion ('of Erechtheus') on the Sacred Rock. The language Euripides uses resembles that of 'sacred laws (*leges sacrae*) inscribed in stone to decree cult practice and the construction of temples within Greek sanctuaries' (Connelly 2014: 138). The language conveys the essence of the self-understanding of the Athenians, which, in turn, informs Connelly's understanding of the Acropolis temples, cults, rituals, and figures on the frieze as depictions of the participants in the parade before the gods (Connelly 2014: 136–175). Greece remains determined to overcome the control that British authorities exert over their identity-forming heritage. Notwithstanding the obvious signs pointing to mimetic contest and the sacred on the pediments, the metopes, and the frieze, however, the importance of sacrifice in ancient Greek religion is consistently underplayed in the restitution claim.

Mimetism was at work in the blame the British Empire cast in the direction of the Ottoman Empire for allowing Elgin's men to remove the Parthenon Marbles, to distract from their own part in the removal. Britain's appropriation of classical Greek sculptures also made it possible for London to cast itself as the reincarnation of ancient Athens and to exude the classical enlightenment of ancient democratic Athens. This interpretation was further cemented by the causal story that the removal of the Parthenon Marbles is justified by the harm they would have come to in situ. The mischievous Turks would have further vandalised them and sold them off, piecemeal, to occasional travellers, and pollution would have sealed their decay. It is a convenient narrative that enables Britain to present itself as a saviour of Western Civilisation (Stahn 2023: 106).

2.4 Competing in restitution, repatriation, and return

It is important for 'ethics' to remain answerable to the ethics of restituting sacred cultural heritage, but the masking, cloaking, and reversal of mimetics pose distinct challenges. Restitution is liable to be used for diplomatic and political point-scoring without the dimension of integrity, in which museums, the wider society, as well as politicians act in accordance with moral principles in cultural exchange (DMB *Care of Collections* 2021: 9). The case of El Negro, whose remains were sent to Botswana despite the lack of any connection with that country, highlights that returns made carelessly may also be wrongful. To force the return of sacred artefacts or human remains without ensuring correct identification of the recipient or their cultural priorities compounds the distress caused by the colonial past. Instead of progressing matters, it humiliates the recipient. Repatriation cannot always be separated from the broader context of reparations and redress (Förster 2020: 110). Reparatory justice demands of living survivors and their descendants, from contexts of generational harm, are on the increase (*Report of the General Assembly-Secretary General on the Implementation of the International Decade for People of African Descent* Doc. No. A/78/317, 18 August 2023, which covers colonialism but also restitution of cultural objects and land: paras 54–56). Simmering frustrations over the larger issue of unresolved reparatory justice can boil over, triggering a 'competition of victims' (Förster 2020: 119). Unless other struggles over historical wrongs and deceit receive proper recognition, repatriation efforts could miss the mark and overly hasty returns can inflict new wounds. Another caution appears in relation to conservation conventions of western cultural institutions, which have impacted on the gathering and interpretation of knowledge by deprived Indigenous peoples. Ceremonial sacred items may appear as 'easy' cases to settle, but their sacrilegious handling includes the use of harmful chemicals to preserve some of these artefacts. It is incumbent on these institutions to communicate that they cannot be used in ceremonies again (Conaty 2015b: 79). Omission of this information raises serious ethical questions.

The interests of the state, an individual, and the Indigenous community that directly has rights under international law may conflict in one and the same claim to cultural objects. In multi-ethnic states comprising Indigenous peoples and minorities, uncertainty as to whom objects must be returned is unavoidable at times. Museums cannot take responsibility for resolving this question on their own. Internal domestic conflict-resolution mechanisms remain under-developed and international mechanisms are being sought (Spitra 2021: 142).

Mimetics foster rivalry also in respect of restitution and repatriation. Continuities of prejudice put hurdles in the way and conventions may stop short of achieving balance. For instance, the process elements of genocide are not fully reflected in the 1948 Genocide Convention. Dichotomisation frequently serves the interests of those controlling difficult heritage. Argumentative contests over title, ownership, and loans, and spats over the classical illustrate the dynamic. Furthermore, historical interpretation may be imbued with mimetism because the opposing sides in the restitution debate use and reverse the same arguments, each for their own gain. No satisfactory resolution of the pernickety title issue relating to the Parthenon Sculptures has been achieved to date. It needs to be made more explicit how tactical arguments on ownership of sacred cultural heritage reflect the dynamics of mimetism. If self-perpetuating loops and indeterminate arguments are made readily identifiable and more obvious, the dimensions of mimetic theory become more visible and a resolution that takeson board the dimension of the sacred, more convincing. These factors are considered in greater detail below.

2.4.1 Rules of war and the obligation to restitute

Hugo Grotius (1583–1645), legend ary international lawyer, jurist, and diplomat, interrogated the lawfulness of war in *De Jure Belli ac Pacis* (*On the Law of War and Peace* 1625). His earlier treatise, *De iure praedae*, was written for the board of the Dutch East India Company (VOC) between 1604–1606. The VOC performed as a governmental body with capacity to import and export to and from Asia and India, wage war with local Indian rulers to expand its Asian trade and conclude treaties (Koskenniemi 2017: 8–9). In *De iure praedae*, Grotius justified the seizure of a Portuguese vessel in the Malay Peninsula. For his detractors, his willingness to serve his client's imperial agenda proved that he was a mouthpiece of Dutch imperialism (Weststeijn 2017: 22). By the time he published *De Jure Belli ac Pacis*, however, his reasoning had shifted. Grotius posited that warring nations had the right to lay waste to enemy property, but things taken in an unjust war must be restored. Devotional works of art ('divine things') had to be spared, especially if the nations at war worshipped the same god and observed the same fundamental laws (Neff 2012: Book 3, Chapter 12, 'Moderation in Laying Waste and Similar Things' para 6). He maintained that, for peoples at peace, legal ownership (*externum dominium*) exists alongside the moral obligation (*interna obligatio*) of restitution. The obligation of restitution extends to all wrongdoings of war. If the reason for war is unjust, so are all resulting activities because of the war's intrinsic injustice. Perpetrators of war, and any person holding objects taken in an unjust war, are duty-bound to return them to the lawful owners who did not agree to the taking and who do not deserve such treatment under the law of nature (Neff 2012: Book 3, Chapter 10, 'Cautions in regard to Things which are Done in an Unlawful War' paras 3–6). Imperialistic expansion and the desire to govern others against their will did not qualify as 'just' (Neff 2012: Book 2, Chapter 22, 'On Unjust Causes [Of Wars]' paras 12–13). The exception of 'things dedicated to sacred uses' granted them a special status that allowed them to be spared during war (Neff 2012: Book 3, Chapter 12, para 6).

The Swiss philosopher, diplomat, and lawyer Emmerich de Vattel (1714–1767) probed the necessity of war and the relationship between *jus in bello* and *jus ad bellum*. A nation that resorts to arms when it has received no injury, nor is threatened with injury, wages an unjust war. The same applies if war is undertaken from motives of advantage without justification. Pondering an emerging rule against wanton destruction and pillage of cultural property by belligerents engaged in conflict on foreign soil, de Vattel became the first legal philosopher to suggest that 'cultural property' is a separate category of property in war. He declared that nothing could be gained from the destruction of public buildings, temples and tombs, and edifices of remarkable beauty (De Vattel 1758 Book 3, Chapter 9, 'Of the Right of War, With Regard to Things Belonging to the Enemy': para 168). Before de Vattel's commentary appeared in 1758, the right to have booty returned, even in a just war, was discredited. Nonetheless, as time went by, the real impact of his theory became more discernible (Cohan 2004: 30). Adjudicators became increasingly willing to affirm the return of art and cultural objects as a normative ideal. The 'Roman right of conquest' was qualified and plundering of artworks and treasures started to decline, only to re-emerge during the French Revolution and the Napoleonic invasions.

Under the law of war, belligerents had to pay compensation for looted or destroyed cultural objects. The 1863 Lieber Code, 1874 Brussels Declaration, and the Oxford Manual of September 1880 are earlier expressions of the rule against plunder which was codifified in the 1899 and 1907 Hague Conventions on the Laws and Customs of War on Land, which proscribe seizure of cultural objects as war booty. Return was not required as part of the protection of cultural objects in armed conflict. Prohibitions on the use of certain methods and means of combat appeared in the 1899 and 1907 Hague Conventions on the Laws and Customs of War on Land. The 1899 Hague Convention entered into force in September 1900, and the 1907 Hague Convention in January 1910. The principle of proportionality permitted only minimum force, consistent with military necessity. Violent means which caused gratuitous suffering or unnecessary harm fell outside the scope (Mattox 2006: 11). The principle of discrimination protected non-combatants by expecting soldiers to distinguish between those actively fighting and others, such as women, children, the aged, the infirm, and wounded soldiers. Aggressors had to pay for the damage wrought on both sides. Conquerors were obligated to return enemy property seized as prizes of war because their unjust acquisition could not be legalised no matter the length of the time that had elapsed since the property was seized. This obligation also applied to property in the hands of those who had acquired it in good faith from the victor (Cohan 2004: 28). The early protection of cultural heritage took the form of an exemption from the right to plunder in armed conflicts, as well as the protection of churches, public buildings, and undefended cities (Article 56 of the 1899 and 1907 Hague Conventions). By these rules, African states would have legitimate claims for restitution of their cultural property and heritage, but distortions of the rules of PublIL became commonplace in the 19th century and the Just War theory fell out of favour (Bush 2002: 2330).

During the interwar years 1919 and 1939, rights to restitution were linked to tiers which differentiated between the 'advanced nations,' the minority groups under League Mandate, non-European people seeking self-determination, and the international community. States in the first tier were given back the most to restore the damage and loss inflicted on them in violation of rules of war. The end of the Second World War saw a return to more sound tenets of international law (Alexandrowicz 1973: 125). The right of European powers to wage war upon each other or upon non-European countries was not subject to limits but the UN Charter established a new paradigm in the law of war with its prohibition of the threat or use of force. *Jus contra bellum* prevents sovereign states from initiating and conducting war of their own volition; it replaced the unfettered *jus ad bellum* by which states were unrestricted in the right to declare war (Article 2(4)). This shift in the law of war ensured decades of relative stability and peace as recourse to violence declined. Superpowers did not come into conflict and states shared a common responsibility for cultural heritage, with the basic obligation to ensure that each people make its contribution to the culture of the world. Since plunder of art and cultural objects was prohibited in wartime, violations required compensation or return. Russian invasions of territories that served as a buffer zone against NATO countries, such as Ukraine, brought an abrupt end to this era of stability.

Instead of advancing the cause of justice and reducing injustice in the world, international law in the 20th and 21st centuries attempted to make war pleasanter rather than prevent it. Unsurprisingly, it failed to function as an instrument of peace or to promote peace and global security.. The ability of 'veto players' to block collaboration has undermined the maintenance of peace and a shared understanding of world events. Their behaviours evoke hostility and paranoia that make unexpected turns in governance ever more likely (US National Intelligence Council, *Global Trends 'Paradox of Progress'* 2017).

The 1954 Hague Convention imposes a rarely used obligation on contracting states to prevent exportation of cultural heritage from any territory under occupation, to seize objects imported from these territories, and to return them to authorities in the former occupied territory when hostilities cease regardless of a possessor's good faith. Indemnity is due to holders in good faith and there is no requirement that the possessor must be in a State Party's territory (First Protocol to the 1954 Hague Convention, I.4). Illegal export of cultural property can occur in both internal and international armed conflicts and may be situated in territories belonging to State Parties or in other territories. Private owners seeking return of any exported cultural objects would require state support, and few states have implemented legislation anticipating conflicts between domestic property and ownership laws on the one hand and domestic law and the provisions in the Protocol on the other.

2.4.2 Uneven scales in respect of a right to restitution

A US court rejected the argument that a Russian soldier or the Russian government might have acquired title to a tiny cuneiform tablet through conquest and as a 'spoil of war.' Excavated in Iraq in the early 20th century, the tablet disappeared from storage during the Second World War. The US Court of Appeals rebuffed the attempt to justify acquisition of title through theft as 'fundamentally unjust' (*In re Flamenbaum* 2013 N.Y. Slip Op. 7510 (N.Y. 2013) 3). The repugnance of a spoils of war justification for colonial-era looting generally remains firmly tucked away under the hierarchy of race in law but the collection and display of war spolia reveals the deep-seated desire to lord over those competing for colonies.

The first international legal standard to abandon the right to retain art trophies that had been seized as spoils of war from European capitals or to oblige return of what had been acquired by treaty from dispossessed countries of origin was set by the Second Treaty of Paris, 1815. It became an important landmark in the evolution of PublIL restitution norms. The extent of the plundered art in France rendered the initiative incomplete, but the Allies remained resolute to repossess the stolen art without diplomatic negotiations. Objections against restitution were disregarded (Gould 1965: 125). At the time, the British delegation's efforts were seen as an attempt to restore the sacred link 'between peoples, territories and cultural objects' (Vrdoljak 2008: 19). In hindsight, it is evident that the colonial powers proclaimed principles of inseparability and protection of cultural objects at the Congress of Vienna but did not apply them to non-Europeans (Stahn 2023: 25–26). The British, for instance, took advantage of the strategic opening that appeared when offers and counteroffers were made with Napoleon involving Egypt, Trinidad, Ceylon, and Malta. Britain rejected the possibility of restitution to Egypt. British demands prevailed and none of the artistic and archaeological loot, deemed to have been taken from an opponent lacking interest in what was in its possession, was repatriated to Egypt. The Articles of Capitulation of Alexandria of 1801 clarified the position of such a 'non-Christian opponent' and brought the French expedition to Egypt to an end. A ban on the looting of cultural property had crystallised with the Second Treaty of Paris in 1815, but the deal struck by the European colonial powers did not include the Ottoman Empire, which was less than an equal of powerful Western European states when restitution was at stake.

'Christian' nations were not averse to taking advantage of so-called non-Christian nations. The glaring omissions in the Final Act of the Congress of Vienna in 1815 benefited the British. The norms regarding the taking of war booty, the protection of cultural property, and military occupation as an act of aggression had been clarified exclusively for European players. Western European states such as France and Great Britain were responsible for the administration of the former colonies of Germany and the territories that formerly belonged to the Ottoman Empire (Spitra 2021: 123). An arbitrary interpretation of the principles of the law of war with respect to war booty precluded their application to non-Christian states. The objective to amass titles was made to look like a mission to 'civilise' but their arbitrary responses towards non-Christian nations were tantamount to breaches of international law (Cohan 2004: 28). Protection by conventional regimes was ruled out even if the coloniser states were States Party because the Hague Conventions are limited in application to situations where all belligerents are State Parties by virtue of the instruments' 'general participation clause.' Formerly colonised countries are not State Parties to the Hague Conventions.

Years later, the conventional stipulations that governed relations between the Christian States of Europe and the Ottoman Empire brought the Ottomans within the 'pale' of the public law of European States (1856 Treaty of Paris; Wheaton 1866: para 13). The Berlin Conference of 1884–1885 suspended the application of PublIL to non-Europeans, however, and the 1919 Peace Conference and the apparatus of the League of Nations overlooked the cultural property and sites of occupied peoples. The domestic laws of Allied colonial governments or settler states had to grapple with the issue (Vrdoljak 2008: 78).

The principle of humanity, which prohibited looting by victorious warring parties, governed relations between European powers. The principle was invoked when it served their strategic interests. Even the enforcement of the ban on the slave trade was sometimes used as a justification for colonial rule (Goldmann 2024: 601). Restitution was ordered to Western European states for losses or damage suffered in violation of the rules of war, but the reallocation of cultural property removed in the colonial context was not part of the post–Second World War restitution programme. The Allies recognised that the return of cultural objects could help to ameliorate the impact of colonial policies, but none of this translated into the Hague codification of the international humanitarian law relating to the protection of cultural property during war (Jakubowski 2009: 142ff).

During the Cold War both the United States and the UK insisted on this uneven approach and opposed the inclusion of restitutionary relief in the 1954 Hague Convention. The Seventh UNESCO General Conference in 1952 moved the restitution provision from the body of the Convention into a separate, optional protocol which States could sign independently. Splitting restitution and protection of cultural heritage during armed conflict into separate instruments was 'contrary to international practice applied since the 1815 Congress of Vienna' and enabled claims for decolonisation and minority protection to continue to be ignored (Vrdoljak 2008: 139–149).

Today, colonialism is notably absent from the list of crimes for which the ICC, ICTY, and ICTR are mandated—genocide, crimes against humanity, and war crimes. Success has eluded calls to recognise American or African Colonisation by European Powers as genocide or Holocaust (Wood 2012: 121).

2.4.3 Misconstruing the belongings of the 'racialised other'

European colonialism bifurcated sociology in the 19th and 20th centuries and continues to divide social scientific knowledge (Virdee 2019: 3–4). By 1880 cultural ideas about groups that shared a common history, a distinctive set of customs or language, had taken hold. National identity became infused with notions about race. By the early 1900s, modernism was preoccupied with the construction of the 'racialised other.' European race study went unquestioned and ethnology and race anthropology-centred disciplines thrived (McMahon 2007: 7). France and Germany contributed to the classification of the races, with support from Britain. Disappointingly, the diversity in western cultures could not prevent their ethnographic knowledge from constituting scientific legitimation for European colonisation (Grimme 2020: 53). Ethnographic museums had to assume responsibility for the prehistory of European man because ethnographic objects were considered inferior to European cultural products, 'primitive' material from cultures with 'no history' and incapable of producing art. (Clunas 1998: 43). 'Anthropology' and 'Oriental Studies' had to focus on anything that Europe did not consider to be of interest. In this constellation of knowledge there was no room for considering the significance of cultural objects for deprived communities. De-historicised museum narratives are the product of a gaze trained on Europe. Many opportunities to fix mistakes and adopt policies and strategies to avoid repeating them have been missed.

Ideas of the Other as a category difference to the Self are socially constructed. As a status that is assigned to people, the Other is a stranger. Certain genres of exhibition, such as the 'cabinet of curiosities,' were used as a technique to construct Otherness. Spolia would be displayed without providing any in-depth information or organisation by chronology, artefact type, or culture of origin (Jenkins 1994). 'Human zoos' portrayed othering in an even more sinister form. Prevalent in the late 19th and early 20th centuries with the explicit and literal purpose of exhibiting Otherness, African and Asian people were displayed in sideshows as well as in ethnographic villages or in study collections. A Brussels World Fair put Congolese people in a simulated zoo environment as recently as 1958. The blatant exhibition of Otherness continues in cultural tourism, television programmes, and museums today (Haughenbury 2016: 4–5). These ideas display cross-cultural differences and shift over time. The effects of colonialism's systematic fragmentation are still evident in the 'disciplinary carve up' of the Indigenous world (Tuhiwai Smith 2021: 31):

> bones, mummies and skulls to the museums, artwork to private collectors, languages to linguistics, "customs" to anthropologists, beliefs and behaviours to psychologists…

Misguided hopes that race science could achieve an archive of the world can be attributed, in part, to the ability of western science to disguise ideology and mask biased subjectivities. The belief that everyone is 'perfect' except for misfits and outcasts preserves western societies' mythical innocence. To counter this propensity, institutions with a stake in the distribution of knowledge—cultural and educational institutions, governments, funders, civil society, and international organisations—should seek common ground between traditional science focused on Indigenous systems of knowledge and systems and western science.

The collective embodiment of rights in sacred ethnographic material, and the obligations embedded in them to see their meaning fulfilled, precludes their permanent transfer, and yet countless ethnographic artefacts circulate on the international art market. The market forces sacred material into the commodification mould. The processes by which the sacred artefacts have been inserted into the market as 'ethnic handcrafts' degrade the material and desacralise their use. The neo-capitalist mindset trivialises the sacred features of traditional ways of life (Champagne 2012: 53). Trivialised as 'art' in a European aesthetic, the sacred must 'pass away.' While many Native Americans choose not to participate in the market economy, there are Indigenous societies that have adjusted over time and prefer to engage with and trade on the market. Sales and exchanges of sacred material amassed during bloody civil wars or at gunpoint elicit a certain consensus regarding market value. Uncertainty surrounding dates and circumstances of removal creates opportunities to paper over the gaps in provenance and achieve a higher sale price. Commercial motivations readily prevail over objections that the trade in sacred objects infringe on the rights to religion, spirituality, traditional knowledge, and education. After all, was 'ethnographic' material not amenable to trade since the 1700s? Has it not become accepted in new westernised contexts?

The lack of awareness and sensitivity to other cultures derives from states having had to fulfil the standard of 'civilised states' to be considered full members of the Universal Family of Nations during the colonial era. Territories that managed to retain their independence were few. They functioned as full members occasionally, when expedient for the colonial powers (Alexandrowicz 1973: 71, 74, 81–82, 90, 113, 117).

2.4.4 Continuities of prejudice

The scholarly search for continuities between the two prejudices of racism and antisemitism has overlooked mimetic desire as a potential connection between the colonial history of murderous racism and the Holocaust (e.g., Kühne 2013: 339ff). When 'force' and its implications are not sufficiently generalised, misleading conclusions must follow. Philosopher Simone Weildedicated the final years of her short life between 1937 and 1943 to colonialism. Her legacy generalised the concept of force in a way that can support the reconstruction of the law governing restitution (Little ed. tr. 2003: 66ff). She emphasised that, while the typology and sequence of effects of the different types of colonialism vary greatly in terms of their particularities, the basic colonial problem was the same in every empire. The attempts to homogenise different cultures into one generated violence, forceful subjugation, and genocide. Weil's anti-colonialist stance had a certain visionary quality that derived from the adverse effect of factory work on her mental faculties and decision-making capacity, her close identification with enslaved persons, and experiences as a member of the Free French Forces in London in 1943 (Little ed. Tr. 2003: 1). Imperial France believed that a benevolent imperial presence could modernise and improve the lives of colonised peoples; and yet the French Empire ruled its colonised peoples by brute force (Little ed. tr. 2003: 65-68). Since the 1950s assimilation policies constellated on insidious forms of indoctrination into European culture have been deployed to counter anti-colonial uprisings (Griffin 1995: 399). Killing an estimated 825,000 Indigenous people during the 'pacification' of Algeria (1956-1958) made the deepest values France claimed to hold seem worthless. The French forces were accused of using 'German methods' and of committing the same crimes as the Gestapo. The conviction that the French Empire imitated the British Empire also took root (von Bulow 2016: 112-113; contra Weil 2002: 147).

The moral flaw inherent in European colonial enterprises is violence. In some locations the dominant polity resorted to military conquest or massacres to appropriate resources, followed by the deliberate undervaluing of peoples and their culture. Local religious practices were dismantled to wear down the resistance of cultural communities to wealth extraction and handing over their most precious possessions which embody their identity. The disastrous impact of changes in ethnic composition, demographics, as well as religious, customary, and cultural value systems, prompted some communities to reproduce the customs of their oppressors, while other communities disappeared altogether (Kautondokwa 2021: 139). The domination of the mental universe of the colonised interferes with their self-definition (wa Thiong'o 1986: 16).

The desire to explore and build trade links also fostered tensions, political dictatorships, and the violent subjugation of entire regions (DMB *Care of Collections* 2021: 24). European powers frequently used force to open ports to 'free trade' and civilisation (Oh 2018: 427). Whatever the tactic—trade, missions, or something other—when the conqueror strives to retain power, the quality of the 'peace' that sets in differs from war only in depriving the conquered of arms (Little ed. tr. 2003: 67). Subjugation is accepted under duress, and only until revenge is exacted (Thompson ed. 2005: 102). Social injustice is fuelled by unwillingness to acknowledge the cultural suppression and violence associated with the projection of racialised ideas onto peoples. Efforts to deny, minimise, or circumvent responsibility for the violence perpetrated may include the suppression of information about the worst excesses, crimes, and abuses during colonialism. Colonial masters exercised the powers of description, administration, classification, and coercion, and set precedents for Nazi 'genocidal thinking' and Nazi crimes (Zimmerer 2004: 64–68).

The hierarchical thinking which mimetism fosters imperils lives. That it threatens human survival on the lower rungs is strikingly evident in the disrespect with which grave robbers in Southern Africa treated the remains of non-Europeans. Khoisan remains from the Cape Khoi San, Nama, Griqua, and Koranna were sold to collections that foregrounded race, typology, and evolution. Many were displayed to symbolise the losses and humiliation suffered by the less powerful (Rassool 2015: 653–655). The colonial elites of Western Europe weighed, classified, and ascribed a hierarchical order to humankind. The indigenous 'non-white inhabitants' of the German colony were not 'citizens'; they were German 'subjects' (Theurer 2023: 1148). The Germans used a hierarchical approach to separate Aryans and non-Aryans in the Third Reich (Bachmann 2018: 334–335). The ideology of the hierarchy of race and its effects bears mimetic traits. Commentators do not always use mimetism to frame their observations, but their reasoning may be in full alignment with a mimetic understanding of history.

Bachmann denies that Germany's colonial policy in Africa served as a blueprint for the industrial-scale genocide of the Third Reich (1933–1945). Apart from the radical exclusion of outgroups deemed as inferior, he fails to see any connection between the genocidal policies of the Kaiserreich in Africa and the Holocaust in German-occupied Europe (Bachmann 2018: 326, 331, 334). Instead, he traces the inspiration for the institutions of the Third Reich to Britain's colonial past rather than to Germany's unsuccessful colonial genocides in Africa (Bachmann 2018: 332). His note that the German war machine came to resemble that of the British Crown's troops during the South African War, and that General von Trotha may have been motivated by a higher pension reward from the Emperor if Berlin could be convinced that genocide had been accomplished, shows awareness of the mimetic dynamic. Nazi bureaucrats generally felt disdain for the catastrophes that led to losses of colonial possessions. The British colonisers inspired in them envy and awe, awakening their mimetic desire.

It is no longer contentious that the Second Reich (1871–1919) experience in German SWA was an important antecedent to Third Reich imperialism, Nazi colonialism, and genocide (Madley 2005: 429ff). German nostalgia for what the African Kaiserreich had achieved in German SWA eroded the moral and political barriers to genocide and the taboos of brutality in Europe. The behaviours of German officials and the state mirrored the bitter hostility of other colonial masters and spurred them to pursue a racially purified 'Aryan' *Volksgemeinschaft* (Kühne 2013: 356). In this sense, the colonial era closely prefigured Third Reich ideas and policies (Madley 2005: 456–457).

2.4.5 The process elements of degenerating rivalry

Mimetics foster rivalries that degenerate into 'absolutely unpredictable, truly undifferentiated violence.' These rivalries may intensify to the point of extermination (Girard 2010: 39; Kearney 1995: 2). Raphael Lemkin (1900–1959) became the first international law scholar to highlight the process elements in genocides in settler-colonial histories. When the Second World War was about to end, Lemkin proposed the adoption of a multilateral convention to criminalise destructive genocidal episodes (Jakubowski 2015: 140). Under examples of 'cultural genocide' Lemkin listed German techniques of occupation such as forbidding the use of a language, compulsory education, and the destruction of national monuments, libraries, archives, museums, and galleries (Lemkin and Schabas 2008: 84–85). The destruction of such tangible and intangible manifestations of group culture destroys the foundations and ways of life of groups. Compellingly, Lemkin identified human life, treasures of art, and historical archives as values that can never be restored once they are lost (Lemkin and Schabas 2008: 95).

In the aftermath of the Second World War, the 1948 Universal Declaration of Human Rights and the 1948 Convention on the Prevention and Punishment of the Crime of Genocide defined the international order. Contracting parties were unwilling to extend the convention's application to the foreign relations of their dependent territories (Article 12). Since the final text of the Genocide Convention limits genocidal practices to the physical–biological destruction of groups and omits cultural genocide, discriminatory policies towards cultural heritage undertaken during the colonial era do not legally qualify as genocidal practices. Colonial powers feared that the international condemnation of cultural genocide could affect Soviet policies of assimilation and the preferred treatment of colonised peoples (Jakubowski 2015: 141–142). Caveats inserted by the United States when ratifying the Genocide Convention in 1988 include that US governmental consent is required to proceed with legal action in the ICJ. This is tantamount to blocking the involvement of the ICJ if any state were to accuse the United States of genocide. It interferes with the evolution of norms and standards that support the implementation of the convention. The concept 'cultural genocide' features in the Final Report of the Truth and Reconciliation Commission of Canada, *Honouring the Truth, Reconciling the Future* 2015. The report defines it as the destruction of the structures and practices that allow a community to continue as a group. The concept 'cultural genocide' has also influenced Sweden and Australia's truth and reconciliation process, but it has not developed into a legal term or an independent crime (Brückner 2019: 45). More recently still the memorial submitted by South Africa in its case against Israel in the ICJ refers to the decimation of libraries, universities and other centres of learning, monuments, and religious sites (*Application of the Convention on the Prevention and Punishment of the Crime of Genocide in the Gaza Strip (South Africa v Israel) Provisional Measures* Merits, 29 December 2023 [2023] ICJ 1, 29).

Arguably, a moral system that maintains societal order and stability, peace, and harmony, has practical functionality. However, societies based on ethically dubious practices such as slavery, which may also serve to achieve 'peace' and order, can be highly functional. This indicates that moral functionalism must refer to more than practical functionality (Flanagan 2016: 154–155). History is not studied to draw moral lessons but to liberalise the mind and inspire direction of the will. Global social and ethical pressures create external processes that help to integrate society, moving it towards reparation and societal restoration. When a damaging event disturbs, changes, or interrupts the course of things, it might be possible and desirable to restore the original, probable trajectory which life would have taken if the damage had not occurred. These processes and responses qualify as 'ethics-based' and cannot be achieved without some self-examination and effort to remove the blind spots obstructing self-knowledge.

Excluding the crime of cultural genocide from the convention means that the international regime for prevention and punishment of genocide precludes important avenues of redress. The proposition that such a claim may derive from the prohibition of genocide 'as an annex' raises the issue of intertemporal law (Thielecke and Geißdorf 2021: 161). Additionally, the 1948 Genocide Convention cannot be remade or amended. Refinement of the concept and definition of an act of genocide can be accomplished only through bilateral negotiation.

International codifications and soft law on the right to reparations in cases where serious breaches of humanitarian law have occurred include a UN General Assembly Resolution that indicates that restitution could be a form of compensation for past harms or offences done to people (Basic Principles and Guidelines on the Right to a Remedy and Reparation for Victims of Gross Violations of International Human Rights Law and Serious Violations of International Humanitarian Law A/RES/60/147, 16 December 2005). The Resolution refers to crimes against humanity and reparation for injury and outlines five types of reparation—restitution, compensation, rehabilitation being individual, and satisfaction and guarantees of non-repetition being structural (Theurer 2023: 1163). States are expected to ensure that victims of crimes against humanity, committed through acts attributable to the state under international law or committed in any territory under its jurisdiction, have the right to obtain reparation for material and moral damages, on an individual or collective basis (at 12.3). This resolution does not specifically address losses suffered prior to or after colonial rule. Whether such obligation is in the making remains contested. The core controversy concerns whether the colonial era violated peoples' rights. Scholars who maintain that a violation of rights exists, tend to support the existence of a legal duty to undertake redress and enter into negotiations on reparations as a form of satisfaction (Theurer 2023: 1162).

Moral standards of behaviour are frequently incorporated into non-binding or soft law. Codes of ethics, policies, and national legislation that support the realisation of cultural rights are common in countries with Indigenous populations. Guidelines and codes of conduct that presume the return of cultural heritage reflect ethics-based thinking and ethical criteria on collection items from the colonial era that correspond to models of responsibility (Stahn 2023: 467). While these guidelines and codes have the potential to refine general principles of cultural heritage law, having a 'moral' obligation implies that the goodwill of the perpetrator determines whether compensation follows or not. The German Parliament issued a statement in the context of the agreement with Namibia indicating that the absence of a legal basis means that Germany will not entertain individual or collective compensation claims of individual descendants of victim groups (German Parliament Press Release 24 March 2023). The initiative prompted the *Swartbooi* case and the Herero and Nama claim for reparative justice. Since '[p]ressures from the outside do not create direct challenges to a moral order,' it is up to those inside the moral order to challenge it (Flanagan 2016: 155–156).

Behaviours that erode legal standards do not release a state from its obligations (Cohan 2004: 30–31). If law and ethics approaches to restitution claims deriving from past injustice can limit mimetism's potential to create normative pressure, it is worth prioritising approaches that encourage expanded human capability. Amartya Sen's theory of justice, which was introduced in Chapter 1, considers what expands human capability in relation to accessible material resources, production, or incomes, what they can do and be, and how they are faring. Arguably, his model would support an assessment of the contribution of restitution to human development and wellbeing. The return of the tangible object alone may 'reduce injustice' in Sen's framework, but justice is being advanced when return revives the spiritual knowledge and cultural practices.

2.4.6 Museum models that cloak 'mummified' thinking

It is challenging to establish a reliable provenance for sacred objects and collections that ended up trapped or 'imprisoned' in vitrines that insist on their 'protection.' Like encamped refugees, they are 'displaced and in between' (Dudley 2018: 53). Their provenance is either 'frozen' in time or the documentation of their provenance doomed to remain incomplete. The labels that assign objects to supposed 'ethnic' or geographical categories may be the only clues remaining (Förster 2021: 107). The record of their legal ownership comprises problematic behaviours that deprived owners, communities, and countries of their most cherished belongings, but these behaviours were not recorded when the theft, seizure or looting occurred.

These frozen provenances have a lot in common with the 'mummified' thinking that thrives in the meeting points between the so-called encyclopaedic museum and the universal museum model. The Napoleonic campaigns that cemented the collections of France inspired museums in Western Europe and England to build up their own 'universal collections' in their national museums along a paternalistic model of universality that reflects a western ontology that favours a European audience. Universal museums, or encyclopaedic museums, exhibit artefacts from a variety of cultures under the same roof (Grau ed. 2021: 1). They aim for a comprehensive overview that contributes to a cross-cultural interpretation of a set of universal cultural values unconfined by borders. Oftentimes they make comparisons and draw conclusions from the overview of cultures on offer. In encyclopaedic museums, education and curiosity provide a licence for extending knowledge of past people based on the data extracted from objects, samples, and remains. The aim espoused by the traditional encyclopaedic museums to achieve 'universalism' in the purported service of all of humanity, has been superimposed on everyone.

The 'universal museum' idea inserts the Parthenon Marbles into world culture, presenting Greek art in chronological narrative among earlier and later world art. Once upon a time, the aim of achieving the widest possible access to educate the public was considered so important that museums readily deployed copies, engravings, and plaster casts (Miniotis 2014: 6). Reconstructions can be made of some of the Parthenon Mables no longer in existence only because Roman copies exist of the original sculptures. Yet this line of thinking no longer appeals. The British Museum has long justified its possession of the original Parthenon Sculptures, which were procured as Enlightenment theory was expanding. The retention of cultural property in univeral museums is supposed to be justified by their pre-eminent position as guardians of the culture of the world. William St Clair, the British historian, famously wondered why univeral museums seem interested in originals only (St Clair 2006: 94). True universalism would place copies of the Parthenon Sculptures in the Duveen Gallery for educational purposes and return the originals to Athens.

The Acropolis Museum opened in 2009, showcasing the Parthenon Marbles in a gallery built to the same dimensions and orientation as the Parthenon, which is in view from the gallery's glass walls. The new Acropolis Museum disrupted the narrative that the British Museum is best placed to tell the 'story' of the Marbles to communities in London and visitors representing all the cultures of the world. The spiritual knowledge of the Parthenon Sculptures can be contemplated in the Acropolis Museum, just as the mummified monk was revered and contemplated in the Puzhao Temple Hall in Yangchun, Fujian, China, built to honour and exalt Zhanggong Zushi. Both temples are places that train the attention on the sacred.

Because 'encyclopaedic' museums bear comprehensive information about a broad category of subjects, they are also burdened with the responsibility to educate and offer new perspectives to visitors. However, they cannot claim to account for the culture of humankind. No encyclopaedic museum has the ability, range, or permission to exhibit such a diverse range of objects without encountering ethical dilemmas. The wide access they offer cannot take precedence over moral and legal notions of ownership (2024 Qingdao Consensus). Universal museums are not truly international; they are western classification exports at best (Curtis 2006: 119). No commitment to relabel museum displays will flick the switch that makes every acquisition ethical, lawful, and 'acceptable.'

Because the 'universal museum' concept has garnered negative attention, many UK museums drop the label while continuing the practice (Byrne 2015: 40). However, universal museums cannot fully advance knowledge, as their status is always under threat from discrepancies in power, memory, and taste in collections. The idea that certain museums are entitled to hold and retain large collections of cultural artefacts for the ultimate good of society is one of the most insidious obstacles to repatriation (Curtis 2006: 120, 125; Janes 2015: 14). Moreover, encyclopaedic museums cannot remain unquestioned repositories while smaller museums make returns. Before the universal museum can meet its self-proclaimed role, it must clarify how objects are sourced, displayed, and their narratives constructed.

Influential legal scholar John Henry Merryman (1920–2015), whose publications dominated law and ethics discourses on the Parthenon Sculptures since the 1980s, highlighted a trifecta of preservation, access, and integrity—so-called 'higher internationalist principles'—to endorse the will of the holding nation while cloaking their mimetic propensities. By 'integrity' Merryman meant that objects should be kept physically as complete as possible within the confines of universal museums, whose position he championed (Merryman 1985: 1919). He was an outspoken proponent of the ontology of an all-encompassing world view of peoples and their cultures and of museums as global resources for the citizens of the world. The origin of cultural objects, the status-changes their collections have undergone after becoming detached from their former cultural context, and the intricacies of domestic ownership rules in an international context, were carefully left out of account, however (Merryman 1985: 1916–1921; Merryman 1986: 847). The Eurocentric ideas which Merryman pushed as 'higher internationalist principles' aligned with his support of the legality of the Ottoman authorities' *ex post facto* approvals to remove the Parthenon Sculptures. He considered it important that the behaviour of Elgin's team was ratified twice over, by additional firmans and the shipment of 40 crates from the port of Piraeus (Merryman 1985: 1899; 1900–1901; reiterated by Herman 2023: 43).

The Ottomans were critical of the conduct of Elgin's team as will be explained (Titi 2023: 74, 79). More important even than directly conflicting evidence are the assertions about the 'legality' of the work claimed prior to its being condemned by the authorities. These are clearly intended to safeguard interests (Rudenstine 2021: 452–453). As a matter of public record during the debate in the Parliamentary Committee, Elgin paid commission and agency for the permissions. Cut glass lustres and firearms were given to the Voivode and the Disdar to ensure a permissive interpretation of the firman (*HC Report* 1816: 143, 146). Elgin's record of expenses, which he kept for his in-laws who financed him, included what was paid to the Disdar and the district governor in Constantinople to release the second shipment of Marbles. The Voivode feared reprimand from his superiors, but his actions went unpunished (Herman 2023: 48). Lusieri's letters to Elgin contain appreciation for the 'money, presents and influence' he made available to allow the team to make headway with the removal of the sculptures (Kakaounaki 2024). Even if Ottoman officials expected gifts to prompt officials to perform their duties, this cannot detract from Elgin's abuse of authority as the British ambassador when bribing officials (Rudenstine 2021: 453–455, 458–459). The factual position, however, is that the Ottoman government considered corruption to be a serious and nagging problem in the 19th century. The anti-corruption and bureaucratic accountability provisions of Ottoman law set a behavioural standard. Bribes were forbidden in the Quran, Sharia law, and Ottoman laws that defined bureaucratic powers and outlawed bribes (Rubin 2011: 45, 114). Merryman concluded however that 'the fact that bribes occurred … is not a significant consideration, particularly in view of the ratification of Elgin's actions by the sultan' (Merryman 1998; Rudenstine

2021: 454). It is a common principle of PrIL that laws concerning public order or social mores are not susceptible to derogation by private agreement. Only if PrIL is sidelined does public policy become 'irrelevant' and the actions of 'rapacious foreigners' metamorphose into 'ratification.' What is more, these Ottoman rules would be pertinent under any choice-of-law rule that pointed to the law of the place where the transfer occurred. Merryman never took an interest in the role and function of secondary legal norms, however, and his selective description of the law left glaring gaps in his argument that the export controls of countries of origin were irrelevant to the restitution debate. Scholars have since pointed out that his arguments gave no account of other tenets of PrIL nor EU instruments, and the 1995 UNIDROIT Convention on Stolen or Illegally Exported Cultural Objects that would be relevant to the discourse (e.g., Papa-Sokal 2009: 237ff).

Greece was relegated to having bystander-status in the 'after-life' of the most of its Parthenon Marbles. Nonetheless, they led and swayed public opinion as a standard framework for legal thinking about the restitution debate, and this is set to continue for as long as no definitive legal argument that qualifies as inherently superior surfaces (Soirila 2022: 4). The legal discourse on the Parthenon Marbles is indeterminate, but the mummified thinking expressed in Merryman's trifecta would have it otherwise. Legal indeterminacy, like normative uncertainty, will breed inaction because it blocks the assumption of institutional responsibility for historical injustice (Prott 2005: 226; Mackenzie et al. 2020: 60–61). The trifecta caught on as a popular ideology that shaped many tactical arguments in support of retention of the Sculptures in Britain, including that they have shaped British culture, defined British identity and community, inspired its arts, civilised British life, and stimulated British scholarship (Merryman 1985: 1915). The National Audit Office warned as early as 1988 that the growth in the size of major collections at museums was inflated and unstoppable. Nonetheless, Merryman habitually defended the outmoded belief that the 'common cultural heritage of all mankind' ought to circulate unhindered and independent from the limits inhering in national jurisdiction and domestic property rights regimes to counter the hoarding tendencies of 'retentionist' source nations and facilitate dialogue among cultures about preservation. Merryman proceeded to denounce retentionism for standing in the way of the international circulation of art for the 'broadest public benefit.' However, his definition of 'retentionist' was entirely self-made. The British Museum exhibits only a tiny fraction of its collection. Instead of making way for claims for restitution to sacred material, Merryman's trifecta mummified the legal discourse, encouraging it to spin in circles. Considered up close, the trifecta recycles violence and perpetuates the might of the powerful.

Displaying cultural objects from different cultures together is supposed to promote intercultural understanding and to humanise what museums do, but museums seldom achieve this (Byrne 2015: 43). Regrettably, the aims of universalism have been used to justify the theft of items of significant cultural value. Arguments against restitution frequently reference the universality of the Declaration on the Importance and Value of Universal Museums (the 'DIVUM'), signed in 2002 by the Bizot Group. The signatories were an exclusive group of antiquities dealers and the Directors of 19 major museums in Europe and North America, but included no museums in Africa, Asia, or Oceania. The DIVUM constructed a 'World or Universal Museum' argument for museums with a similar history (text reproduced in Curtis 2006: 125–126; Gorman 2013: 76). It declares that, while requests for repatriation had become an important issue for museums 'objects acquired in earlier times must be viewed in the light of different sensitivities and values reflective of that earlier era.' This sentiment erects a 'firewall' between colonial takings and modern return practices (Stahn 2023: 425). The DIVUM generally discourages repatriation claims for their narrow nationalism and the political impulses they represent. It condemns those claiming restitution as hostile to art collections across the globe. Handing back cultural heritage to their rightful owners would supposedly lessen the significance they have gained whilst in the custody of western museums.

The DIVUM leans heavily on institutional authority to affirm a colonial present but lacks legal authority. A self-important declaration of power that questions the connection between cultural heritage and human rights can be expected to lack normative effect, especially when issued by a self-appointed group (Byrne 2015: 25). The declaration garnered considerable traction with the support provided by influential authors such as John Merryman, however.

The DIVUM's take on the legality of ownership and control of cultural property is a tailored justification of the signatories' possession and retention of cultural objects obtained through colonial rule. In attempting to procure exemption from having to recognise cultural rights, the DIVUM assumes the status of contemporary successor to exploitative colonialism that endorses the power imbalances underpinning the collecting practices of yore. Assuming that universal museums are best placed to house diverse collections, it dismissed the need forfurther contextualisation of the collections, and advocates setting aside of national claims. The DIVUM fully absorbed Merryman's problematic dichotomy. To dismiss the effects of removing cultural material from colonies that depended on it, attributes a certain effect to mimetics.

Motivated by a wish to steer clear of 'retrospective politics' the signatories have continued to highlight the ideals that underlie the universal museum at UNESCO bi-annual meetings (Gorman 2013: 80; Byrne 2015: 26). The signatories consider current perspectives risky for historical analysis of the colonial question. However, there is no denying that repatriation demands have become political acts by which Indigenous peoples seek to reclaim their cultures and pride (Supiot 2007: 97). Repatriation as resistance may result in redress and a more secure future for many communities. The lack of progress with reburial of ancestral remains and 'sacred' material continues to be a source of great frustration. Overall, the pace remains slow.

2.4.7 Limitations and dangers of dichotomisation: cultural nationalism/internationalism

Merryman's persistent defence of a free market in cultural property was supposed to offer great liberalisation for the exclusive benefit of the destination market (e.g., 1985: 1880ff; 1986: 831ff). He pitted 'cultural nationalism' (cultural property should return to country of origin) against 'cultural internationalism' (cultural property should move freely around the world and be widely accessible as a global public good). The importance of returning heritage to communities opposed to display was diminished. Merryman accentuated only the positive in 'internationalism' while dwelling on the negative aspects of 'nationalism.' To prioritise the legally cognisable international interest in cultural property of museums, he took issue with so-called 'blanket' state ownership laws for undiscovered archaeological finds and the strict export restrictions they relied upon for purposes of their claims. Consequently, source nations and communities who claimed back their heritage or waged re-unification campaigns were cast as being bent on serving their exclusive subordinate national interests in a politically motivated manner. Neither the homogenisation of the world nor the idea that universal museums hold heritage in trust for the world, will neutralise nationalist agendas.

Appeals to 'internationalism' and 'cosmopolitanism' created hide-outs for exploitative dealers and collectors to bring antiquities and ethnographical material to museums in market states (Chechi 2014: 302–303). The flaws of Merryman's framework became strikingly obvious in the Parthenon Marbles dispute. Given the powerful competitive spirit that raged over antiquities among museums in and beyond Britain, the juridical framework of circulation that supports art loans is hardly the most appropriate conceptual framework to apply. The moral responsibility evoked by the Parthenon Sculptures does not derive from free market sentiments, and efforts to separate out ownership and possession in legal terms to resolve the dispute have always run aground.

Most cultural policies necessarily encompass elements of both 'cultural nationalism' and 'cultural internationalism.' A middle ground between them was available all along in the rules and principles contained in primary and secondary EU law, PrIL, and international law jurisprudence. For instance, choice-of-law rules of PrIL for property and other categories of legal disputes are both national and international in character. Splitting them in two excluded discourses supporting restitution because splitting entrenches the unequal power relations of the colonial era, favours wealthy nations on the demand-side of the trade in cultural objects, and discounts moral benefit as a factor in an ethico-legal framework. Efforts to refrain from impoverishing countries of origin, empower them to resist the illicit trade in antiquities, and avoid the chaos of undocumented and illegally excavated and smuggled antiquities are not prioritised. Yet smuggling has increased as tourism and travel have become easier and more widespread (Greenhalgh 2019: 518–523).

Decades before the DIVUM was published, and starting in the 1960s, the 'New Museology' movement encouraged museums to contribute more broadly to society. It set out to make museums more democratic, accessible, and inclusive. The resources of museology (collection, conservation, scientific research, restitution, diffusion, creation) were to be transformed into workable instruments that could be used in the service of specific social contexts and projects. The aims and function of museums were considered ripe for renewal, and the nature of the processes by which knowledge is produced and reproduced in museums were considered important (*International Movement for a New Museology (MINOM)* 1984 Declaration of Quebec Basic Principles of a New Museology 2010: 23–24). While the idea behind a 'new museology' cannot be traced back to any ethical precept or principle as such, an ethics of responsibility and reciprocity is found at the centre of the idea. Adherents supported collaborations between source cultures and museum organisations, and encouraged engagement with source communities (Lynch 2011: 151). The 'new museology' brought the social function of museums into view and considered their role in addressing social and economic disparities (Labadi 2017: 1).

Intended to serve as the foundation for the British Museum's ideas of ownership and control of cultural knowledge, the DIVUM justified the version of the truth in which artefacts unethically collected are merely 'displaced' from their original source. This version exempts universal museums from responsibility for theft and trade in stolen goods that helps them prolong the benefits of cultural tourism. Yet the core ethos of the museums of the 21st century, to increase the cultural intelligence of visitors, does not aim to instil superiority in western cultural institutions (Hicks 2020: 19). The idea of the widest possible access and preservation of static materiality stands in stark contrast to well-considered policies that foreground the purpose, function, and obligations inhering in ethnographic material. The stale and circular moralist arguments that draw on 'cultural nationalism' and 'cultural internationalism' add traction to mimetics. Creating and serving only the niches which the universal museum's visitors and academic communities prefer has become unacceptable.

One of the crucial questions hovering in the background concerning the Parthenon Sculptures is who has title to them.

2.4.8 The crucial question of title to the Parthenon Marbles—is it colonial era?

The respective testimonies of Hunt and Elgin are an informative starting point for the question of title. Hunt claimed to have persuaded the Caimacan to issue a document allowing Elgin's team to draw, excavate, erect scaffolding and 'take away some pieces of stone with old figures or inscriptions' from the Acropolis. He testified that he procured for Elgin many inscriptions and detached pieces of sculpture. He also averred that the Voivode extended the Porte's authorisation out of respect for Elgin (*HC Report* 1816: 1816, 145, 146). Lord Elgin claimed that the Ottoman authorities authorised the stripping of the sculptures from the Parthenon. The Greeks did not have powerful allies who could bring to the world's attention that Lord Elgin and his team were depriving them of their cultural heritage, and thus it was not considered odd that the Greeks had no say in the removal of the Sculptures (Hitchens 1997: 49). Willing to blur boundaries in his testimony before the Parliamentary Committee, Lord Elgin insisted that he had permission to 'draw, model, remove and excavate.' The Committee queried the word order. Permission to 'excavate and remove' would carry a very different meaning (*HC Report* 1816: 35–36).

Ottoman officials in Constantinople attempted to regain control of the removal of fragments and pediments; they condemned the dismantling of the Parthenon and sawing off the backs of thick slabs as unauthorised and gave orders to cease (Rudenstine 2021: 452–453). A ban on further removals brought Lusieri's work to a standstill in 1804. The Voivode issued a prohibition on furthering the excavations in 1805. Another prohibition followed by order of the Porte to prevent the Sculptures from setting sail in 1809 (De Lathuy 2018: 20–21). The Select Committee of Parliament did not discuss whether the occupying power had the legal capacity to agree to the Marbles' removal. It made no effort to obtain the document from Ottoman officials in Athens and it did not communicate with Ottoman officials in Constantinople. It did ask Lord Elgin if he had disclosed his intention to establish a private museum to the Ottoman government (*HC Report* 1816: 49). Elgin insisted that he only expanded the scope of his project when it became clear to him that the unique treasures were in danger (*HC Report* 1816: 40–41). The version delivered by the Earl of Aberdeen was that, had Lord Elgin not 'secured' the Parthenon Sculptures, the French might have removed them (*HC Report* 1816: 7, 124). Elgin swore that he had not been actuated by 'motives of private emolument.' Privately, however, his desire for personal and familial aggrandisement and glory was confirmed in a letter he wrote to Lusieri in 1801, stating that he wanted to collect as much marble as possible for his ancestral home and to multiply the marble ornaments decorating 'Broomhall House.' Concerns over saving cultural heritage or the encouragement of arts and architecture in England were hardly uppermost.

The question of whether the Parthenon Sculptures form part of the collections of the British Museum dangles against a backdrop of unanswered questions of provenience and provenance. Assuming the Sculptures were Elgin's rightful property, they are legitimately owned by the British Museum because Elgin's good title over the Marbles could transfer ownership to the Crown and confer the right to sell them. If Parliament investigated Elgin's actions in 1816 and found them sound, the British Museum holds valid title. The British Museum Act 1963 precludes the Trustees from returning them without passing a de-accession law, and their fate is in the hands of the British Parliament (Carruthers 2005: 124–125). If Elgin's title was defective, the Crown has defective title. According to the common law principle *nemo plus juris ad alium transferre potest quam ipse habet*, the right of the Crown to the Marbles would be no better than Elgin's right to them. In addition to *nemo dat quod non habet*, a principle of common law incorporated in the Sale of Goods Act 1979 (s 21, with exceptions applying where the seller and the buyer can transfer legal title), international soft law and unratified treaties would prompt reconsideration (Woodhead 2023: 66–74). The 1816 Act vesting title in the Trustees of the British Museum, would be a state sanctioning improper acquisition and the abuse of rights to gain ownership over culture within Europe (Stahn 2023: 118; Titi 2023: 121–122). If the British Museum did not acquire title, the Trustees would be competent to return them.

The late Greek Minister of Culture Melina Mercouri officially requested the restitution of the Parthenon Marbles in 1983. Her vision for the reunification of Athens' archaeological sites bred reluctance to agree to any deal that fails to recognise the Marbles as 'stolen.' Stressing that the occupying power authorised the sculptures' removal and remained passive in the face of the conduct of Elgin's men, no concessions were made that evidence for this is conflicting. Since the Greek government does not recognise in the British Museum any right of possession or ownership, and cannot be expected to accept anything less than full repatriation by the UK. Greece considers the firman to have been made up by Hunt and Elgin. Even if the firman were genuine and the permission granted by the Ottomans real, the removal remains unlawful since the occupying force was not the real owner, had no right to give the Marbles away, and granted the Athenians no say in their removal.

One year after Mercouri's official request, the British Museum added legal and political components to their standard defence, indicating legal acquisition under the laws in force at the time, and legal ownership by the Trustees (Stamatoudi and Korka 2013: 46). For the museum's spokespersons, the 'legality' of the removal and transportation, and the lawfulness of its ownership, are justified by the Sublime Porte's firman of 1801. The framework of English law does not permit a public museum to return objects from its collections. This banner ensures that the status quo remains undisturbed.

Notwithstanding the unanswered questions of provenience and provenance, Parliament approved the purchase on the assumption that the Parliamentary Committee ruled the removal of the Marbles proper. The British Museum relies on the same assumption (British Museum website 'The Parthenon Sculptures: The Trustees' Statement). The circumstances in which Elgin removed the Marbles from the Acropolis and the question as to whether he had obtained them lawfully, were not expressly included in the brief of the Parliamentary Select Committee. While competent to seek advice on the correct application of legal principles in the case, Parliamentary committees cannot determine or verify title. Its primary task was to examine whether and at what price Lord Elgin should be able to sell his collection to the UK government (Titi 2023: 100). The shipments did not incur customs tax upon entry into British waters, but how this affected the price and payment remain unclear.

Contemporary best practice standards do not conclusively clarify the ethical, moral, and legal aspects of transfers and ownership history in this instance, but legal doublespeak obscures the fact that the UK's claim to title is clouded by the absence of a diligent investigation (Rudenstine 2000: 3–4; Rudenstine 2021: 420, 452). Tactical arguments that the law confirms that the activities of Elgin's team were 'entirely legal' cannot render the matter fully confirmed and proven. Even on a presumption that an Act of Parliament establishing valid title in respect of foreign cultural heritage must be valid because the legitimacy of the institution would be challenged if not, the issue of whether the British Museum has acquired ownership of the Parthenon Sculptures remains contested. It lies central to the dispute (Machado Haertel 2021: 492).

Standing in the way of return of the Parthenon Sculptures are argumentative impediments that proliferate. For instance, assertions that Ottoman officials ratified the removals can be based on the theory that extensive interpretations given to narrowly worded authorisations may be condoned or ratified subsequently. Approval to embark the antiquities collected was also an approval of the actions that preceded embarkation, and in permitting Elgin's shipments of the Marbles, the Ottomans approved or condoned their taking. Among the glaring problems with the 'retroactive ratification theory' is the fact that Ottoman officials in Constantinople condemned the behaviours of Elgin's team in 1804; in 1809, they ordered Elgin's workers to cease and asserted that they lacked permission to undertake the work.

2.4.9 Spats over the classical

Western Europe self-identifies with a classical past, the wonders of ancient antiquity, and the Parthenon Sculptures as the crowning glory of classical architecture in the West. Several European museums ascribe narratives to Greek monuments that reveal a similar intense nostalgia for a link with the classical past (Connelly 2014: x, xiv). Classical Greece and ancient Athens are celebrated as representative of the zenith of humanism, reason, and democracy. The argument that the Parthenon Sculptures have a special character as the great symbol of democracy contributes to self-identification, projection, and imitation which obscure their true and original meaning. Their British setting have occasioned multiple spats over the Classical.

Paparrigopoulos presents the ancient–medieval–modern history of the Greek nation in *History of the Hellenic Nation from Ancient Times to the Present* (1886). Not one of the eight volumes supports the idea that contemporary Greeks stand apart from the heritage of an ancient culture they have no direct lineage to. The argument that many modern Greeks are not the descendants of the ancient Greeks merely confirms that the Athenians are central to the question of the permission for the removal of the Parthenon Marbles.

Every Greek government since the new nation of Greece was formed in 1833, has prioritised the legacy of the Athenian golden age. The ideology of the classical past continues to shape the contemporary sense of identity of the Greeks (Loukaki 2008: 45). The Bavarian monarchy stood ready to invest in ancient Greek culture and from 1832 onwards took active steps to link classical antiquities such as the Parthenon Marbles to Greek nationhood. Greece's sense of itself as the cradle of European civilisation prompted it to consider ancient Greek works a 'unicum.' This special character was reserved for classical works alone (Voudouri 2008: 129). From 1837 onwards, efforts were made to cleanse Greece of material evidence of its pre-classical ancient Greek past. Post-classical monuments were neglected, and Byzantine, Venetian, and Ottoman monuments destroyed. Ancient Greek civilisation was reshaped and revitalised by its interaction with Christianity during the Byzantine Empire. This influence did not disappear. In 1899, stricter legislation was adopted for objects of 'medieval Hellenism' to stop Europe's markets from turning into 'auction-houses for Greek antiquities.' The West has devalued the Byzantine element as decadent, preferring to see ancient Greece as a symbol of European roots, but the Greek nation identified with both the classical Hellenic and the Byzantine period of Greekness (Loukaki 2008: 45–56; Kynourgiopoulou 2011: 158).

From the aforesaid it follows that both Greece and Britain attach significance to the revival of the classical age in the arguments they present. For Greece, the basic thrust of its argument that the Marbles belong to the national cultural heritage of Greece, and that Greece has a natural right of ownership to them, has not changed since they were taken. The British side sees only what flatters its own self-image.

Its aspirations connect with the birthplace of direct democracy, which was practised in Athens. Imperialistic image-making recalls its superiority in its power relations. From this vantage point, the imitative architecture of the British Museum is a striking historical and situational irony. Since British people do not derive their sense of self from what the Marbles represent in the way the Greeks do, the claim that the Parthenon Marbles are defined by British identity is a reversal of truth.

2.4.10 Loans: a sensitive point

Cross-border art loans are a form of modern cultural exchange in which possession is transferred for purposes of research (e.g., authentication), assessment before purchase, or exhibition. Exhibitions enable information-sharing and stimulate revenue for the borrowing institution hosting the exhibition, while travelling exhibitions provide wider access to the objects on display and may provide opportunities for scholarly research. Frequently there may be expectations of a lucrative commercial exchange if one or both parties intend to derive a right, interest, profit, or benefit from the arrangement. Lending institutions may fund the exhibitions or receive income or another type of benefit from them. Wider publicity enhances the economic value of items, for instance (*Kamidian v Holt and Others* [2008] EWHC 1483 (Comm)). The agreement between collectors and lending institutions is typically documented as a contract. A sophisticated contract might extend the loan agreement beyond the physical corpus of what is on loan, to include, for example, intellectual property rights.

The lender state may gain 'soft power' from the information that is shared as part of non-commercial cultural exchange. The borrower will not necessarily request the lending institution for a confirmation of title if it is keen to promote the cultural exchange, but the exchange may be jeopardised if the title position is unclear. While the loan is under way, a third party might step forward asserting a right of possession or ownership superior to that of the borrower. Third-party title claims can be costly and time-consuming. The risks for lending institutions differ depending on whether the loan is concluded between private parties, between states for a non-commercial and official purpose, or between private enterprise and public entities. Since seizure and suit while an object is on loan erodes any return guarantee, the risk of seizure or suit for the borrower for the duration of the loan may be limited by legislation that renders arrest or specific restitution temporarily unavailable while a declaration of title or damages could be available during the event.

The PrIL questions arising in the context of loan agreements are numerous. Anti-seizure legislation does not hold up against UNESCO or UNIDROIT treaty obligations to return a cultural object to the territory it was illegally removed or exported from, but it is important to strike the right balance between claimant's interests; interests of states in cultural exchange; and public interest in access with regard to the legal and ethical standards governing ownership. The PrIL dimension determines whether the arrangement constitutes a contract (classification); whether the contract exists (which law governs its existence); whether the contract is valid (which law governs its formal validity and its intrinsic validity); and what the position may be in respect of an elective or accessory contract (which law governs these aspects for an insurance contract).

Whereas loans are contractual arrangements, ownership concerns property relations, which take priority over most contractual agreements. Some loans pave the way for restitution through the cultivation of mutual understanding over time. For instance, many sacred medicine bundles have been restored, and loans preceded the legislative reform that was needed to operationalise restitutions. Loans and conditions imposed on loans paved the way for repatriation in Alberta, the only province in Canada to recognise through law 'the right of first nations peoples to retrieve sacred material from public collections' to continue their traditional spiritual practices (Conaty 2015a: 37). The Royal Alberta Museum (at the time the Provincial Museum in Alberta) started with occasional short-term loans to the Blackfoot community in 1977. Because of concerns over casual loans inviting museum liability, the Glenbow Museum in Calgary proceeded to conclude a memorandum of understanding with the Blackfoot Nation despite the legal restriction under the Historical Resources Act of 1973 that provincial resources belonged to all the people of Alberta, and all archaeological materials and similar items belonged to the province and to the people (Conaty 2015b: 111; Weasel Head 2015: 169). The Glenbow Board of Governors approved the return of numerous sacred objects to the Blackfoot Confederacy in 1999 but the Alberta Government blocked the returns with a claim of ownership in respect of the Glenbow's collection. A search for more formal ways to organise requests for loans led to the drafting of a coherent loan initiative to deal more uniformly with loans of ceremonial objects. Consultations with the Canadian Blackfoot followed in 1998. Work on the formulation of criteria and procedures for loans to First Nations and tribal communities culminated in the legalisation of the repatriation of First Nations sacred ceremonial objects and Blackfoot objects by means of the First Nations Sacred Ceremonial Objects Repatriation Act (FNSCORA F-14 RSA 2000) and the Blackfoot First Nations Sacred Ceremonial Objects Repatriation Regulations 96/2004.

The legislation applies to the return of sacred objects that are currently vital to the practice of First Nations ceremonial traditions but does not apply to human remains. Opinions differ on the extent to which the FNSCORA has provided an appropriate level of care for culturally sensitive knowledge. Nonetheless, it signifies the progress made since the Indian Act of 1876 prevented Indian chiefs and councils from receiving repatriated objects and put an end to the obligation of tribes to return sacred medicine bundles to the museums when loans expired. These impositions breached the normal cultural protocols for this sacred material and were deeply disrespectful of the source communities.

Loans enable objects that are owned by encyclopaedic museums to be seen in their country of origin. However, an art loan cannot transfer ownership and does not qualify as a form of restitution. Loans only draw attention to their imperial backdrop, for encyclopeadic museums may stand on their right to own and control them. Temporary in nature, they permit relatively few people to see and learn from the items. Even a permanent loan does not allow the deprived owners and impoverished states to make their own decisions on whether to loan their artefacts to museums in other countries (AFFORD Institute 2020: 18).

Since the 1990s, museum officials in Africa have developed a decisive preference for the restoration of ownership over institutional cooperation through travelling exhibitions and loans with western museums. The restoration of ownership in the form of property rights to African states confirms their independence and control over their heritage and futures. Legal ownership and control of cultural heritage by the community that produced and wove their lives around it, is crucial to the right to determine its preservation. It impacts the group's cultural identity and development (Vrdoljak 2008: 196–197). A refusal to restore ownership can be construed as a refusal to acknowledge the capacity of an independent state to assume responsibility and care for its heritage and past. The new standard of justice cannot be met by loans that fail to replace ownership. It is met by permanent returns alone (Grechi 2021: 154).

The Parthenon Marbles have never been loaned to Athens. In December 2014, after advancing the excuse that the Marbles were too fragile to travel and could not be safely shipped to Greece in 2004, the British Museum organised the loan of the Parthenon's pediment sculpture of the river god Ilissos to the Hermitage in St Petersburg, Russia. At the time of the loan, Moscow's Russification policies were aimed at the annexation of regions in the Crimean Peninsula. Its support for pro-Russian separatists ignited tensions. The loan contradicted the British Museum's original claims and incited anger, not least because it seemed like an attempt to persuade the world that the British Museum has the power to maintain its control over every Parthenon Marble in its possession. Sending Ilissos to a country which had violated international law only a few months prior, endorsed a delinquent regime; it insulted the Greeks as well as those who have suffered at the hands of the Russian regime. The timing of the loan raised the question whether it was a tactic of diplomacy or a message that the relationship with the Hermitage Museum enjoyed higher priority than the Acropolis Museum. In March 2015, just months after loaning Ilissos to Russia, the British government issued a delayed response declining a 2013 invitation extended by UNESCO to join a mediation process over the Parthenon Sulptures, denying that the museum was 'a government body.' Both the government and the trustees extolled the benefits of loans as a compromise that 'solves' disputes, yet title was set to remain with the British Museum's Trustees. Any loan which the British Museum may claim they will consider would be managed and monitored heavily and would be nothing like a full return to the people and the place they were taken from.

Parliament's concern for retaining the Parthenon Marbles shaped the British Museum Act 1963, which permits the trustees to disengage from claims for restitution and the government to refuse to discuss return. Parliamentary debates confirm awareness that it is up to individual national museums to determine their response to restitution claims but legislation prevents them from removing objects from the national collection (Hansard HC Deb. vol. 672, col. 722, 2 March 2020; Hansard HL Deb. vol. 818, cols. 1396, 8 February 2022).

The former British chancellor and chair of the British Museum, George Osborne, proposed a plan in 2022 to ensure that the Greeks would return any Parthenon Sculptures that were loaned to Athens by building gradual trust with a series of loans, without expecting Greece to renounce its claim or to accept a 'loan' of what they consider to be Greek property. A lending scheme that rehouses some of the Marbles in Athens would see the British Museum ship to Athens potentially one-third or more of the Marbles for a period of decade or more, and Athens would loan significant ancient Greek artefacts to London as a type of insurance. Upon expiry of the loan, the Parthenon Sculptures would be returned to London and a bigger portion would be simultaneously sent to Athens. With confidence in the deal increasing over time and a legal agreement that would not force Athens to accept the British Museum's ownership on principle, the expectation was that several Parthenon Sculptures would be rehoused in the Acropolis Museum and that the sculptures would ultimately be restored permanently in Athens. De-accessioning would not take place, but at the same time, returning the Sculptures to London would be unlikely, leaving the British Museum Act 1963, and its general bar on de-accession, unimpaired. Later reports indicated that the British Museum was working with Greece to create a broad and lengthy cultural agreement that would include an interchange and rotation of historical artefacts between Greece and the British Museum which would see some of the Marbles coming home. A wave of optimism swept through the media in the first weeks of 2023. However, the likelihood that Greece would never return them should they be sent led to sharp criticism by a member of Parliament that the idea was a 'legal fiction' that does not align with the museum's statutory duty. He called on museums to resist restitution (Harris 2024).

Sharing the Parthenon Sculptures between London and Athens based on a loan, as the Parthenon Partnership seems to suggest, potentially jeopardises any future claim for their repatriation as stolen objects. Itwould force Greek officials to accept British ownership of the Marbles. Many Greeks would not reconcile themselves with a partial return that implies that their culture can be loaned or that ownership lies with the British Museum. For them, the Parthenon Marbles dispute cannot be resolved without resolution of the ownership issue. A loan agreement only changes the power relations that predominated in the colonial era if a museum of a former colonial power becomes the borrower of the cultural material. The role of property law in fostering colonialism, as well as the relationship between loan practices and western preferences for the distribution of cultural material, adheres to the 'modern museum-as-lender' idea.

The Arts Council of England (ACE) updated its advice on restitution policies and guidelines for museums on 5 August 2022 (ACE *Restitution and Repatriation: A Practical Guide for Museums in England*). Its advice suggests that loans, rights of access, and shared legal ownership are reasonable outcomes of restitution claims. In this regard the ACE follows the Museum and Galleries Commission's 2000 *Restitution and Repatriation: Guidelines for Good Practice* and makes no attempt to update or align the perspective with the new conception of justice. This sense of justice no longer aspires to long-term loans and forms of sharing that allow museums to retain ownership of objects and the power to discontinue loans. What would keep a loan arrangement for the Parthenon Sculptures from being interpreted as tacit agreement that the UK owns them?

2.4.11 Argumentative contests over ownership: mirroring and turn-around

Mimetic competition in legal argument undermines the normative force of the restitution argument. The rivalry between proponents and opponents of return (as opposed to non-return) plays out in inverting and flipping or turning around the argument to mirror oppositeness. Kennedy originally highlighted the pattern of argumentation and the dialectic pitfalls which arguments and counterarguments evoke (Kennedy 1991: 75ff). The erosion which this patterns of legal argumentation caused has delayed the resolution of the Parthenon Sculptures dispute. The effect was not quite the same in the dispute concerning the dispersed Benin Bronzes. They are indicative of the readiness of museums in Europe to restitute heritage looted during the colonial era.

The historical injustices involving the slave trade history of the Benin Bronzes and victimisations carried out by local rulers in the past were invoked to resist efforts to remedy the looting perpetrated by former colonial powers against those local rulers (Stahn 2023: 511). In October 2022, the Restitution Study Group, a US-based NGO promoting slavery justice, lodged a complaint seeking to enjoin the Smithsonian Institution from transferring title in the Benin Bronzes. Their argument in the class-action lawsuit played different types of coloniality and injustice against each other. It maintained that most of the Benin Bronzes in the Smithsonian's collection should stay in the United States for the benefit of American citizens who are the descendants of enslaved peoples trafficked by Benin royalty and kidnapped and enslaved by European slave-traders. The Smithsonian opposed the claimants' request and the motion to dismiss was granted on 14 October 2022 (*Deadria Farmer-Paellmann and Restitution Study Group v Smithsonian Institution*, Emergency Motion for Temporary Restraining Order and Preliminary Injunction, Civ No. 1:22-cv-3048, D.D.C 7 October 2022). The court expressed doubts over the procedural requirements and the merits of the case. The decision in the civil trial highlights the boundaries of the court's subject-matter jurisdiction. Standing to sue requires a concrete injury to connect the claimants and the ancestors they claim were sold as slaves, but the claimants' connection was not of this type. Already in 2006, in a suit instituted to redress harms to third parties (the ancestors of Farmer-Paellmann and others), the 7th Circuit Court of Appeals held that any legal wrong committed against the claimants would not be a wrong to any living persons 'unless they were somehow the authorised representatives to bring suits on behalf of their enslaved ancestors' (*In Re African-American Slave Descendants Litigation, Appeals of Deadria Farmer-Paellmann et al. and Timothy Hurdle et al.* 471 F.3d 754 (7th Cir 2006)). The *ultra vires* claim failed because the Smithsonian is explicitly empowered to 'transfer' works in its collection (Smithsonian Institution, National Museums and Art Galleries, 20 U.S.C. para 80m(a)(2)).

The Smithsonian proceeded to transfer ownership as planned on 11 October 2022, and three days later the court denied the claim for an emergency temporary restraining order because it was impossible to grant relief. The case had to be dismissed. A broad interpretation of the complaint may have avoided mootness issues, but standing to pursue their claims would still be insurmountable. If standing to sue could be established, claimants still failed to assert any valid causes of action to challenge the Smithsonian's decision to transfer the Bronzes. In March 2022, the Smithsonian vowed to relinquish ownership of 39 Benin Bronzes and return them to Nigeria. In a ceremony held at the NMAfA on 11 October 2022, ownership of 29 Benin bronzes was transferred to the National Commission for Museums and Monuments in Nigeria. The turn-around of the Restitution Study Group did not meet with success but the potential for an argumentative contest in relation to colonial era removals is demonstrated.

The University of Cambridge received approval from the Charity Commission to repatriate its 116 Benin Bronzes to Nigeria. In August 2022, London Horniman Museum decided to return 72 Benin City objects and the Charity Commission authorised it (Herman 2021: 97). Oxford also promised returns. The Bristol and the Hancock Museums offered to make returns to Benin and the University Museum of Aberdeen in Scotland broke ranks with the UK government when it returned a sculpture of a Benin king on 28 October 2021. Provenance research was undertaken for another 20 Benin Bronzes in the Smithsonian's National Museum of Natural History (Press release 11 October 2022). The Joint Declaration on the Return of Benin Bronzes and Bilateral Museum Cooperation signed by the governments of Germany and Nigeria on 1 July 2022 envisages the transfer of ownership to Nigeria of 1,130 items in collections held by, among others, the Linden Museum in Stuttgart and Berlin's Humboldt Forum. Stahn cautions that Germany's position on the Benin City Bronzes may trigger a race for the return of cultural heritage (Stahn 2022: 52). He observes that a new competition may develop between cultural institutions or states that seek prestige and public acclaim rather than to rebalance relationships. If repatriations degenerate into a competition or a 'cosmetic self-purification ritual,' there would be limited hope of achieving internationally recognised criteria of return, procedures for the handling of claims, modalities of provenance research and/or practices of re-engagement, or practices of re-engagement with sufficient transparency and due diligence in the private sector. Researchers may not be permitted to perform sufficient analysis of dislocated human remains and belongings. This situation will heighten the risk of rushed and insensitive returns.

The pattern that legal argument follows in the dispute concerning the Parthenon Sculptures also promotes understanding of how mimesis plays out in legal argument as well as in the reasoning behind the moralistic reactions to restitution claims. Legal argument invokes evaluations norms, facts, and other factors that may encourage dialectical exchange with and between different communities, or between the Self and Other. In PrIL, this exchange may be with the forum/foreign courts, or application of the *lex fori*/*lex causae*, which is PrIL's language for differentiating the 'Other.' While PrIL language is not intended to homogenise the 'Indigenous experience,' legal argument about the secondary legal norms of ownership of cultural property and heritage may still degenerate into maxims and countermaxims that operate like sound-bites.

When legal precepts are non-determinative, there is a risk of smothering novel ideas about non-legal factors as well as extra-judicial principles that may bring about settlement for designated categories of cultural material (Childress III 2011: 4; Chechi 2008: 180). The introduction of a factor external to the system of law could cut through the loop made up of equally ranked principles. Whereas the sacred is frequently referred to in the context of restitution and repatriation, the different understandings that attach to the meaning lead to different outcomes. No scholarly treatise identifies a non-legal factor that elevates the dialectic in cultural heritage disputes to a plane where resolution of the Parthenon Sculptures dispute comes into full view.

2.4.12 Limited mandates in ADR

A deadlock ensued in the dispute concerning the Parthenon Marbles when UNESCO invited Britain to the table on behalf of the Intergovernmental Committee for Promoting the Return of Cultural Property to its Countries of Origin or its Restitution in Case of Illicit Appropriation (ICPRCP) in 2013. Mediation procedures commenced at the 19th session in 2014 but, by the time the 20h session took place in 2016, the UK had declined the invitation and rejected these overtures. Greece distanced itself from 'legal action,' opting for diplomatic and political channels. Scholars consider the potential of lawsuits in the courts of England and Wales, the European Court of Human Rights, and the European Court of Justice to be low and have turned their attention to the possibility of the UNGA or UNESCO seeking a favourable advisory opinion from the ICJ (Titi 2023: 206; Wadsworth 2023: 148–149). The ICJ has heard a small number of cultural heritage cases to date. The UK restricts the jurisdiction of the ICJ to disputes arising after 1987, however (Titi 2023: 202). The PrIL implications of cases are rarely confronted in English courts. A stronger convention on expatriated cultural property is mooted as a more viable option (e.g., Wadsworth 2023: 149–150).

The intergovernmental ICPRCP was established as a UNESCO advisory body to allay the frustrations of newly independent states with a conventional framework that did not apply retrospectively. Greece and Benin are members of the ICPRCP, but Britain is not. The ICPRCP mandate is to facilitate mediation and conciliation, exercise moral pressure, and adopt recommendations. As an ADR mechanism that promotes bilateral negotiations under the aegis of the ICPRCP, the success of any claim depends on the will of states to cooperate towards a mutually agreeable solution (Machado Haertel 2021: 500). The interstate nature of the ICPRCP makes for a 'state-centric' approach which scholars consider one of its main limitations (Stahn 2023: 369). The ICPRCP has never attempted to act on claims for human remains or in respect of Nazi looted art, but the Parthenon Marbles dispute has been a standing item on the ICPRCP agenda since Melina Mercouri officially requested their restitution in 1983. A request to UNESCO followed to add the matter in 1984. Calls for dialogue and intensified efforts within the ICPRCP framework were renewed in 2018 and 2019. A 2021 decision stated that the UK has an 'obligation' to return the Marbles and must proceed to a bona fide dialogue with Greece (ICPRCP Twenty-second Session, 27–29 September 2021, ICPRCP/21/22.COM/Decisions, Decision 22, COM 6, para 7).

On the recommendation of the ICPRCM the Greek Prime Minister has been treating the Parthenon Marbles dispute as an intergovernmental issue that comes under the remit of the Prime Minister in Britain. The ICPRCP considers the case a dispute between nations but the impasse between the British Museum and the UK government has long been mutually convenient if not symbiotic. Successive British prime ministers have insisted that the future of the Marbles is not a matter for ministers but for the British Museum, which has deflected the British government's responsibility to respond to claims onto the British Museum's Trustees (e.g., para 19, Report of the Secretariat on the follow-up to the recommendations and decisions adopted during the Twenty-second Session CPRCP/22/23.COM/5.Rev). The ICPRCP's position that it is not a dispute between museums as the Conservative British government ardently made it out to be, is connected to its structure and mandate. Only states can bring a claim or have sitting at the ICPRCP.

States are not obliged to bring cases or implement its recommendations. They use it as a podium to state their claims rather than resolve their disputes (Campfens 2019: 97; Chechi 2014: 104–106). The Conservative UK government did not assume responsibility for clarification of its position in that forum and the British Museum deployed arguments to cause delays and encourage refusals of restitution requests. The structure of the ICPRCP promotes the marginalisation of legal engagement with past takings. The voices of cultural communities are neither prioritised nor heard (Stahn 2023: 368). Commentators conclude that, while the ICPRCP's efforts to promote cooperation between the parties have not led to the restitution of the Parthenon Sculptures nor generated consensus between the parties, they exposed the lack of meaningful engagement with Greece's claim (Machado Haertel 2021: 500).

The ICPRCP's involvement has not advanced the case of the Parthenon Sculptures housed in the British Museum. The limited mandate of the ICPRCP leaves it incapable of countering the normative workings of mimesis. Consequently, the body is not expected to play a significant role in future returns of colonial collections (Stahn 2023: 370).

2.5 Reining in mimetic competition and counter-balancing mimetic contests

This study foregrounds cases that highlight an elemental intuition that easily slips into 'circular reasoning.' Shapiro acknowledges this risk of slippage in relation to cultural property and heritage. Unfortunately, he does so only in a broad manner that remains in the realm of the unspecified. Placing the focus on removals that are 'inherently insulting and potentially capable of destroying a people's continued existence,' Shapiro approximates a workable definition of the 'sacred.' The sacred exudes an 'axiomatic' or 'self-defining' quality as peopleconsider it to be 'inherently connected to them in some inalienable way'. Possession by another individual, museum, or nation is 'diminishing and inequitable'—its loss leaves a residue that fosters rancour in the relations between the dispossessed and those currently in possession (Shapiro 1998: 96).

Not every cultural object is sacred and cno common understanding has been achieved across the social sciences and humanities. Girard's conception of the sacred turns on a general unified explanatory principle at the foundation of human culture: desire and sacrifice. It aspires to a common, global view that integrates the tangible and the intangible. Is there a real possibility of agreeing that this integration is crucial? The sacred carries obligations to see its meaning fulfilled; the obligations inherent in it spur action when decontextualisation drains the material of meaning.

2.5.1 The elusive common understanding: concealed from human consciousness or part of praxis?

Girard's sweeping anthropology of religion and historical analysis of what communities hold sacred highlights the myth of expulsion and sacrifice of the scapegoat which informs the laws that govern rivalry. He focused on the structural function and meaning of the scapegoat ritual, around which early human societies spontaneously united in times of chaos and disorder. The projection of collective envy, rivalry, and hostility onto the sacrificial victim—be it an innocent outsider or a convenient scapegoat who provides the channel for their violence—engenders solidarity around the common act of persecution. When transferred onto the alien shape of the scapegoat, uncontrolled violence can be 'confronted and propitiated' (Cayley ed. 2019: 16). Allowing competitive humans to achieve reconciliation through solidarity, hostilities may cease, and vengeance is prevented (Girard 2010: x–xi; Kearney 1995: 1).

The ritual establishes spaces for non-violence in a culture without which no community can survive and no society can become better integrated. This understanding supports the definition of 'sacred' as that which offers protection and sanctuary to the vulnerable in society, enabling its survival and growth (Cayley ed. 2019: 16).

Controversially, Girard hypothesised that sacrifice—a means by which the relationship with the sacred is managed—is the only mechanism able to control the impulse to violence. Since the conflict between rivals flows from imitation, he presented violence as inescapable except through awareness and understanding of the 'laws' that govern it.

Girard and Fanon shared many ideas about mimesis. They were contemporaries with close ties to France. Girard was born in Avignon, France, in 1923 and Fanon in the French colony Martenique in 1925. Both considered scapegoating the origin of the impulse to violence and release the only way to achieving freedom from hatred, but their mimetic theorems diverge on the inevitability of violence (Kirwan 2009: 106).

Fanon attached modern meaning to the word 'scapegoat' which aligned with the ordinary use of victim of arbitrary, irrational cruelty. He maintained that violence ceases to be an unconscious drive and becomes a 'colonised man's praxis' whereby he liberates himself through violence against the coloniser. Causing the coloniser's death prevents the colonised man's return to the colonial system. This is 'the absolute praxis'—not just essential, but also inevitable (Fanon 2004: 44). This perspective implies that colonised people will always turn the brutality and violence perpetrated against them onto the coloniser. The dynamic of victims turning into killers is exemplified by the rising nationalism of countries that had no fiercer desire than to shake off the yoke of British imperialism. It may also play out in societies overwhelmed by identity politics. People considered to be 'non-African' are actively scapegoated in South Africa, for instance (Lagardien 2022: 57).

Girard's understanding of the scapegoat mechanism differs from Fanon's. Girard takes mimetic theory in a very different direction. The promise of peace and global justice within the theory is not always properly acknowledged. For Girard, 'scapegoating' is not arbitrary cruelty, but rather society's first line of defence against itself. The scapegoat channels a community's aggression onto an arbitrary victim or group to prevent that aggression from overwhelming society (Kirwan 2009: 26). Importantly therefore, the sacrifice of a scapegoat is the way out of the violence trap. Girard's paradigm is more hopeful than Fanon's in that humans are capable of a shift in consciousness that permits them to see through their own self-deception. When the subconscious desire to have what the other has, is brought into full awareness, the desire fades, and the need for a scapegoat disappears (Cayley ed. 2019: 25). With harmony, stability, and peace restored in the wake of the ritual sacrifice, the community may forget its hatred. They may also achieve more than maintaining harmonious social co-existence. in Girard's theory mimetic rivalry conceals itself from human consciousness. His reasoning is confirmed by the ignorance and unwillingness of world leaders to acknowledge that violence builds a worldwide, unbridled empire that constantly reproduces itself (Girard 2010: x). Further confirmation can be found in the narratives of historical, religious, and ethnic belonging invoked by political leaders, non-state movements, militias, and terrorists to solidify legitimacy and justify their supposed agency (e.g., Rosén 2017: 15). Girard never denied people's capacity to choose against violence and in favour of normative evolution, but intimated that it is exceptional. They need to surmount recurring cycles of bloodletting but illusions prevent them from achieving this (Kearney 1995: 2).

Observing the colonial era removals of ethnographic material from colonised populations, historians and art historians may be inclined to consider the object first, and then analyse the human desires converging on the object. The anthropology of mimetic rivalry erupting into a sacrificial conflict and the 'sacred' speaks to an inverted order. The mechanism described by Girard suggests that it is not the intrinsic value of the object that inspires the struggle, but the value which violence bestows on the object and the longing for its return by the dispossessed. The inversion renders the tragic rivalry dynamic more poignant (Girard 1972: 144). The French invasion of Algeria in 1830 and other conflicts in the Middle East and North Africa confirm the inverted understanding. Al-Mahdi, the Islamist rebel convicted for smashing Muslim shrines in Timbuktu in 2016, was sentenced to nine years in prison for the intentional destruction of cultural heritage under the 1998 Rome Statute of the ICC (Art 8(2)(b)(ix); *The Prosecutor v Ahmad Al Faqi Al Mahdi, Judgment and Sentence*, 27 September 2016, ICC-01/12-01/15; *The Prosecutor v Ahmad Al Faqi Al Mahdi, Reparations Order*, 17 August 2017, ICC-CPI-20170817-PR1329). The court took note of efforts to prevent the people of Timbuktu from practising their faith and culture, as well as the emotional and symbolic value the mausoleums held for them (*The Prosecutor v Ahmad Al Faqi Al Mahdi, Judgment and Sentence* paras 78 and 80). If the al-Qaeda leader or the Islamist rebel is the surrogate victim, peace is possible precisely because the violent impulse in the community is displaced by them.

It is easy to see that rules, norms, and technologies can affect restitution outcomes, but the challenge is to see if our knowledge can be organised in a way that can transform our understanding of restitution of sacred cultural heritage and the law. Once the structure of the competitive urge and the nature of what it demands are grasped, the stages of the theory's natural unfolding can be investigated. Can it be taken on board in legal processes as the legal ground in restitution claims? Consecutive chapters of this study and a follow-up study on restoring the law of restitution, are constructed on the premise of the potential of the 'sacred' to arrest the normative thrust of mimetism and brute force and to transform our level of knowledge about this capacity.

2.5.2 Transformative impact of sacrifice

The sacred may inspire certain ethical behaviours, but the mythology of sacrifice also points to the transformative impact of what tends to remain concealed. The one interpretation of the act of dismemberment of the Parthenon Sculptures that is impervious to appropriation, distortion, and negation, is the sacrifice of the Athenian people. The monuments, tombs, and temples dedicated to the heroes of Athens and their associated rituals brought Athenians into direct contact with their ancestors, reminding them of 'the values on which their communities were founded' (Connelly 2014: xxii). Men went to war, but the only way maidens could win honour was by being willingly sacrificed to win the favour of the gods. Connelly theorises that, if the ancient Athenian consciousness is to be properly understood, the philosophical and the spiritual cannot be kept separate. Emphasising that the Acropolis temples attested to the 'all-consuming' compulsion of ancient Athenians—the most ardently religious among all Hellenes—to retain favour with the gods, she frames their religiosity as symptomatic of their egocentrism when faced with continuous threats of war, violence, and death (Connelly 2014: xix–xxii). Sacrificing one's life for the common good was the ideology that promoted solidarity among all Athenian citizens (Connelly 2014: 145–147). Athena wins the contest for patronage of Athens but the tensions with Poseidon do not dissipate andAthena's and Poseidon's progeny continue the battle for supremacy. Praxithea, wife of King Erechteus loses one member of her family to human sacrifice, and her entire family ends up dead. For the ancient Athenians sacrifice was part of life.

The evidence spurs new questions and methods that take account of the continuity of the sacred space in the temple's northern peristyle. This space predates the construction of the Parthenon. The Acropolis temple was not just a sanctuary for Athenians—it was the ultimate place of sanctity (Connelly 2014: 40, 43). There is a great irony in the open acknowledgement of the sacred dimension of the Parthenon Sculptures soon after their removal. In a letter to Lord Elgin dated 15 October 1815, his private secretary at the Constantinople embassy, William Richard Hamilton, wrote as follows: '[the Parthenon Sculptures] are considered so sacred a property, that no direct or indirect means are to be allowed for their being conveyed elsewhere than where they came from' (Hitchens 1997: 48).

Reunifying all remaining parts with the temple they were created for, is high on the list of Greek aspiration, given that they were removed from one integral work of art namely the temple dedicated to Athena and a sanctuary for Athenians to observe sacred rituals (Stuart and Revett 1762; Beard 2002: 133). Astonishingly, however, the law and ethics discourses about the repatriation of the Parthenon Sculptures have not yet homed in on the fundamental sacrality of the Acropolis temples. The repatriation debate is not a feature of Connelly's study, and her interpretation of them does not differentiate between the 'religious' and 'the sacred.' The 'sacred' is intrinsic to the Parthenon Marbles and the systems of knowledge they contain but their 'sacred' character is rarely pursued in repatriation discussions. Certainly, the original, authentic, sacred meaning of the subject matter of the Parthenon Frieze is not at the heart of the dispute where it belongs, nor is the argumentative contest about uncovering its essence. A satisfactory settlement will remain elusive until both Greece and Britain foreground the sacred character and function of the Parthenon Marbles in their respective assertions.

It is vital to find a way to differentiate the 'religious' and 'the sacred'.. One of the differences that can be indicated at this stage is religion's deification of the victim for saving them from their internecine rivalry (Kearney 1995: 1). If the community believes that peace was restored by transcendent power, the transcendence may be attributed to the 'sacred.' The Christian faith's attribution to the sacrificial lamb have drawn its believers to enact and re-enact this reverence. Christianity also undermined the origin of the scapegoat mechanism in ancient Hebrew ritual (Cayley ed. 2019: 1, 21, 27). This history points to the 'religious' but not to the 'sacred.' Bloody colonisations were perpetrated at the hand of nominally Christian states. Once the Latin American republics separated from the monarchies of Spain and Portugal, achieving independence between 1808 and 1824, extreme violence was unleashed on South and Central America. The secular crisis of order that followed was conditioned by exceptionally high levels of state-centred or 'public' violence (Holden 2020: 490–509). The new mimetic rivalries that emerged culminated in the ensuing world wars.

2.5.3 Can pressure to decouple law and ethics be resisted?

The Greek philosop hers adopted an expanded approach to legal questions, integrating liability and responsibility in their legal opinions and texts. They extended the legal question of liability to the moral question of responsibility when they transferred purely legal opinions recorded in laws and practical legal texts into much broader philosophical, ethical, and religious contexts (Winiger 2018: 51). Notions of 'responsibility' and 'liability' are not integrated in modern Western European liability laws. This makes them poorer in comparison even if the Greeks never reduced their law to a system and did not know 'jurisprudence' as we know it today (Jones 1956: preface).

In a multicultural context, moral systems interact, and the virtues, values and norms that define one worldview may be entirely incongruous with those informing another, with neither one being 'better' or 'truer' (Flanagan 2016: 46). An individual with better resources to solve a problem might prevail over those with less. The interaction may introduce novel possibilities leading not to radical change, but to incremental adjustments of norms, values, and practices (Flanagan 2016: 155). Radical shifts may also follow, for cultural restitution claims may have moral benefits that outweigh other ideas of maximising benefit. Through 'exploring the space of moral possibility,' one may arrive at a respectful understanding of 'what people are doing inside other forms of life' and the willingness to consider whether different ways of thinking and doing are good (Flanagan 2016: 144). A moral position on the question of restitution of cultural property may become externalised in the political space, where it can manifest either as a newly created legal norm or in opposition to the formation of a legal norm. It may manifest also in the process of adjudication as a ruling based on a value judgment (Zeidler 2016: 111–112). Observance of legal norms indicates where the legal norm is to be found, and compliance may well follow not because the law declares a duty to comply, but because of the force of the ethical claim it is making (Glenn 2011: 251).

Ancient Greek and Roman codes acknowledged the spirit in things before the distinction between personal law and real law emerged (Godelier 2002: 27). The earliest remedies of Greek law in respect of interference with legal interests in land and movables were personal and delictual in character rather that proprietary. Encroaching on someone's property was considered an infringement on their personality or 'being' (Jones 1956: 202).

The identification of person and property is no longer a feature of modern law and yet law uncoupled from ethics may erode the legitimacy of the law. Prior to the Holocaust (Return of Cultural Objects) Act of 2009, the prohibition on disposal in UK law included Nazi-looted art. The reluctance of the UK Parliament to amend the restrictive legal framework of its national museums and galleries necessitated the promulgation of a new separate piece of legislation to enable restitution. The Commission for Looted Art in Europe brought a claim against the trustees in 2002 based on the allegation that the Gestapo had taken Old Master drawings from Arthur Feldmann during the Nazi occupation of Czechoslovakia in 1939, which the British Museum acquired in the 1940s. The dilemma was that the statutory power existed to authorise a payment out of charity funds where there was a moral obligation to return works of art to their true owners, and charitable trustees were competent to consider 'moral claims' against them; yet Section 3(4) of the British Museum Act 1963 seemed to prevent the recognition of implied exceptions. This created uncertainty over whether a moral obligation could justify overlooking the prohibition on dispositions, enabling restitution to Feldmann's heirs in the absence of an express statutory exception. The ruling reached in *Her Majesty's Attorney-General v Trustees British Museum* ([2005] Ch 397) was to the effect that statutory authority was needed to permit a divergence from statutory obligations imposed on the trustees by an Act of Parliament, and a third party who establishes title in separate proceedings could entitle the trustees to transfer the drawings. Without it, the attorney general would exceed the scope of his authority by returning items in a museum's collection. Barring the trustees from restituting the drawings was an abject failure to interpret the British Museum Act in a manner that aligns it with a basic moral position on the Holocaust.

Having the option to cling to the strictures of national museum legislation creates scope to exclude ethical considerations in decision-making. This adds a significant legal obstacle to claims for the return of the Parthenon Sculptures. Statutory principles and regulations (*lex*) that seek to exclude moral, ethical, and non-legal considerations may produce harsh results. Collection items may not be de-accessioned from holding institutions without a legal basis, but German policies recognise that a statutory right may exist for governing bodies with the capacity to authorise de-accessions of property on ethical or moral grounds even if there is no legal obligation to do so (DMB *Care of Collections* 2021: 85).

'Hard cases' are not necessarily connected with law presently in force. They may emerge against a backdrop of lack of regulation; regulation that missed the mark; or conflicting legal principles, highlighting the acute pressure points that require society's attention. The tension between the law as it is and as it ought to be endures when law is structured in a way that does not favour recognition of a legal obligation to return. The need to create new law is felt even as positivist legal conceptions suppress political and moral conversations regarding ownership of the Parthenon Sculptures. The British government finalised its policy position on international property transfers in a letter signed by the Minister for Arts and Heritage, Lord Parkinson of Whitley Bay, to the Chairman of the Charities Commission, Mr Orlando Fraser KC, on 31 January 2024, stating that:

> [N]ational museums and galleries should continue to be bound by their governing legislation, precluding them from resolving to restitute objects from their collections other than in the limited and specific circumstances expressly provided for in legislation.

Any charity seeking to transfer ownership of an object to its country of origin 'will have to seek approval from the Charity Commission (as they currently do).' Scope for international transfers of material located in national museums is limited, therefore. This makes it too easy to forget the history of restitution and to present it as either a new idea or a 'culture war' that invokes random and untested principles.

The British Museum is supposed to operate independently from government and free from political interference (*Hansard HC* Deb. vol. 672, col. 722, 2 March 2020 col. 727). In practice, however, the British Museum receives most of its funding from the government and 15 of up to 25 of its trustees are appointed by the Prime Minister and four by the Secretary of State for DCMS. Given that most trustees are appointed by and accountable to the government, the 'independence' of the museum exists only in an exceedingly narrow sense, namely in relation to how the chair is elected (British Museum website under 'Governance'). The institution cannot hope to escape political oversight (Harris 2024). If it were 'independent' in its decisions on de-accessioning or restitution, the government would not interfere with governance and curatorial freedom in so-called 'arms-length' cultural bodies. The government does not directly control decisions concerning the collections of British museums, but its control over subsidies carries a risk of funding cuts if repatriation decisions affected income streams or the wider economy negatively.

Every country has its own regulatory framework that enables museums to take decisions involving their collections. Even within the same country certain museums may have greater autonomy than others. National museums governed by statute, university museums, museums run by local authorities, museums established as companies, and museums established as charities, all have different responsibilities. In the United States, all but the most problematic cases of de-accession by an institution have been resolved through negotiation rather than by courts (Paterson 2014: 275–277, 294). De-accession rules and norms for museums based in the United States and Canada are derived from the rules of equity concerning charitable institutions, including the fiduciary obligations of those who control them. The common law determines whether a museum is deemed in law to hold its property for a charitable purpose for the benefit of the public. The traditional responsibility to enforce charitable trusts or gifts rests with the attorney general of the jurisdiction where the charity is located. For these institutions, de-accessioning is a process.

The criteria and procedures that promote ethical responses in the NAGPRA across all federal agencies and museums receiving federal funding do not apply to the Smithsonian, and consequently, the Smithsonian catalogued the Native American remains and cultural items held in its collections as it saw fit (Smithsonian National Museum of the American Indian, Repatriation Policy 2014). Prior to 2021, the museums and research facilities of the Smithsonian were not subject to a uniform standard of repatriation. This policy gap fostered delays with returns. To promote a more unified institution-wide restitution policy for each of the Smithsonian museums, an Ethical Returns Working Group was set up in 2021, and it published the Shared Stewardship and Ethical Returns Policy on 29 April 2022. All Smithsonian museums adopted this guidance on unethically sourced cultural heritage. Items that were stolen, taken under duress, or removed without the owner's consent are considered unethical acquisition. The Directive issued shortly after contains de-accessioning and disposal grounds such as 'ethical returns'; 'repatriation,' and instances where an insufficient relationship exists 'between a collection item(s) and the mission, programmatic goals, or the collections stewardship plan of the collecting unit, such that the item would be better placed elsewhere' (Smithsonian Directive 600, 12 May 2022: 8.1.2).

UK museums are in a different position. Most UK museums are constituted as charities registered with the Charity Commission. They are set up for the benefit of the public and not for trading. Government-subsidised museums include those governed by local authorities which are obligated to keep collections intact and are precluded from modifying their collections. They share a civic foundation that invokes statutory prohibitions to de-accessioning. Despite de-accessioning being a healthy practice of collection management, national museums do not always announce their decisions and the administrative steps taken to remove a museum's legal ownership in respect of an object or a collection. Decisions about restitution in the UK often lie with local councils and museum trustees whose interests are likely to co-incide with those in national government. Their obligations to keep their collections intact under the domestic legal framework impede the return of looted artefacts to their countries of origin. The autonomy of regional and non-national museums and institutions is comparatively greater compared to national museums; they remain free to determine whether to transfer ownership or repatriate items under UK property laws (Museums Association *Supporting Decolonisation in Museums* 2021). Non-national institutions have a clearer pathway and greater legal certainty in decisions concerning restitution if they have a 'returns policy'.

UK universities are free to repatriate collection items. University collections have been pro-active in arranging the return of secret, sacred, and ceremonial items and human remains ever since 2019. The Oxford University museums and libraries adopted new procedures in 2020 which brought a welcome change to its repatriation ethics. The Procedures for Claims for the Return of Cultural Objects acknowledge already existing rules such as the Return of Cultural Objects Regulations of 1994 and demonstrates empathy with the traditions and procedures of source communities who have been impacted by the loss of their cultural property (Oxford University Procedures for Claims for the Return of Cultural Objects). When processing a request for repatriation, several factors are considered, i.e., the circumstances of acquisition; the relationship of claimant to the object(s) being claimed; whether the object had been taken under duress or in an apparently legal transaction that involved use of force or coercion; and if the object was communal property acquired from a person or persons of that community not authorised to give or sell it (clauses 2.1 a; 2.2 a).

The policy vacuum left by the Conservative UK government has been filled by an NGO that is dedicated to expanding contributions by the diaspora to African development, the African Foundation for Development Institute (AFFORD Institute). It investigated the question of the restitution of African artefacts and human remains with the intention to complement outdated museum policies and stop information gaps. Its *Return of the Icons: The Restitution of African Artefacts and Human Remains Project Mapping Report* (2020) reveals that museum professionals are reluctant to speak on the record because of the rancorous debate conducted in the local and national media in response to proposed returns of African artefacts (AFFORD Institute 2020: 30). The normative environment in which to fill gaps in museum de-accessioning policy is hostile in part because privacy rights have been augmented by stealth. This trend interferes with open dialogue and constructive debate, and undermines freedom and democracy. Frank Weasel Head admitted to using the term 'long-term loans' when meeting with British museum workers, because '[w]e cannot really use the word "repatriate" in England without raising alarms' (Weasel Head 2015: 176).

The AFFORD Institute took charge of art restitution for the all-party parliamentary group on African reparations 'African Restitution (APPG-AR)' (AFFORD Institute 2020: 14). Chaired by a Labour MP in the British Parliament, the APPG-AR was a platform for the debate concerning the restitution of artefacts looted by Britain in the colonial era to African countries. It encouraged audits and catalogueing what collections hold and regulating the ownership and distribution of digital rights in African heritage (APPG-AR webinar 20 April 2022). These activities will likely continue under the new Labour government.

National Museums Scotland is subject to a statutory bar on de-accessioning objects and de-accessioning restrictions in the statutes of national museums and galleries limit the capacity to make decisions to repatriate based on property rights (Last 2007: 140). The ability of a museum to de-accession human remains may also be restricted. Claims must be instituted by legal persons and entities and must have endorsement from a National Government or recognised National Agency (Museum) supported by a National Government, as well as a community descended from those to whom the remains are ancestral (*Human Remains in Collections Policy of National Museums Scotland*, March 2016 updated 2021: para 6.2). The constitutional documents of a museum or conditions imposed upon a gift or bequest of human remains could also hold restrictions (Whitby-Last 2011: 34–35). There is scope to argue that the terms of the prohibition on de-accession do not cover human remains because they are not objects in which property vests. In addition, the approval of the Scottish Ministers may be secured under Section 8(3)(d) of the National Heritage (Scotland) Act 1985. The museum sector in Scotland has constructed its own active repatriation history since 1990 with a notable focus on the return of ancestral remains (Curtis and Scholten 2022: 427–442). Based on the absence of a repatriation provision in Scottish law, cultural institutions and local authorities have exercised their discretion to take decisions to repatriate material from 'world culture' collections originating from North America, Africa, and elsewhere. For example, Glasgow museums returned a notable number of stolen items such as the famous Lakota Ghost Dance Shirt, a protective talisman. The Aberdeen University museum, a university collection outwith the national portfolio, has amassed commendable experience of repatriation, including, in 2003, with what was catalogued as a 'Headdress' but which belonged to a sacred bundle of the Kainai. The governance framework of regional and university museums in the UK accommodates restitution policies that incorporate ethics and enable de-accession and voluntary return agreements. Nonetheless, many human remains are listed in the Human Remains Collections from outside the United Kingdom of National Museums Scotland (e.g., on the NMS website dated 31 March 2020).

While the constraints of legislative de-accessioning provisions no longer set a realistic moral standard for museological aspirations, a coherent policy for the British museum sector seems out of reach at times.

The modern tendency to specialise on either the law or the ethics side makes it harder to cross the 'divide' to integrate models of responsibility. The legal paradigm of restitution is not a complete paradigm. Ethical considerations supplement it, as happens when the term 'repatriation' is used for returns made to the community of origin based on a moral obligation (Last 2007: 128). If the primary concern is about returning something to its true owner, there is also a symbolic process to be completed by its source community to re-appropriate the material. In the United States, ethical considerations frequently inform the processing of repatriation requests. The contribution and value of repatriation requests tend to be recognised as they can inform the procedures of return and allow shifts in institutional policymaking to occur. More important than the number of transfers from a museum collection is the compilation and sharing of actionable information (Jacobs and Porter 2021: 533). The definitions of 'sacred' material found in both NAGPRA and Alberta's provincial First Nations Sacred Ceremonial Objects Repatriation Act (FNSCORA) illustrate the way in which free-floating discretion by government officialscan be controlled. The NAGPRA defines sacred objects as ceremonial objects required by recognised traditional religious leaders to practice traditional Native American religion (s 3(2)(c) NAGPRA). The most recent amended regulations declare that, '[w]hile many items might be imbued with sacredness in a culture, this term is specifically limited to an object needed for the observance or renewal of a Native American religious ceremony' ('Definitions' para 10.2, 43 CFR Part 10 Regulations for Repatriation of Native American Ancestors and Objects 2024, 88 FR 86518 of 13 December 2023). The traditional ceremonies of Native Americans have ritual qualities that have religious significance or function in the continued observance or renewal of such ceremony. Proposing that all sacred objects have a religious character but not all religious items qualify as sacred, the NAGPRA protects the sacred, not the religious (NAGPRA 25 USC 3003 (d)(3); Echo-Hawk 2002: 104). The FNSCORA protects the sacred in objects vital to a First Nation to practice sacred ceremonial traditions (Article 1 (e) FNSCORA). This legislation systematises issues in a way that refutes the idea of animism or disregards the spiritual and personal significance of cultural heritage (Coody Cooper 2008: 65; Conaty 2015a: 55, 63). This situation would lead to a 'hard case' because of the complexity of the cultural material in question. Complex objects may be described in various ways by altering one's view of the significance of descriptions of their component features, or by adopting a different perspective. Their component features characteristically compete with one another to influence application of concepts such as 'distributive justice,' which may depict equality of welfare but perhaps also of resources (Hurley 1989: 46–47).

Transnational cases, in which legal rules come into conflict with rules belonging to another recognised normative order, deserve special treatment as a category of 'hard cases.' The criteria for ethical judgments in transnational cases require clarification, but no ready-made answers are available. Ethical reasoning may open the way for an acceptable and defensible judgment and change the status quo only if the conflict between two opposites can be reconciled. On the one end there is hard, uncompromising law that is still law (*dura lex sed lex*), and on the other end there is unjust law that is no law at all (*lex iniustissima non est lex*). Adjudicators may look towards principles and policies that aspire to justice (*jus*), beyond rules (*lex*), legal norms, and potentially applicable systems of law, creating a normative environment that is supported by a model of responsibility for sacred material.

2.5.4 Understandings of ownership

Understandings of ownership from the Roman and later European nation-state legal systems underpin many facets of European property laws. These understandings inform the European perspective on how cultural property and heritage are to be protected, administered, and preserved. Sir Henry Maine's notable insight, that proprietary rights originated in the joint ownership practised in ancient societies, rather than in individual ownership in Roman jurisprudence, has far-reaching implications for discourses on restitution and repatriation (Maine 1861: 153).

A common ownership lens draws attention to the need to preserve peace and order amid individual demands for the material things of the earth, for they are imbued with scarcity value. The competition for resources could spark conflict and therefore some system of allocation is required. To assign ownership to objects that are found in a public area, philosophers of old famously argued that an implied agreement exists amongst individuals that occupation or possession of the thing makes it the private property of the occupant. This thinking gave rise to the principle of first occupation. Resources could be allocated to whomever had first occupation (Panesar 2000: 116, 120). Grotius argued that the earth's resources were given to humankind in common, and the 'first state of ownership' in common was followed by the distribution of private property and ownership based on the occupation theory (Neff 2012: Grotius Book 2, Chapter 2 'Of Things which Belong to Men in Common': paras 2–3). Blackstone theorised that all was a gift of the creator held in common as public stock; from this stock everyone took 'to his own use such things as his immediate necessities required' (Blackstone 1979: 1765–1769; Panesar 2000: 115–116). The communal conceptions of property are visible in the social, cultural, and community institutions that are viewed as gifts from the creator (Champagne 2012: 41–42). They shape the conception of obligations in gift economies which illustrate the *quid pro quo* understanding of ceremonial gifts shared across ancient societies. The argument that the structure of the law supports a duty-oriented conception in gift economies is investigated further in a follow-up study on restoring the law of restitution.

The legal terminology of restitution debates invites semantic, conceptual, and legal disagreements over the substantive issue of ownership. Polarised narratives about morality and the law, private and public law, contracts and property, the 'commercial' and the 'non-commercial' are imprinted on European thought (Godt et al. 2022). The (private or civil) law on restitution is structured differently across Common law systems, but also between Common law and Civil law systems. Even when different legal systems belong broadly to the same 'legal family,' their knowledge practices differ. Unsurprisingly, the study of collection histories does not always lead to similar or shared understandings of the facts of sales by community members lacking the authority to sell. If debates about rightful ownership take the western private property construct as their starting point, legal technicalities will likely determine what constitutes rightful ownership because sales of human remains and object-beings challenge individual ownership. Tribal property systems consider animate objects to be neither property nor art, but in courts located on the demand-side of the trade, conceptions of private and public will likely predominate. Consider sacred medicine bundles, for instance. They are communal or tribal property according to traditional practices. Different forms of ownership co-exist in them. The Piikani, Kainai, and Siksika of the Blackfoot established corporate entities to satisfy the legal requirement for repatriation of their bundles and to meet museums' criteria to receive restituted material. However, tribal property and the implications of the stewardship of the collective imply more than what the continuing rights of the community or a rights framework conveys. The changes which some Indigenous communities have made to their way of life cannot be assumed to follow along the same pattern as in western societies. Theories of modernisation and development do not provide ready explanations for these patterns either (Champagne 2012: 47). The portrayal of history as continued advancement fails to acknowledge the urgency of restoring and re-unifying heritage (Spitra 2021: 121–122).

Rights and their presumptive power form part of the theoretical framework relating to the restitution of the cultural function, value, and meaning of sacred cultural property and heritage removed from erstwhile colonies, but no rights framework can provide an adequate restitution theory on its own. The ownership of cultural objects bestows power and wealth In many relational ontologies the worlds of matter and spirit are inseparable. For instance, all knowledge and experience are drawn together in a moral universe to establish the life path of the Sioux (Stewart-Harawira 2005: 36–37). Intertwinements in the subject–object relationship make it harder to untangle norms and rules from the social life (and agency) of cultural objects. The life of the material object cannot be translated into enforceable rights or duties in claims for restitution of sacred material and human remains.

Assuming for argument's sake that a property rights framework is the most appropriate legal basis for restitution claims for sacred material or human remains removed in the colonial era, a constructive starting point would be determinations about property that are pertinent to colonial era removals. These determinations may be that compulsory acquisition of property rights is to be compensated, or that profits received without justification and at another's expense are to be restored, or that no one may profit from their own unlawful conduct (McBride and Steele 2018: 113). As far back as 23 BC the person in possession of a stolen slave had a legal duty under Mesopotanian law in Eshnunna to return that slave. Since the power of property can benefit heritage and communities, the two should not be opposed. Scholars have noted how unproductivethe interaction between property law and heritage treaties is (Lixinski 2019a: 64). Discarding conceptions of property will be at the claimants' risk, for the foundations of property conceptions as regards heritage matter for the success of restitution claims. Disciplinary hostility between law, heritage, and museum studies iundermines efforts of cultures that prioritise the cultural life of sacred material heritage over conservation (Lixinski 2019a: 54–57). Nonetheless, awareness of the potential property has to dilute the communities' control over their own cultural heritage is vital, as 'property' rules may require communities to return their own cultural material to cultural institutions (Lixinski 2019a: 50). Western conceptions of property may preclude courts from recognising the authority of community members to handle, care, and transfer 'title' in medicine bundles under customs or the 'protocols' of First Nations and Native American Tribes, for instance (Simpson 1996: 195–196). That the 'civilising' mission works hand in glove with a western conception of rights is an alarming possibility that cannot be ignored (Anghie 1999: 80).

2.5.5 Setting aright colonialism's damaging impact on the language of return

In *The Leviathan* (Chapter XLVII: 636), Thomas Hobbes attacked what the 'Schoolmen' taught at Universities—'frivolous Distinctions, barbarous Terms, and obscure Language.' The will to power employs language to serve its ends. The reconstruction of the domains affected requires great care.

The five conventions governing cultural property and heritage exhibit 'the progressive abandonment from one treaty to the next of the terminology of property' (Lixinski 2019a: 50). The progressive terminological switch from cultural 'property' to 'heritage' has lent more visibility to the connection between material objects and their associated intangible cultural processes (Zeidler 2016: 59). 'Cultural heritage' recognises the social value which cultural property has for communities and its role in shaping cultural identity. The language of heritage promotes awareness of the many key values of cultural heritage and the importance of ensuring that multiple stakeholders participate fully and effectively in decisions implicating their own heritage (Lixinski 2019a: 27). Nonetheless, cultural property is the principal material component of the concept of cultural heritage. Physical cultural heritage may encompass material objects, artefacts, and even digital artefacts, and intangible heritage is embodied in people, and not in inanimate objects (Byrne 2015: 9). Protection of non-material cultural heritage is most frequently accomplished through its material products (Zeidler 2016: 59, 61). The knowledge humans gain about material objects is the result of both human and material agency. Virtual access cannot provide access to all the intangible qualities derived from such cultural property and heritage in its original, authentic setting. Both human and material agency contribute to the knowledge that humans gain about material objects.

While the 'sacred' is all-encompassing in an Indigenous world view, the secular conception often lumps it in with umbrella terms such as 'cultural heritage,' which affects how a case is handled. For sacred objects and material that should never have been accessioned into museum or antiquities dealers' collections, the duty-oriented conceptions of communal responsibility are inextricably wound up with rules deriving from 'Persons' and 'Things' as separate categories of rules. A close connection exists in law between gift and ownership, and further complexity is introduced by the intermingling of freedom and obligation in the giving of gifts (Hyland 2009: paras 24, 1355). For example, in English law, a gift implies ownership on the part of the giver. Special doctrines govern cases in which a non-owner gave away another's property. The legal adage 'no one can give what they do not own/have' (*nemo dat quod non habet*) captures the idea that a buyer receives only such title as the seller conveys, and that, generally, the buyer cannot receive title superior to that of the seller (Roodt and Carey Miller 2013: 1).

The Latin word *restitutio* means return or restoration. A 'restitution claim' may refer to a claim proffered in a lawsuit in jurisprudential terms, or more broadly, to every demand relating to the return of cultural property based on a restitution argument. The National Policy (South Africa) on the Repatriation and Restitution of Human Remains and Heritage Objects (2021: 8) defines restitution in terms of 'the restoration of something lost or stolen to its proper owner, for instance, the return of heritage objects to their community of origin.' Replacing what was destroyed or taken with an identical item could make good on the loss of wealth suffered by the victim. When an object or property item itself cannot be returned, the damage caused to the aggrieved party can be repaired or the owner can be compensated for their loss. Restitution extends also to claims for the return of state and private property looted or taken illegally during armed conflict and making up for damage inflicted upon one state by another by returning plundered property (Zeidler 2016: 27–28). More than any other term, 'restitution' relays that a state owns up to its participation in confiscation, spoliation, theft, coercion, and relinquishment due to missionary zeal, as well as forced sales and sales under duress. 'Restitution' is the preferred way to serve justice to former owners (or heirs) who have been deprived of their property rights in circumstances of extreme past injustice (Veraart 2015: 212).

Repatriation derives from the Late Latin *repatriare*—to go home again: to restore to the country of origin, the place of allegiance or spiritual home. The two meanings can be linked, as when a legal claim is raised after non-performance of an agreement (Zeidler 2016: 46). The National Policy (South Africa) on the Repatriation and Restitution of Human Remains and Heritage Objects (2021: 8) defines repatriation as the return of human remains and heritage objects from another country to their country of origin. Repatriation claims to 'sacred' objects may come from a community of origin within the same or another state. These might be claims to enable transmission of its culture to future generations, complete the historical record, restore its cultural identity, etc. Repatriating is not only to return cultural material to their homes, but also to complete and re-appropriate their original meaning (Effiboley 2020: 73, 76). For many Indigenous peoples, the very language of 'repatriation' signals an inalienable birth right to their most significant cultural artefacts; they consider their claim to be self-defining and axiomatic. Transferring these artefacts outside of the Indigenous community or away from the spiritual leader responsible for their care breaches cultural protocol. The sacred character of the artefact constitutes the ground of the claim to have it returned.

The 2022 African Union Model Law on the Protection of Cultural Property aims to assist Member States to develop and strengthen their national legislation on the protection of cultural property and heritage and to facilitate the return of illicitly trafficked cultural property from Africa. The Model Law defines 'repatriation' as 'the process of retrieving and returning illegally acquired cultural property and heritage to its country or place of origin.' Article 27 acknowledges that restitution relates to movable cultural property and heritage stolen or otherwise taken out of the country without authorisation or illegally exported from the national territory. In the event of a claim for restitution of cultural property and heritage that has been duly bought or transferred in good faith by a third party, the possessor must return it to the community of origin or National Body (Article 27.2). This formulation reflects an understanding of 'restitution' as a specific legal remedy of giving back to claimants what had been stolen from them, to restore them to their original position and provide reparation for injury (a meaning that is common in Civil and Common law systems). The Model Law's definition of 'restitution' refers to 'payment of compensation and restoration of cultural property and heritage to its original condition' and yet Article 27 advances a more inclusive interpretation that does better justice to the concept. The Model Law would become uniform law if Member States were to incorporate the model into their domestic legal frameworks.

2.5.6 Application of standards set in uniform law even when not strictly binding

It is not necessary to have ratified a convention before a state may benefit from the standards set by it. Dutch courts have relied on the reasoning that contemporary principles of justice and equity justify the non-applicability of statutes of limitation in relation to colonial crimes committed in the war of independence of Indonesia between 1945 and 1949. They have provided redress in circumstances where victims have been precluded from making claims under colonial structures and were able to demonstrate continuing harm. Victims have been held to have valid claims against the former colonial power based on criteria of 'reasonableness and fairness' and reasoning that, if a state has been complicit in grave violations and barred victims from claims, it may be prevented from invoking such bars to responsibility in good faith (*The Hague Court of Appeal, Children of Executed Men in South-Sulawesi v The Netherlands*, Case No. 200.243.525/01 (1 October 2019); *The Hague Court of Appeal, Heirs Java Torture Victim v The Netherlands*, Case No. 200.247.634/01 (1 October 2019); European Convention on the Non-Applicability of Statutory Limitation to Crimes against Humanity and War Crimes (1974), United Nations Convention on the Non-Applicability of Statutory Limitations to War Crimes and Crimes Against Humanity (1968); Article 7 of A/RES/60/147, 16 December 2005, Basic Principles and Guidelines on the Right to a Remedy and Reparation for Victims of Gross Violations of International Human Rights Law and Serious Violations of International Humanitarian Law).

2.6 Case studies

The mummified thinking that sustains the after-effects of European trade colonialism leaves a grim legacy of colonial geopolitics in the form of a colonial 'jurisprudence of power'. The Buddha Mummy and the Parthenon Marbles disputes shed light on the fundamental problem of fragmentation within and between legal systems and norms which make restitution so hard to achieve. The problem manifests across the levels and layers of the discourse:

- at the level of the material frame of reference and methodology of materiality;
- at the level of systems of knowledge associated with the material in question;
- in subject specialisms and within the structure and method of international law, where the 'sacred' is lumped in with 'cultural heritage';
- in the realm of human rights, where vaguely defined rights that grant governments discretion to ignore or prioritise 'religious freedom';
- in dichotomies such as science/sacred; form/substance; and
- in the gatekeeping functions ascribed to time.

Paradigmatic cases make this fragmentation more noticeable and impart depth clues pointing to the model of responsibility that would support transnational restitution claims associated with the removal of sacred material during the colonial era.

2.6.1 The case of mummified monk Zhanggong Zushi

Given the virtually unlimited demand for curiosities by collectors specialising in sacred objects, it is not surprising that mummies regularly exceed their high price estimates at auction. Their exhibitions in museums draw big crowds. Where versions of market overt remain in play in transit jurisdictions, unlawful export and sale accelerate the commodification of sacred material. The principle legalises the trade in stolen cultural property. The litigation in *Village Committees v van Overeem* concerns a Buddha statue encasing the human remains of a medieval self-mummified monk from the Song Dynasty. The litigation links the influence of colonial powers in global trade with post-colonial illicit antiquities trade. The theft, trafficking, and sale of the Buddha Mummy follows the imprint of European trade colonialism of high-value antiquities that attract sophisticated criminals whose networks exploit the history of privacy in the art sector. These criminals employ third-party intermediaries to launder the proceeds of their criminal activity (Financial Action Task Force Report *Money Laundering and Terrorist Financing in the Art and Antiquities Market* 2023: 4, 9, 11, 14). The Buddha Mummy was taken from Fujian in China, smuggled via Hong Kong, and traded and transported into the Netherlands in the final years of Britain's 99-year lease when Hong Kong was a British colony with semi-autonomous status in China. The theft and export of these artefactual human remains did not occur during colonial conquest, but the direction of the illicit trade and flow of cultural material are predictable after-effects of colonial expansionism. Hong Kong's art and antiquities market has been bolstered by the intensification of restrictions on the sale of art and antiquities in Mainland China, cementing its reputation as both transit and market state for the illicit trade in antiquities obtained from Mainland China and elsewhere in Asia (Murphy 1993; Gallagher 2017: 486). The expansionist agenda is no longer labelled 'colonial,' but *de facto* dependencies that develop under the banner of 'free trade' continue through arrangements between commercial actors and institutions. The trafficking of the mummified monk coincides with global trends in the illicit trade in culture.

The classic trade enclave of Hong Kong has long facilitated Western European control without those powers having to establish formal rule (Zimmerer 2021: 96). Free ports were part of the trade with ancient China since the 9th century BC (Lavissière and Rodrigue 2017: 5). A pivot of European expansionism that remains anchored in an imperial age, the geographic position and logistics infrastructure of the Hong Kong free port eases the transit of cultural material across state borders as a connecting point between the Asian antiquities trade and prime destinations in Europe and America. It is an ideal location for buying stolen cultural objects (Gallagher 2017: 479ff). The border between Hong Kong and mainland China runs in the middle of the Shenzhen River. Passport clearance continues while administrative quarantine of goods is theoretically possible but in practice, the border is permeable. It allows fewer administrative controls and less rigorous checks for cross-border movement is simply another aspect of market activity (Gallagher 2017: 486). The combination of storage facilities at the free port and the time factor also means that statutory limitations or acquisitive prescription provisions in Civil Codes may be circumvented to guarantee that restitution proceedings cannot succeed.

Free ports function like 'locks' since they can be used to transform illegal activity into lawful activity. This serves the schemes of 'rapacious foreigners' who use smuggling networks to maximise their profits. Demand is transferred directly to the port, where sellers are under no obligation to exercise or prove due diligence for the items they are selling (Bull 2009: 30). As soon as goods enter the port, shipping, customs, wholesaling, and retail functions are conducted openly and legally at major venues and elite shops. Sales are made directly to collectors, tourists, and dealers in locations across the west (Alder and Polk 2002: 35, 39). Having few controls on imports, export papers can be obtained for items leaving the port to lend a 'veneer of legitimacy' that will 'help eventual import into a destination country and placement on the market' (Mackenzie et al. 2020: 45). Being a most convenient transition point for stolen and illicitly excavated antiquities transiting into market states where they can be sold legally, Hong Kong lends itself to purchasing sacred cultural material and arranging their transit.

When Oscar van Overeem, Dutch private collector of Chinese art and antiquities, purchased a Buddha statue in the mid-1990s, he thought it was a neglected, damaged Ming statue. Restoration work undertaken in 1997 revealed the human skeleton inside, a very rare mummy from the Song Dynasty with a high market value. Van Overeem agreed to put it on a travelling exhibition in exchange for its inclusion in a Mummy Research Project at the Reiss-Engelhorn Museum in Mannheim.

After the 2014 *Mummies—overleven na de dood* (Mummies—surviving after death) exhibition, the mummies were sent to the Natural History Museum in Budapest, Hungary, for the 'Mummy World' exhibition. In 2015, the statue commanded major media attention. A resident of Yangchun, the village from which the statue had been stolen in 1995, recognised the Zhanggong statue while browsing the news on his smartphone (Chen 2022: 275). By March 2015, photos of the statue and x-rays had reached the inhabitants of Yangchun. Van Overeem withdrew the statue from the Budapest exhibition when the story reached the press. The case caught the attention of the international community in 2016. Van Overeem maintained that he bought his statue in mid-1996 in Amsterdam and later exchanged it for other statues with an (unnamed) Chinese collector who wished to remain anonymous (Min Min Final 2022: sub 'Trial court's fact findings' paras 4 and 5; *NL Times* 17 July 2017). He refused to disclose the particulars of the transaction and the whereabouts of the statue.

Legal frameworks prohibit the destruction of cultural heritage and regulate their export, illegal transfer, and trafficking. In respect of the transfer of movables, diverse principles govern consent and delivery. The principles of unity and separation and of causality and abstraction underscore the legal diversity in play. Legal diversity in property law complicates harmonisation efforts across European jurisdictions (Drobnig 2011: 1004). Created to establish a common European conceptual framework, a Study Group on a European Civil Code worked on a Draft Common Frame of Reference (von Bar and Clive (eds.): 2010). The DCFR provides a comprehensive model of the law of obligations. However, the law of property is dealt with in a fragmented way. Whereas the transfer of ownership of movable assets, security rights and trusts are included in the scope of the DCFR, the transfer of immovables is not (Akkermans 2012: 201).

The US Safeguard Tribal Objects of Patrimony Act was signed into law on 21 December 2022, to prevent the international export of cultural items prohibited from trafficking under the NAGPRA and the Archaeological Resources Protection Act (ARPA), and to facilitate the international repatriation of any items taken illegally. A Native Working Group comprising representatives from Indian tribes and Native Hawaiian organisations will advise on the voluntary return of cultural items and the elimination of the illegal trafficking of these items in the US and internationally under the ARPA. The group can request the Department of Justice and the Department of State to take legal or diplomatic actions to obtain and return cultural property. This body has an opportunity to work actively towards the principle of the comity of nations, but it remains to be seen whether it will contribute to legal evolution in the field. Final regulations to improve implementation of NAGPRA took effect on 12 January 2024 (Native American Graves Protection and Repatriation Act Systematic Processes for Disposition or Repatriation of Native American Human Remains, Funerary Objects, Sacred Objects, and Objects of Cultural Patrimony, 13 December 2023).

Human rights attract much interest as factors that could resolve ownership disputes involving sacred cultural material. Obtaining consent from Indigenous communities when dealing with their ancestors' remains recognises Indigenous ownership and stewardship under their customs, traditions, and laws. Affected communities deserve to be consulted and the Free, Prior, and Informed Consent requirement ('FPIC') complied with by researchers and companies who perform research with Indigenous resources (Human Rights Council Report 2020: para 41). States must consult and seek the FPIC of Indigenous peoples, ensuring participation through their own representative institutions (Human Rights Council Report 2020: 89).

Museums must avoid getting caught up in competition between different communities to make progress with restitution. Focusing on national heritage exclusively will exacerbate the gaps that already exist in conceptions of responsibility. Interpretation of the consequences of colonial events and the authority of those who determine which collection items have special significance for source communities cannot necessarily be determined within historical or contemporary legal frameworks. Legal frameworks do not locate to whom sacred material ought to be restituted, and the efforts museums undertake to determine with whom return is to be negotiated are easily befuddled by mimetics. Both sides will require representation. It is vital to keep government officials at the right levels of state informed about processes, because their decisions will determine the direction returns may take.

Possessors who consider themselves 'owners' may choose to deploy provenance and legal arguments in ways that avert legal liability to continue enjoying the fruit of colonial exploitation. Compilation of an exhaustive inventory allows provenance to be determined with certainty, but this does not automatically constitute a critical reading of provenance. Critical provenance research could re-align and enhance museum data; broaden participation; and join-up research to counter the loss of information through carelessness, indifference, or superior mindsets. It is vital to ascertain with whom to negotiate the process to be able to anticipate the recipients' priorities and collaborate with parties and experts from source countries. Many western institutions remain unable to accept local decisions about restituted cultural heritage and tensions persist over who is authorised to conduct restitution discussions (e.g., DMB *Care of Collections* 2021: 87). German museums have outlined the importance of establishing contacts with representatives and the knowledge holders, elders, and practitioners of Indigenous systems of knowledge to allow for active and respectful collaboration (DMB *Care of Collections* 2021: 46–48). Research integrity requires acknowledgement of their involvement in the research process. Objectification of the object may also carry over in legal argument on the application of the choice-of-law rule in question and the juridical framework it supposedly unlocks. PrIL's public policy exception may halt or interrupt circulation, but in the usual order of things, profits count for far more than sacred tradition (Greenblatt 1991: 53).

Provenance may play out in a complex interaction between law and ethics. The first evidence of a less fragmented and more holistic approach in an international civil claim involving involuntary loss of the sacred associated with the colonial era is found in the parallel litigation and competing outcomes reached regarding the Buddha Mummy in the Netherlands and China. The Chinese cases highlight the significant potential for co-ordination that exists amid the fragmentation within and between legal systems and norms which makes restitution seem unachievable. The issue of ownership was among those addressed in the final ruling of the Fujian Higher People's Court. The court also paid attention to the legal basis for return. These aspects will be analysed in a follow-up study. The Chinese cases also highlight the 'connectivity' of the PrIL toolbox—its tools of legal reasoning and the ways in which the toolmakers have arranged them in different toolboxes for different purposes—to extra-legal factors such as provenance and the sacred as well as the standards in (non-binding) uniform law. The Amsterdam court's attentional failings in respect of the interaction between law and facts affected how it viewed provenance and the allegation that there were two different statues.

Normative conflicts may be precipitated by competing judgments emanating from courts at opposite ends of the world. PrIL techniques control the conflict of litigation—international parallel proceedings resulting in divergent and competing rulings in different venues that produce normative conflict (McLachlan 2009). The Fujian Higher People's Court confirmed the Sanming trial court's approach to the issue of the identification of the Zhanggong Zushi statue. It rejected the dealer's submission that he bought a different statue than the Zhanggong Zushi statue (Min Min Final 2022: sub 'On the question of whether it should be returned'). To date no attempt has been made to have the final Chinese ruling enforced by a court in the Netherlands, despite this seeming a logical step towards achieving justice. The example of the mummified monk draws together property and heritage, yet this union is not necessarily productive from the perspective of repatriation. The focus must necessarily turn towards human responsibility for decisions concerning restitution and non-restitution. Successful transnational recovery of stolen cultural relics must overcome hurdles posed by time, distance, and material changes, in addition to distinct differences in the legal and ethical frameworks in an EU state's court and courts located in a third state.

The committees argued before the Amsterdam District Court that the Buddha is collectively owned, it was removed without authorisation, and its theft violated their right to religious freedom (first hearing of 14 July 2017). After the initial Amsterdam hearing, the village committees amended the particulars of their claim to three main points, namely (a) that van Overeem acted in bad faith as he had failed to conduct (provenance) research prior to acquiring the statue; (b) that the Dutch Burial Act 1991 applied and precluded property rights in human remains; and (c) that an exchange agreement concluded between van Overeem and a third collector was invalid, unlawful, and contrary to public order, and that an order to disclose the name of that party should be issued because he had removed evidence (the statue) from the court's jurisdictional reach. Essentially, the timeline of the chain of custody was uncertain, as were the dates on which van Overeem acquired and allegedly relinquished possession. Proof of purchase was never produced, nor was any form of certification of the transaction provided or even the date and place of its changing hands supplied.

The village committees wanted to use the Amsterdam proceedings to have the identity of the person who obtained the Buddha Mummy from van Overeem disclosed, but their request did not yield results. Van Overeem's response to the villagers' case was brief, stating that the claimants were not natural or legal persons and could not act in legal proceedings, and that there were in fact two different statues, since the statue he had owned before exchanging it was already in Amsterdam by mid-1995, before the Zhanggong mummy was stolen from the village (*Amsterdam District Court, Village Committee of Yangchun and DongPu v Oscar van Overeem* 12 December 2018, para 3.3). The court's refusal to recognise the committees as juristic entities with proprietary rights to the Buddha Statue endorsed van Overeem's first line of defence, namely that standing to sue for recovery was lacking. Group claims for repatriation typically require representatives or institutional structures to whom objects may be transferred (Last 2007: 137).

The principal reasoning of the Amsterdam Court, published in 2018, was that Dutch law and jurisprudence applied and that the forum law allows civil proceedings to be brought by natural or qualified legal persons; and the village committees that instituted proceedings had not clarified their legal capacity as special legal persons under Article 96 of the General Rules of the Civil Law of the Peoples' Republic of China. The court rejected the legal opinions of Chinese lawyers that the respective village committees qualified as legal persons. The villagers' legal representative cited these opinions as proof that the village committees meet the requirements. While the court acknowledged that exceptions may apply when effective legal protection cannot be ensured in another way, it reasoned that procedural difficulties are unavoidable if there is uncertainty about who is bound by the ruling, against whom to seek execution of a cost order, or if a party is unsure about the identity of an opposing party. The court held that the claimants did not convince the court that this was indeed the case (*Amsterdam District Court, Village Committee of Yangchun and DongPu v Oscar van Overeem*, para 4.2).

The Fujian Higher People's Court held that the argument that the Dutch Civil Code should be applied in the case lacks a factual and legal basis and cannot be substantiated (Min Min Final 2022: sub 'On issues concerning the applicable law'). Both the intermediate and higher court in China respected notions of private property rights in adversarial legal proceedings. In China, historic human remains found in tombs or other religious sites are protected as cultural relics that, if privately owned, may be traded provided export has been authorised by customs authorities (Liu 2017: 232). Since the encased mummy's exportation was never authorised, it must have been smuggled into the Netherlands, and the Fujian Provincial Higher Court treated it as such (Chen 2022: 285). This approach equates illegal export to theft, whch aligns with the 1995 UNIDROIT Convention. The people of Yangchun have the right to the return of the relic of the monk's remains, which were never intended to be sold on the international art market and were not authorised to be removed from Chinese soil, and yet the difficulty in ascertaining the status of the committees before the Dutch court interfered with their exercise of rights and precluded a finding on their right to institute civil proceedings. This technicality absolved the court from having to rule on the merits of the case and relieved it of its responsibility to consider the proprietary basis of their claim. The court denied the village committees the right to proceed with an action to recover their sacred mummified monk and ordered them to pay costs (*Amsterdam District*

Court, Village Committee of Yangchun and DongPu v Oscar van Overeem, paras 4.2.6 and para 4.3).

Offering van Overeem protection of privacy in his business transaction serves only to hide illicit trafficking and theft. In proceedings brought to enforce a judgment from another Member State in the EU, a court may be asked to grant a domestic freezing order against the property of the party against whom enforcement is being sought. Such a provisional measure would apply to property located within the forum's territory (Hartley 2009: 442). Any measures that would have precluded exchange agreements with other collectors for the Buddha Mummy or gave cause to seek disclosure of the name of a party with whom a defendant concluded exchange agreements, would have been in order. Search orders may be granted against defendants in civil proceedings, allowing a litigant to search the premises of a named person to obtain evidence to support the claimant's case (either ongoing or planned). *Ex parte* injunctions restraining further activities under complaint are usually included (Hartley 2009: 463–467).

Restitution claims cannot move forward if courts use legal reasoning to suppress context as the case in Amsterdam shows. Depletion of substantive normativity in adjudication provides scope for smuggling networks to maximise opportunities at the local level. An entry point for the public policy of returning stolen and illegally exported artefacts to their countries of origin could have been supplied if the court considered where to draw the dividing line between substance and procedure. It may have found reason to require the collector to verify the incongruent provenance, and to establish connections between the facts and the social life of villagers with the object. However, policy issues in the cultural sphere were not considered because the procedural barrier which the Dutch court erected around cultural traffickers disallowed questions of a substantive nature. Consequently, the juridical framework in which law expresses itself could not be identified. Evidently, PrIL is easily co-opted to serve the commercial paradigm of the juridical framework of circulation of goods instead of the juridical framework of exception, despite human remains and sacred cultural material deriving from colonial contexts being in private hands. Amidst so much uncertainty over potential outcomes, the pathways to repatriation remain obscured. The interaction between PrIL and ethics requires support when historical injustices are remembered and re-assessed. PrIL is bound to struggle to keep up with these complex intermixing contexts when a human subject takes the form of physical object, as in the example of the mummification of the monk. The potentially applicable legal norms do not automatically converge when changes occur in the material world. Moreover, the fragmentation that mars instruments of uniform law can easily carry over into the treatment PrIL gives to the time factor. The timelessness of the 'sacred' necessitates closer investigation of an alternate chronosophy of the 'imprescriptability of the sacred'.

Attention has already been drawn to the new antinomies and disempowering side effects of human rights doctrine and discourse and there is more to say about this (Stahn 2023: 392). Restitution offers ways to apprehend the lessons of history, provided that a balance can be struck between the factual circumstances and the voices of those affected when addressing questions about responsibility and sphere of influence. Consequently, the historicisation of PrIL assumes importance (Banu 2022: 385). Since critical provenance research taps into diversity of opinion, ideological frames of reference, world views and expressions, it could contribute to breaking down the boundaries between disciplines and forms of expertise. This prepares the ground for the process of re-unifying fragmented records. Decisions to repatriate human remains are inherently political and moral and do not rest with provenance researchers, however (Winkelmann 2020: 45–46). In some situations, for example, the permission from direct descendants, and not just interested communities, is required for sampling of human remains (National Policy (South Africa) on the Repatriation and Restitution of Human Remains and Heritage Objects of 2021).

More light must be shed on the sacred dimension of the mumified monk. Does this dimension resonate with Girard's theory? Zhang Qisan readied himself for the 'next stage of existence' by the rites of the Ch'an School of Buddhism, which is associated with polytheistic values. Training by this School leads the embodied consciousness and intelligence of the practitioner towards 'absorption' ('dhyana'), a state that is beyond the senses and the reasoning mind (also known as 'Zen'). The intangible qualities of the mummified monk—his spirituality, patience, devotion—mark his remains and their encasement as 'sacred.' Behaviours that honour the sacred—such as rituals—introduce a 'slowness' in the responses to bodily and sense perceptions that nurtures community. There is also great sacrifice in the discipline of the spiritual tradition Zhang followed, and the contribution which mummified monks made to the economies of their monasteries.

The encasement of human remains differs from other burial practices. The tangible property (artefact) comes to embody the sacred over time. Besides being a skilled local healer who drew on a deep knowledge of botany and Chinese herbal medicine, Zhang Qisan was also trained up to control the manner and timing of his death (Liu 2017: 227). The preservation of the body in self-mummification depends on the flesh of the Ch'an practitioner collaborating with the process (Sharf 1992: 6). Certain processes were perfected by the tradition to support the flesh in the mummification process such as wrapping the monk's body in lacquer-soaked hemp cloth (Sharf 1992: 6; Robson 2003: 151–152). Like the bodies of the Patriarchs who were considered reservoirs or 'fields of merit,' Zhang's body remained intact (Sharf 1992: 6). The self-transformation ritual, which lasted approximately seven years, was concluded between 1022 and 1155 AD. A mashed paper statue was made more than a century after the mummification, in 1292, to hold his body (Bruijn et al. 2015: 337ff). The lacquering, gilding and adornments of the case were intended to preserve the sacred icon (Sharf 1992: 22). The attention which devotees have lavished on Zhanggong Zushi and the sacrifices made to him in the village temple where the statue was enshrined, have been consistent for centuries. The Ch'an tradition of self-mummification has fallen into disuse, but it was common for relics of the practice to be integrated in Ch'an rituals and ceremonies in medieval China. The case illuminates the tension between science and the sacred. The Buddha Mummy was the only one available for scientific research in the west in 2014. Scientists at the Meander Medical Centre in the Netherlands vied for the opportunity to conduct research on it. A computed tomography (CT) scan, an endoscopy of the thoracic and abdominal cavities, as well as bone samples were taken. Imaging showed the paper scrolls printed with ancient Chinese characters that had replaced the organs, and the iron rod inserted to support the spine and neck. Carbon-14 dating established the top layer of clothing to the Ming dynasty (1368–1644); the inner layers of the textile shroud to between 1272 and 1284; and the remains to between 1092 to 1149. The inscription on the bolster identifies the figure as a prelate from a Buddhist monastery identified by a name which the villagers believe to have been conferred on Zhanggong Zushi when he crossed into the 'next stage of existence' (Bruijn et al. 2015: 340).

The sacred is present in the cultural knowledge of the tradition of self-mummification. The Ch'an practitioner's sustained attention over several thousand days. They undergo consecutive stages in their diets and levels of physical activity to start the mummification process from the inside. When ready they lock themselves in a stone tomb barely larger than body-size, and a small air tube is provided for the tomb. When the bell that let the outside world know that the monk was still alive stopped ringing, the tomb would be sealed for the final thousand day-period. If found in a preserved state, the body would be removed from the tomb and the monk raised to the status of Buddha. If the body had decomposed, the monk would be resealed in his tomb, respected for his endurance, but not worshipped. Monks whose bodies failed to mummify were later incinerated (Faure 1994: 159).

Whether the Ch'an Buddhist tradition of self-mummifications was based on free decisions of individual monks in the Song Dynasty is a historical and cultural question with potential normative implications. Faure poses the question concerning ritual suicides (Faure 1994: 161). It would be easy to dismiss the tradition of mummified monks as 'consenting sacrifices' or religious extremism, but there is no historical evidence to indicate that the monks were subjected to pressure from their spiritual communities. Duress would conflict with the personal, mental, physical, and spiritual commitment required to achieve self-mummification. Nonetheless, the monks may have tried to meet religious expectations, recommitting to their deepest intentions and practice each day.

The villagers' submission to the Amsterdam court included an argument that the unauthorised removal of the mummified monk violated their right to religious freedom. Human rights were originally conceived of as powerful legal claims, but they encompass so much that they end up being indeterminate or inconclusive, which undermines the claims. Importantly, rights based on freedom of religion are meaningless when the state was not directly involved in the theft, smuggling, or looting of the cultural material and human remains. Moreover, attempts to enforce rights based on religion encounter practical challenges at the state, group, and individual level. The right of a people to their own artistic, historical, and cultural wealth may foster an expectation that it would impart a right to assert the primacy of a spiritual claim over a commercial one, yet this is rarely achieved in practice. Human rights are not 'rights' in the strict sense at the constitutional (domestic) level. They are akin to 'open phrases' or 'empty signifiers' for which appropriate full phrasing with more substance may yet be found; their realisation depends on the right conditions (Van der Walt 2018: 67). As one would expect, the religious freedom argument garnered no traction.

Cultural normative systems co-exist with state law or municipal regulations, and these normative systems—made up of informal non-religious community norms, customary norms, or religious norms—enjoy protection under the right to freedom of thought, conscience, and religion in Article 9 ECHR (David 2020: 147, 153). Freedom of religion arguments cannot supply a convincing legal basis for a restitution claim, however. PrIL must be called on to refine the human rights argument. A separate 'category' of material that would shape existing PrIL choice-of-law rules in restitution claims is not needed, but the formulation of the rule must be adjusted to liberate the emancipatory power of the sacred. Overall, the normative phenomena of legal rights appear to be less relevant to the question of restitution. More is at stake than just an identifiable person with human rights. The origin of obligations intrinsic to gift economies needs to be acknowledged. The origin of obligations in ancient societies points to the role of 'responsibility' in normative ethics. Duty-oriented conceptions of communal responsibility are discussed in more detail in a subsequent study.

2.6.2 Application of convention standard as an expression of policy

Legal remedies are steadily developing for cultural property claims in the framework of conventions and treaties but as with the cultural property and heritage conventions, will take effect in states only after signing and ratifying the convention. For claims that intersect with the colonial era, the addition of the most recent Council of Europe Convention on Offences relating to Cultural Property will not change much (signed 19 May 2017, entry into force 1 April 2022). The common standard for criminal law set in this new development is due care and attention. States must ensure that the acquisition of stolen cultural property, where the unlawful provenance is known, constitutes an offence under their domestic law, and that placing such material on the market is prohibited. In this way the convention harmonises differences in criminal legislation regarding the illegal trafficking of cultural objects. It criminalises the different components of the trafficking in cultural property and will facilitate cooperation among the signatory states to target the activities of international crime rings. It is already in operation in states such as Cyprus, Greece, and Italy.

The Netherlands signed the 1995 UNIDROIT Convention in 1996 but in 2004 the Dutch government decided not to accede; instead, it ratified the 1970 UNESCO Convention (van Woudenberg 2016: 122). Important features of the 1995 UNIDROIT Convention were incorporated into Dutch law in full alignment with secondary EU law. Ratifying the 1970 UNESCO Convention and implementing internal legislation according to both Conventions without adopting the UNIDROIT Convention, is referred to as the '1970 Convention plus' option (Schneider 2016: 157). Implementation legislation in respect of the 1970 UNESCO Convention introduces a limitation period of 75 years as the absolute maximum for most categories (art 3:310 (a) of the Dutch Civil Code; Campfens 2021: 218).

China concluded bilateral agreements with several states to curb illicit transfer, import and export of cultural property, but the Netherlands do not count among them (People's Republic of China, National Report for UNESCO, *Implementation of the 1970 Convention on the Means of Prohibiting and Preventing the Illicit Import, Export and Transfer of Ownership of Cultural Property 2011–2015*). China acceded to the 1970 UNESCO Convention on 28 November 1989 but Dutch accession followed only on 17 July 2009. The mummified monk's removal date precedes Dutch accession to the UNESCO Convention by approximately 14 years. China acceded to the 1995 UNIDROIT Convention on Stolen or Illegally Exported Cultural Objects in May 1997, which is approximately two years after the removal of the Buddha Statue. The convention seemed unavailable to support China's restitution claim but the ruling of the Fujian Province Higher People's Court (2021 Min Min Final 19 July 2022) invoked and upheld the standards set by both the 1970 UNESCO Convention and the 1995 UNIDROIT Convention. The full implications of this ruling for the illicit trade in sacred artefacts removed during the colonial era will be set out in a follow-up study.

2.6.3 The Parthenon Sculptures claim

The Parthenon Sculptures are frequently differentiated from other Greek works of art based on the powerful meanings they carry as masterpieces of classic art and as archaeological messengers from the Acropolis. Greece re-iterated its arguments in favour of the reunification of the sculptures with the Parthenon structure during the Twenty-second Session of the ICPRCP in Paris in 2021. It argued that the Marbles dispute must be distinguished from the removal of colonial objects from Africa because they are fragmented and dispersed sculptures belonging to one work that needs reunification in Greece. Reliance on exceptionalism on this basis is unhelpful.

Their taking and unlawful sale bear a distinctive colonial imprint, yet Greece's claim does not capture the link between the inequality inherent in retaining the Parthenon Sculptures in London and the anti-colonial discourse over artefacts looted from Africa. Greece's position on the outside of 'Europe,' on the western fringe of the Ottoman Empire, was leveraged in some quarters to support Lord Elgin's removal of sculptures and other items from the Parthenon on the Acropolis in Athens (Gunning and Challis 2023: 563). David Wilson, the director of the British Museum at the time, deployed the notion of ownership rights anchored in the colonial era in 1985. He argued that Greece was a 'Third World country' and the Greeks a formerly colonised people. As a tack to justify the plunder of the Greek past, Greece was placed in an impossible position, lodged between the standard for civilisation and democracy yet looking to Europe's beneficence for its survival because of its status as an Oriental vassal (Kynourgiopoulou 2011: 161).

Complex colonial relationships surrounded the removal of the Parthenon Sculptures. Greece's status cannot be considered in splendid historical isolation. The Sculptures were taken from Athens by colonial powers, their taking and unlawful sale bear a colonial imprint, and the dynamics of the extraction of the Parthenon

Marbles resembled those relating to other complex material such as the sacred medicine bundles. When a brig commissioned by Elgin carrying sections of the Parthenon frieze and 16 boxes of antiquities, sank off the island of Kythera in 1802, colonial mechanisms were called upon to salvage them. The many Marbles absent from the Parthenon were among the myriad of collectables whose emplacement in the British Museum was facilitated by colonialism. Even if the repression of Greek culture and social practices is not apparent, Greek political life during the revolution was a mirror image of the three major powers which the political parties of the day considered best placed to help Greece most—the English party (1825–1873), the French party (1824–1865), and the Russian party (1827–1865). The Treaty for the Pacification of Greece between France, Great Britain, and Russia of 6 July 1827 was intended to halt the oppression of Greece and re-establish peace. Greece itself was not a party to this treaty, which reflected paramount European commercial interests in the fledgling state. The threat of colonial power impacted the assertion of claims for restitution by European nations as much as by Indigenous communities (Zimmerer 2021: 98). Much like the Greek demands for their Parthenon Marbles, African demands for restitution are also being continually restated. What is more, the calls for re-unification of the Marbles in Athens echo the need of Native Americans for spiritual completion. Nonetheless, Greece has not framed its claim concerning the extraction and exportation of the Parthenon Marbles as the colonial era theft it represents.

The Athenians' Association, an advocacy group active in the field of protection and maintenance of the monuments and works of art connected with the history of Athens, launched the first legal bid for restitution of the Parthenon Sculptures in 2016. The case brought before the European Court of Human Rights did not reach merits (*Syllogos ton Athinaion v United Kingdom*, Application No. 48259/15, First Section, 31 May 2016; ECHR 23 June 2016). The suit was instituted against the UK based on a suite of rights under the European Convention of Human Rights (ECHR): the right to respect for private life (Article 8); the right to respect for its conscience (Article 9); the ability to access cultural information about the history of the Marbles and of Athens (Article 10); the denial of a remedy (Article 13); and interference with its proprietary right to access the whole monument (Article 1 of the First Protocol to the Convention). The Athenians' Association argued that the combined effect of these provisions implied that Greece had a right to demand that the UK government join mediation. The Court disagreed. The Athenians' Association was not the Greek state and cannot bring a claim for return of the Marbles on behalf of Greece, nor could it base a claim on any rights under the ECHR or its associated protocols. The Court declined to proceed to the merits and held all the claims inadmissible *ratione materiae* (i.e., based on subject matter). If Greece were to institute proceedings on behalf of the City of Athens, its argument would require refinement, given that time assumes a gatekeeping function.

2.6.4 Time's gatekeeping function

The principle of intertemporality and expired periods of limitation introduce hurdles to successful restitution claims (Labadie 2021: paras 9, 10, 18, 27). The intertemporality principle of PublIL stands in notable contrast to the natural law theories that view law as unified and capable of transcending both time and space (Oh 2018: 419). Non-retrospectivity and limitation periods pose formidable hurdles for colonial era and Indigenous restitutions and may rule out older claims. The principle of non-retroactivity pulls against the consideration of present-day values and norms in the interpretation of the conventional framework for cultural property and heritage in restitution claims in regards to a different era.

It cannot be assumed that the justifiability of an acquisition or transfer of property can be determined conclusively at the date of acquisition on transfer without regard to social changes over time. The proposition that a just or unjust acquisition in 1890 would remain a just or unjust root of title today, is utopian. Honoré asserts that colonies and slavery plunge legal title into permanent uncertainty which cannot be clarified even by rules of lapse, expropriation, and compensating compulsory acquisition of property rights (Honoré 1987: 218–220).

In *Syllogos*, the Court identified the removal of the Parthenon Sculptures by Elgin's men as the underlying cause of action, which would require it to apply the principles of the ECHR retrospectively. Article 7.1 of the 1950 ECHR contains the general rule of non-retrospectivity which is clarified regarding liability in Article 7.2, to ensure that no doubt could be cast on the validity of prosecutions of crimes committed during the Second World War after the war ended. Article 7 applies to the offences as defined and their corresponding penalties, meaning that, when a crime has been committed under the general principles of law recognised by civilised nations, penalties cannot be applied retrospectively (Council of Europe, European Court of Human Rights, *Guide on Article 7 of the European Convention on Human Rights* updated on 31 December 2019: para 58 refers to the *travaux préparatoires* to the Convention). The European Court of Human Rights considered it unnecessary to assess a conviction for war crimes committed during the Second World War under Article 7.2, because the relevant acts constituted an offence under 'international law' within the meaning of Article 7.1. Thismeaning was understood as referring to customary international law, in particular the Laws and Customs of War (*Kononov v Latvia* [GC], Application No. 36376/04, ECHR 17 May 2010; Council of Europe, European Court of Human Rights, *Guide on Article 7* 2019: para 58). Applying this legal position would indicate that the action brought by Syllogos ton Athinaion was no longer timely.

Proof may be required that the retention of a particular cultural object by a museum constitutes a continuing violation of a person's right to enjoy their culture (Byrne 2015: 15). Proof is challenging to provide, however. Wide variation is to be expected between the recognition accorded to cultural rights in the museums sectors of the United States as opposed to England, for instance. Certain interpretations of colonial law may promote harsh results, e.g., that the expropriation of property does not constitute a continuing wrongful act, but that it is merely the effects of the expropriation that persist (Crawford 2002: 136). To circumvent the retrospective application of the ECHR, Greece would have to convince the European Court of Human Rights that the persistent refusal to agree to mediation constitutes an ongoing or continuing violation (Wadsworth 2023: 144). However, the Court declined to consider whether continuing possession by the British Museum constituted an ongoing violation of Greece's rights in the case at hand. The human rights thrust of the claimant's argument in the *Syllogos* case could not suspend the power hierarchies of the colonial era. The will of the UK, the holding nation, prevailed.

2.6.5 Difference between Dutch policies and guidelines and ACE guidelines

Since the ruling in the Buddha Mummy case, the policy position in the Netherlands has evolved. Having reached an intermediate phase in the development of new rules for the return of colonial cultural objects, it provides an instructive model. The Minister of Education, Culture and Science in the Netherlands, Ingrid van Engelshoven, requested the Dutch Council for Culture to establish an Advisory Commission in 2020, and it issued an Advice on Colonial Collection: A Recognition of Injustice when the brief had been completed (Dutch Council of Culture, *Colonial Collection: A Recognition of Injustice*, The Hague, January 2021). The *Report on the National Policy Framework for Colonial Collections in the Netherlands* (2020) contains recommendations that were developed jointly with source countries. The handling of requests for the return of cultural objects was conceived of as an ethical question, and ethical handling would have to be respectful of the standards and principles of international humanitarian law and the codes of ethics of international social organisations.

In a response to the initiative taken by the Dutch Council for Culture, the Ministry of Education, Culture and Science published its *Policy Vision on Collections from a Colonial Context* on 29 January 2021. The *Policy Vision* adheres closely to the recommendations comprising the policy framework, but its categorisation has been refined to clarify legal and ethical implications. The first category relates to cultural objects taken away involuntarily from a former Dutch colony. 'War booty' are to be returned unconditionally if the country of origin wishes a return to be made. The export regulation in Article 4.22 of the Heritage Act of 2016 would not apply in these cases. The second category refers to cultural goods with special significance to the country of origin but with undetermined provenance or a record of ownership that does not indicate involuntary loss of possession. These cultural goods are to be returned conditionally if preservation and access can be maximised. The interests of the countries and communities concerned are to be balanced and the legal regime of the Dutch Heritage Act adhered to. The third category concerns cultural objects from former colonies of other colonial powers such as Sri Lanka or Nigeria, for which the Minister will make a judgment call whether to rectify an injustice that was not caused by the Netherlands, but regarding which the Netherlands is the only one in a position to rectify it. The *Policy Vision* also highlights the NIOD Institute for War, Holocaust and Genocide Studies, the *Nationaal Museum van Wereldculturen* and the *Rijksmuseum*, who were requested to develop a methodology for provenance research and who published their final report in March 2022 (Pilot Project Provenance Research on Objects of the Colonial Era (PPROCE); *Policy Vision* of 2021: 8). Ministerial assurances have been given that requests for the return of ancestral remains will receive the highest priority (*Policy*

Vision of 2021: 6). The vision does not deal with colonial archives. The Minister has no direct say about objects owned by municipalities, provinces, universities, missionary organisations, or private possessors. Return requests must come to an independent assessment advisory committee. A request will only be heard if made by a state via the appropriate diplomatic channel.

Whereas the Dutch policies and guidelines pull law and ethics together, the 2022 ACE Report declares that the guidelines do not change any policy or legislation. This statement in the ACE guidelines resists the normative effect of soft law. Furthermore, the simplified 'map' of the technical procedure and the steps to be taken towards dispute resolution in the ACE guidelines leave their rationale and ethos unclear. No guidance is provided on cases in which ethical claims compete. The inherent complexity of restitution policy is neither acknowledged nor reflected.

The normative environment calls for improvement at the macro-level. This would necessitate far-reaching theoretical and practical reforms (Stahn 2022: 59).

2.7 Conclusion

While the Parthenon Sculptures impart a profound identity-forming function for Athenians—one which allows their continued participation in the construction of identity—Chapter 2 ventured beyond its 'identity' and 'heritage values.' It brought the genealogical origins of the Parthenon and its sculptures into focus. It connected colonial collecting practices and restitution practice with the sacred. The sacred is not a by-product of violence, war, and death; what confers on material a sacred status are practices that interrupt the cyclical repeat patterns of subconscious mimetic desires to possess more than or be superior to others at all cost. Chapter 2 also mapped some of the artificial analytical distinctions, conceptual fragmentations, and dichotomies that fuel mimetics.

Mummies of the spiritual masters are frequently disputed commodities. The case involving the mummified monk encased in a Buddha statue evokes numerous competitive elements. The rivalrous classification between 'faith in' the 'sacred' and the science features prominently in the ensuing litigation. The fundamental problem of fragmentation arises at virtually all levels: that of the material, the knowledge system at work in the intangible Ch'an tradition, the language, human rights approaches, terminology, and definitions.

Potential exists for restitution, repatriation, and reparation claims in respect of sacred cultural material to overlap with claims for reparative justice. The claims advanced by the Ovaherero and Nama are instructive on the historical context of these claims and the normative leverage they possess. Claims for reparative justice bring law face-to-face with its own complicity in historic injustice. Questions of legal liability, moral and ethical responses, practical solutions, and effective mechanisms for dispute settlement affect the legal strategies and techniques which parties adopt. The focus of this study does not lie with questions of state responsibility and accountability. Consequently no attempt is made to provide an overview of claims for compensation for historic wrongs and attempts to determine whom or which juridical persons to persecute or exonerate.

Human rights bolster protection for Indigenous peoples. It may support the multiple cultural and historical meanings of their cultural material, the restorative possibilities of objects as cultural agents, and restorative policies based on cultural rights (Soirila 2022: 12). Nonetheless it would be naïve to focus only on efforts to expand on rights and freedoms. External restraints on rights are vital to keep in check the propensity to blame others for our misery. Human solidarity, communitarian relationships, and the ethical duties which the functions of shared human nature presuppose, are as important as an expansion of freedoms.

In international civil proceedings, adjudicators draw from law in the transnational realm as well as from extra-legal expectations in the social realm. A non-legal factor based on a common understanding held across the humanities and social sciences could effectively steer legal decision-making in ways that primary and secondary legal norms cannot support on their own. It seems reasonable to expect that the integration of legal and non-legal factors would better support adjudication and law reform for restitution.

Bibliography

African Foundation for Development (AFFORD) Institute. *Return of the Icons: The Restitution of African Artefacts and Human Remains Project Mapping Report* Compiled by Paul Asquith 2020.

Akkermans, Bram. 2012. 'Property Law and the Internal Market' in Sjef van Erp, Arthur Salomons & Bram Akkermans (eds.) *The Future of European Property Law* Munich: Sellier European Law Publishers 199–246.

Alder, Christine & Kenneth Polk. 2002. 'Stopping This Awful Business: The Illicit Traffic in Antiquities Examined as a Criminal Market' *Art Antiquity & Law* 7(1): 35–53.

Alexandrowicz, Charles Henry. 1973. *The European-African Confrontation: A Study in Treaty-Making.* Leiden: A.W. Sijthoff.

Anghie, Antony. 1999. 'Finding the Peripheries: Sovereignty and Colonialism in Nineteenth Century International Law' *Harvard International Law Journal* 40(1): 1–80.

APPG-AR webinar 20 April 2022 <https://www.youtube.com/watch?v=u8x5OU4V378>.

Arts Council England. 2022. *Restitution and Repatriation: A Practical Guide for Museums in England*, 5 August 2022 <https://aim-museums.co.uk/guidance-restitution-repatriation-released-arts-council-england>.

Bachmann, Klaus. 2018. *Genocidal Empires: German Colonialism in Africa and the Third Reich* Frankfurt/Main: Peter Lang.

Banu, Roxana. 2018. *Nineteenth Century Perspectives on Private International Law* Oxford: OUP.

Banu, Roxana. 2022. 'Teaching by Historicising Private International Law' *International Journal of Law in Context* 18(4): 383–392.

Basic Principles and Guidelines on the Right to a Remedy and Reparation for Victims of Gross Violations of International Human Rights Law and Serious Violations of International Humanitarian Law A/RES/60/147, 16 December 2005.

Beard, Mary. 2002. *The Parthenon* London: Profile Books.

Blackstone, Sir William. 1979. *Commentaries on the Laws of England, Vol II* Chicago: University of Chicago Press.

British Museum website. n.d. 'The Parthenon Sculptures: The Trustees' Statement <https://www.britishmuseum.org/about-us/british-museum-story/contested-objects-collection/parthenon-sculptures/parthenon>.

Bruijn, Eric, Amelie Alterauge, Stephanie Zesch, Ben Heggelman, Sylvia Mitschke, Francesca Coletti, Wilfried Rosendahl, Albert Zink & Vincent van Vilsteren. 2015. 'Die Mumie in Inneren–eine übermodellierte Mumie eines buddhistichen Mőnchs' in Alfried Wiexzorek, Michael Tellenbach & Wilfried Rosendahl (eds.) *Mumien: Der Traum vom ewigen Leben* (Reiss-Engelhorn-Museen: 2. teilweise überarbeitete Auflage) Darmstadt: gGmbH und WBG 337–342.

Brückner, Wenke. 2019. '"Cultural Genocide" and the International Criminal Court: The Possibilities and Limits of the Protection of Cultural Heritage' in Alessandro Chechi & Marc-Andre Renold (eds.) *Cultural Heritage Law and Ethics: Mapping Recent Developments* Genève: Schulthess 45–68.

Bull, Toby. 2009. 'Lack of Due Diligence and Unregulated Markets: Trade in Illicit Antiquities and Fakes in Hong Kong' in Noah Charney (ed.) *Art and Crime: Exploring the Dark Side of the Art World* Santa Barbara: Praeger 26–38.

Bush, Jonathan A. 2002. '"The Supreme... Crime" and Its Origins: The Lost Legislative History of the Crime of Aggressive War' *Columbia Law Review* 102(8): 2324–2424.

Byrne, James G. 2015. *Factors Determining the Repatriation of Cultural Heritage from Museums; the Place of Cultural Rights in British Museums Practice* Master Thesis, SOAS University of London.

Campfens, Evelien. 2019. 'The Bangwa Queen: Artifact or Heritage?' *International Journal of Cultural Property* 26(1): 75–110.

Campfens, Evelien. 2021. *Cross-Border Title Claims to Cultural Objects: Property or Heritage?* PhD Thesis, Leiden University (Meijers-reeks Eleven).

Carruthers, Janeen. 2005. *The Transfer of Property in the Conflict of Laws: Choice of Law Rules in Inter Vivos Transfers of Property* Oxford: OUP.

Cayley, David (ed.). 2019. The Ideas of René Girard: An Anthropology of Religion and Violence Interviews Broadcast on 'Ideas', 5–9 March 2001, CBC; Amazon.

Champagne, Duane. 2012. 'Indigenous Self-government, Cultural Heritage and International Trade: A Sociological Perspective' in Christopher B. Graber, Karolina Kuprecht & Jessica C. Lai (eds.) *International Trade in Indigenous Cultural Heritage: Legal and Policy Issues* Cheltenham: Edward Elgar Publishing 31–58.

Chechi, Alessandro. 2008. 'The Return of Cultural Objects Removed in Times of Colonial Domination and International Law: The Case of the Venus of Cyrene' *The Italian Yearbook of International Law Online* 8(1): 159–181.

Chechi, Alessandro. 2014. *The Settlement of International Heritage Disputes* Oxford: OUP.

Chen, Zhen. 2022. 'Is a Mummy a Person or a Property: The Classification and Choice of Law of Cultural Objects in Private International Law' *The Chinese Journal of Comparative Law* 10(2): 274–296.

Childress III, Donald Earl. 2011. 'Introduction' in Donald E. Childress III (ed.) *The Role of Ethics in International Law* Cambridge: CUP 1–8.

Clunas, Craig. 1998. 'China in Britain: The Imperial Collections' in Tim Barringer & Tom Flynn (eds.) *Colonialism and the Object: Empire, Material Culture and the Museum* London: Routledge 41–51.

Cohan, John Alan. 2004. 'An Examination of Archaeological Ethics and the Repatriation Movement Respecting Cultural Property (Part Two)' *Environmental Law and Policy Journal* 28(1): 1–115.

Conaty, Gerald T. 2015a. 'The Development of Museums and Their Effects on First Nations' in Gerald T. Conaty (ed.) *We Are Coming Home!: Repatriation and the Restoration of Blackfoot Cultural Confidence* Athabasca, Edmonton: AU Press 37–69.

Conaty, Gerald T. 2015b. 'Niitsitapiisinni: Our Way of Life' in Gerald T. Conaty (ed.) *We Are Coming Home!: Repatriation and the Restoration of Blackfoot Cultural Confidence* Athabasca, Edmonton: AU Press 71–117.

Connelly, Joan Breton. 2014. *The Parthenon Enigma: A Journey into Legend* New York: Alfred A. Knopf.

Coody Cooper, Karen. 2008. *Spirited Encounters: American Indians Protest Museum Policies and Practices* Lanham, Maryland: AltaMira Press.

Crawford, James. 2002. *The International Law Commission's Articles on State Responsibility: Introduction, Text and Commentaries* Cambridge: CUP.

Curtis, Neil G.W. 2006. 'Universal Museums, Museum Objects and Repatriation: The Tangled Stories of Things' *Museum Management and Curatorship* 21(2): 117–127.

Curtis, Neil G.W. & Steph C. Scholten. 2022. 'Repatriation from Scottish Museums: A Short Report' *Santander Art and Culture Law Review* 8(2): 427–442.

David, Valeska. 2020. *Cultural Difference and Economic Disadvantage in Regional Human Rights Courts: An Integrated View* Cambridge: Intersentia.

Declaration on the Importance and Value of Universal Museums. Text reproduced in Neil G.W. Curtis (2006) 'Universal Museums, Museum Objects and Repatriation: The Tangled Stories of Things' *Museum Management and Curatorship* 21(2): 125–126.

Dedering, Tilman. 1999. 'The Prophet's "War Against Whites": Shepherd Stuurman in Namibia and South Africa, 1904–7' *The Journal of African History* 40: 1–19.

Deliss, Clémentine. 2021. 'Manifesto for the Right of Access to Colonial Collections Sequestered in Western European Museums', in Dan Hicks, Priya Basil, Haidy Geismar, Marlene Kadar, Emeka Ogboh, Fernando Domínguez Rubio, Clémentine Deliss, Nicholas Mirzoeff, Bonita Bennett, Ciraj Rassool & Ana Lucia Araujo *Necrography: Death-Writing in the Colonial Museum* British Art Studies 26 February 2021 Issue 19 London: Paul Mellon Centre for Studies in British Art 15-21.

De Lathuy, Philippe. 2018. *The Parthenon Marbles: A Landmark Case for the Future of the Repatriation Movement*, LLM Thesis by Research, University of Ghent.

Department of Sports, Arts, and Culture. 2021. National Policy (South Africa) on the Repatriation and Restitution of Human Remains and Heritage Objects <https://www.westerncape.gov.za/assets/departments/cultural-affairs-sport/draft_national_policy_on_the_repatriation_and_restitution_of_human_remains_and_heritage_objects.pdf>.

De Vattel, Emer (Joseph Chitty ed 1834 Online 2015). 1758. *The Law of Nations or the Principles of Natural Law* Cambridge: CUP.

Drobnig, Ulrich. 2011. 'Property' in Arthur Hartkamp, Martijn W. Hesselink, Ewoud H. Hondius, Chantal Mak & C. Edgar du Perron (eds.) *Towards a European Civil Code* 4th ed Alphen aan den Rijn, the Netherlands: Wolters Kluwer 1004–1023.

Dudley, Sandra H. 2018. 'The Buzz of Displacement: Liminality Among Burmese Court Objects in Oxford, London and Yangon' in Paul Basu (ed.) *The Inbetweenness of Things: Materializing Mediation and Movement between Worlds* New York: Bloomsbury Academic 38–56.

Dutch Council of Culture. 2020. *Report on the National Policy Framework for Colonial Collections in the Netherlands* <https://www.raadvoorcultuur.nl/documenten/adviezen/2020/10/07/summary-of-report-advisory-committee-on-the-national-policy-framework-for-colonial-collections>.

Dutch Council of Culture. 2021. *Colonial Collection: A Recognition of Injustice* The Hague <https://www.raadvoorcultuur.nl/english/documenten/adviezen/2021/01/22/colonial-collection-and-a-recognition-of-injustice>; <https://www.raadvoorcultuur.nl/english/documenten/adviezen/2020/10/07/summary-of-report-advisory-committee-on-the-national-policy-framework-for-colonial-collections>.

Dutch Ministry of Education, Culture and Science. 2021. *Policy Vision on Collections from a Colonial Context*, 29 January 2021 <https://open.overheid.nl/repository/ronl-d9b39619-d475-436c-aedd-0451cfc6bdb9/1/pdf/rapport-beleidsvisie-collecties-uit-een-koloniale-context.pdf>.

'Dutch Collector Faces Chinese Villagers in Lawsuit over Buddha Statue' *NL Times* 17 July 2017 <https://nltimes.nl/2017/07/17/dutch-collector-faces-chinese-villagers-lawsuit-buddha-statue>.

Eaton, Natasha. 2018. 'Colonial Iconoclash: Mimetic Rivalry, Collecting and Idolatry Between India and Britain' in Benedicte Savoy, Charlotte Guichard & Christine Howald (eds.) *Acquiring Cultures: Histories of World Art on Western Markets* Berlin: De Gruyter 31–46.

Echo-Hawk, Roger. 2002. *Keepers of Culture: Repatriating Cultural Items under the Native American Graves Protection and Repatriation Act* Denver: Denver Art Museum.

Effiboley, Emery Patrick. 2020. 'Reflections on the Issue of Repatriation of Looted and Illegally Acquired African Cultural Objects in Western Museums' *Contemporary Journal of African Studies* 7(1): 67–83.

Fanon, Frantz. 2004. *The Wretched of the Earth* (tr. Richard Philcox 1963) New York: Grove Press Inc.

Farneti, Roberto. 2013. 'Bipolarity Redux: The Mimetic Context of the "New Wars"' *Cambridge Review of International Affairs* 26(1): 181–202.

Faure, Bernard. 1994. *The Rhetoric of Immediacy: A Cultural Critique of Chan/Zen Buddhism* New Jersey: Princeton University Press.

Financial Action Task Force. 2023. *Report on Money Laundering and Terrorist Financing in the Art and Antiquities Market* https://www.fatf-gafi.org/content/dam/fatf-gafi/reports/Money-Laundering-Terrorist-Financing-Art-Antiquities-Market.pdf.coredownload.pdf

Flanagan, Owen. 2016. *The Geography of Morals: Varieties of Moral Possibility* Oxford Scholarship Online.

Förster, Larissa. 2020. 'The Face of Genocide' in Cressida Fforde, Timothy McKeown & Honor Keeler (eds.) *The Routledge Companion to Indigenous Repatriation* London: Routledge 101–127.

Förster, Larissa. 2021. 'Legal Questions from the Perspective of Social/Cultural Anthropology' in DMB *Guidelines for Care of Collections* Berlin: German Museums Association 165–168.

Gallagher, Steven. 2017. '"Purchased in Hong Kong": Is Hong Kong the Best Place to Buy Stolen or Looted Antiquities?' *International Journal of Cultural Property* 24(4): 479–496.

German Museums Association (DMB). 2021. *Guidelines for German Museums: Care of Collections from Colonial Contexts* 3rd ed, April 2021 <https://www.museumsbund.de/wp-content/uploads/2021/03/mb-leitfaden-en-web.pdf>

German Parliament Press Release 24.03.2023 <https://www.bundestag.de/presse/hib/kurzmeldungen-939936>

Girard, René. 1972. *Violence and the Sacred* (tr Patrick Gregory) Baltimore: The Johns Hopkins University Press.

Girard, René. 1982. *Le Bouc Emissaire* Paris: Editions Bernard Grasset.

Girard, René. 2010. *Battling to the End: Conversations with Benoit Chantre (Studies in Violence, Mimesis, and Culture)* (tr Mary Baker 2007) East Lansing: Michigan State University Press.

Girard, René. 2013 (tr. Malcolm B DeBevoise). *The One By Whom Scandal Comes*. East Lansing: Michigan State University Press.

Glenn, H. Patrick. 2011. 'The Ethic of International Law' in Donald E. Childress III (ed.) *The Role of Ethics in International Law* Cambridge: CUP 246–270.

Godelier, Maurice. 2002. 'Some Things You Give, Some Things You Sell, but Some Things You Must Keep for Yourselves: What Mauss Did Not Say about Sacred Objects' (tr. Nora Scott) in Edith Wyschogrod, Jean-Joseph Goux & Eric Boynton (eds.) *The Enigma of Gift and Sacrifice* New York: Fordham University Press 19–37.

Godt, Christine, Geertrui Van Overwalle, Lucie Guibault & Deryck Beyleveld. 2022. *Boundaries of Information Property, The Common Core of European Private Law Series vol 4* Cambridge: Intersentia.

Goldmann, Matthias. 2024. 'The Ambiguity of Colonial International Law: Three Approaches to the Namibian Genocide' *Leiden Journal of International Law* 37: 580.
Gorman, Joshua M. 2013. 'Universalism and the New Museology: Impacts on the Ethics of Authority and Ownership' in Janet Marstine, Alex A. Bauer & Chelsea Haines (eds.) *New Directions in Museum Ethics* New York: Routledge 76–89.
Gould, Cecil. 1965. *Trophy of Conquest: The Musée Napoléon and the Creation of the Louvre* London: Faber and Faber.
Grau, Donatien (ed.). 2021. *Under Discussion: The Encyclopedic Museum* Los Angeles: Getty Research Institute.
Grechi, Giulia. 2021. 'Whose Heritage? Restituire. Verso una Nuova Etica Relazionale' in *Decolonizzare il Museo. Mostrazioni, Pratiche Artistiche, Sguardi Incarnati* Milan: Mimesis Edizioni 153–162.
Greenblatt, Stephen. 1991. 'Resonance and Wonder' in Ivan Karp & Steven D. Lavine (eds.) *Exhibiting Cultures: The Poetics and Politics of Museum Display* Washington DC: Smithsonian Institution Scholarly Press 42–56.
Greenhalgh, Michael. 2019. *Plundered Empire: Acquiring Antiquities from Ottoman Lands* Leiden: Brill.
Griffin, Rayanne J. 1995. 'Sacred Site Protection against a Backdrop of Religious Intolerance' *Tulsa Law Journal* 31(2): 395–419.
Grimme, Gesa. 2020. 'Systemizing (sic) Provenance Research on Objects from Colonial Contexts' in Philipp Schorch (ed.) Special Issue on Sensitive Heritage: Ethnographic Museums, Provenance Research, and the Potentialities of Restitutions, *Museum and Society* 18(1) 52–65.
Gruber, Manuel. 2019. 'Time for a Reappraisal? The Intertemporal Principle of International Law Examined' *Australian International Law Journal* 26: 91–109.
Gunning, Lucia Patrizio & Debbie Challis. 2023. 'Planned Plunder, the British Museum, and the 1868 Maqdala Expedition' *The Historical Journal* 66(3): 550–572.
Hansard HC Deb. vol 672, col. 722, 2 March 2020.
Hansard HL Deb. vol 818, cols 1396, 8 February 2022.
Harris, Gareth. 2024. 'UK Politician Says Liberal Progressives Running Museums Must Resist Restitution' *The Art Newspaper* 8 April.
Hartley, Trevor C. 2009. *International Commercial Litigation* Cambridge: CUP.
Haughenbury, Sarah. 2016. *A Spectacle of the Odd: Constructing Otherness in the Odditoriums of Ripley's Believe it or Not* Master of Arts in Anthropology, University of South Carolina.
Herman, Alexander. 2021. *Restitution: The Return of Cultural Artefacts* London: Lund Humphries.
Herman, Alexander. 2023. *The Parthenon Marbles Dispute: Heritage, Law, Politics* Oxford: Hart Publishing.
Hicks, Dan. 2020. *Brutish Museums: The Benin Bronzes, Colonial Violence and Cultural Restitution* London: Pluto Press.
Hitchens, Christopher. 1997. *The Elgin Marbles: Should They be Returned to Greece?* (with essays by Robert Browning and Graham Binns) London: Verso.
Hobbes, Thomas. 1651. *Leviathan* Minneapolis: First Avenue editions.
Holden, Robert H. 2020. 'Violence, the State and Revolution in Latin America' in Louise Edwards, Nigel Penn & Jay Winter (eds.) *The Cambridge World History of Violence* Cambridge: CUP.
Honoré, Tony M. 1987. *Making Law Bind: Essays Legal and Philosophical* Oxford: Clarendon Press.
Human Remains in Collections Policy of National Museums Scotland, March 2016 updated in 2021 <https://www.nms.ac.uk/about-us/our-organisation/policies-and-reports/collections-policies/>.
Human Rights Council Report, *Repatriation of Ceremonial Objects and Human Remains under the UN Declaration on the Rights of Indigenous Peoples*, A/HRC/45/35 21 July 2020.

Hurley, Susan L. 1989. *Natural Reasons: Personality and Polity* Oxford: OUP.

Hyland, Richard. 2009. *Gifts: A Study in Comparative Law* Oxford: OUP.

ICPRCP. Twenty-second Session, 27–29 September 2021, ICPRCP/21/22.COM/Decisions, Decision 22. COM 6.

ICPRCP. Twenty-second Session, 27–29 September 2021, ICPRCP/22/23.COM/5.Rev.

ILA Committee on the Participation in Global Cultural Heritage Governance, Resolution 01/2022, Lisbon, 19–24 June 2022, 1.

International Movement for a New Museology (MINOM) 2010. 'Declaration of Quebec Basic Principles of a New Museology 1984' Sociomuseology IV, Cadernos de Sociomuseologia 38: 23–24.

Jacobs, Jordan & Benjamin W. Porter. 2021. 'Repatriation in University Museum Collections: Case Studies from the Phoebe A Hearst Museum of Anthropology' *International Journal of Cultural Property* 28(4): 513–550.

Jakubowski, Andrzej. 2009. 'Return of Illicitly Trafficked Cultural Objects Pursuant to Private International Law: Current Developments' in Ana Filipa Vrdoljak & Francesco Francioni (eds.) *The Illicit Traffic of Cultural Objects in the Mediterranean* (EUI Working Paper 2009).

Jakubowski, Andrzej. 2015. *State Succession in Cultural Property* Oxford: OUP.

Janes, Robert R. 2015. 'Prologue' in Gerald T. Conaty (ed.) *We Are Coming Home!: Repatriation and the Restoration of Blackfoot Cultural Confidence* Athabasca: AU Press 3–20.

Jenkins, David. 1994. 'Object Lessons and Ethnographic Displays: Museum Exhibitions and the Making of American Anthropology' *Comparative Studies in Society and History* 36(2): 242-270.

Jones, J. Walter. 1956. *The Law and Legal Theory of the Greeks: An Introduction* Oxford: Clarendon Press.

Kakaounaki, Marianna. 'A Greek Archaeologist's Dig into the Elgin Archive' *Kathimerini* 2 April 2024.

Kautondokwa, Nehoa Hilma. 2021. 'Curating with Communities: A Collaborative Partnership between the Museums Association of Namibia and Namibia San Council' in DMB *Guidelines on Care of Collections* Berlin: German Museums Association 136–139.

Kearney, Richard. 1995. 'Myths and Scapegoats: The Case of Rene Girard' *Theory Culture and Society* 12(4): 1–14.

Kearney, Richard. 2003. *Strangers, Gods and Monsters* London: Routledge.

Kennedy, Duncan. 1991. 'A Semiotics of Legal Argument' *Syracuse Law Review* 42(1): 75–116.

Kirwan, Michael. 2009. *Girard and Theology* London: T&T Clark.

Koskenniemi, Martti. 2017. 'Introduction: International Law and Empire–Aspects and Approaches' in Martti Koskenniemi, Walter Rech & Manuel Jiménez Fonseca (eds.) *International Law and Empire: Historical Explorations* Oxford: OUP 1–18.

Kühne, Thomas. 2013. 'Colonialism and the Holocaust: Continuities, Causations, and Complexities' *Journal of Genocide Research* 15(3): 339–362.

Kynourgiopoulou, Vasiliki. 2011. 'National Identity Interrupted: The Mutilation of the Parthenon Marbles and the Greek Claim for Repatriation' in Helaine Silverman (ed.) *Contested Cultural Heritage: Religion, Nationalism, Erasure and Exclusion in a Global World*. New York: Springer 155–170.

Labadi, Sophia. 2017. *Museums, Immigrants and Social Justice* London: Routledge.

Labadie, Camille. 2021. 'Decolonizing Collections: A Legal Perspective on the Restitution of Cultural Artifacts' *ICOFOM Study Series* 49(2): 132-146.

Lagardien, Ismael. 2022. *Too White to be Coloured, Too Coloured to be Black: On the Search for Home and Meaning* Cape Town: Melinda Ferguson Books.

Last, Kathryn V. 2007. 'Cultural Pluralism and the Return of Cultural Heritage' in Stephen Tierney (ed.) *Accommodating Cultural Diversity* Burlington: Ashgate 123–143.

Lavissière, Alexandre & Jean-Paul Rodrigue. 2017. 'Free Ports: Towards a Network of Trade Gateways' *Journal of Shipping and Trade* 2: 1–17.

Lemkin, Raphael & William Schabas. 2008. *Axis Rule in Occupied Europe: Laws of Occupation, Analysis of Government, Proposals for Redress* 2nd edn., Clark, New Jersey: The Lawbook Exchange, Ltd.

Lord Parkinson of Whitley Bay, the Minister for Arts and Heritage. Letter dated 31 January 2024, to Mr Orlando Fraser KC, the Chairman of the Charities Commission <https://assets.publishing.service.gov.uk/media/65bb826acc6fd6000d5dbe32/31.01.2024_Letter_from_Lord_Parkinson_to_Orlando_Fraser_-_s15-16-accessible.pdf>.

Little, Janet P. (ed and tr). 2003. *Simone Weil on Colonialism: An Ethic of the Other* Lanham, Maryland: Rowman & Littlefield Inc.

Liu, Zuozhen. 2017. 'Will the God Win?: The Case of the Buddhist Mummy' *International Journal of Cultural Property* 24(2): 221–238.

Lixinski, Lucas. 2019a. *International Heritage Law for Communities: Exclusion and Re-Imagination* Oxford Scholarship Online.

Lixinski, Lucas. 2019b. 'A Third Way of Thinking About Cultural Property' *Brooklyn Journal of International Law* 4(2): 563–612.

Loukaki, Argyro. 2008. *Living Ruins, Value Conflicts* London: Routledge.

Lynch, Bernadette T. 2011. 'Collaboration, Contestation, and Creative Conflict: On the Efficacy of Museum/Community Partnerships' in Janet Marstine (ed.) *The Routledge Companion to Museum Ethics: Redefining Ethics for the Twenty-First Century Museum* London: Routledge 146 –163.

Machado Haertel, Letícia. 2021. 'The Past, Present: The Parthenon Sculptures Dispute as an Example of the ICPRCP's Role on Claims Barred by the Non-Retrospectivity of the 1970 UNESCO Convention' *International Journal of Cultural Property* 28(4): 479–504.

Mackenzie, Simon R.M., Neil Brodie, Donna Yates & Christos Tsirogiannis. 2020. *Trafficking Culture: New Directions in Researching the Global Market in Illicit Antiquities* London: Routledge.

Madley, Benjamin. 2005. 'From Africa to Auschwitz: How German SouthWest Africa Incubated Ideas and Methods Adopted and Developed by the Nazis in Eastern Europe' *European History Quarterly* 35(3): 429–464.

Maine, Sir Henry. 1861. *Ancient Law* London: JM Dent & Sons Ltd.

Mattox, John. 2006. *Saint Augustine and the Theory of Just War* London: Continuum.

McBride, Nicholas J. & Sandy Steele. 2018. *Great Debates in Jurisprudence* (2nd ed) Great Britain: Palgrave.

McLachlan, Campbell. 2009. *Lis Pendens in International Litigation* Leiden: Martinus Nijhoff Publishers.

McMahon, Richard. 2007. *The Races of Europe: Anthropological Race Classification of Europeans 1839–1939* PhD Thesis, European University Institute.

Merryman, John H. 1985. 'Thinking About the Elgin Marbles' *Michigan Law Review* 83(8): 1880–1923.

Merryman, John H. 1986. 'Two Ways of Thinking about Cultural Property' *American Journal of International Law* 80(4): 831–853.

Merryman, John H. 1998. 'Leave the Marbles Where They Are!' <https://library.biblicalarchaeology.org/article/leave-the-marbles-where-they-are/>.

Miniotis, John Nicholas Saunders. 2014. *Defining the Characteristics of the Universal Museum: Missions, Collections, and Size* Master of Arts, University of Washington.

Murphy, David J. 1993. 'The People's Republic of China and the Illicit Trade in Cultural Property: Is the Embargo Approach the Answer?' *Asia Pacific Law Review* 2(2): 53–69.

Museums Association. 2021. *Supporting Decolonisation in Museums* <https://media.museumsassociation.org/app/uploads/2021/11/02155426/Supporting-decolonisation-in-museums.pdf>.

Neff, Stephen C. (ed and annotated). 2012. *Hugo Grotius on the Law of War and Peace* Cambridge: CUP.

Oh, Si-Jin. 2018. 'Historical Injustice in East Asia: A Case for Interspatial Law' *Pacific Focus* 33(3): 414–433.

Oughourlian, Jean-Michel. 1991. *The Puppet of Desire* Stanford: Stanford University Press.

Oxford University Procedures for Claims for the Return of Cultural Objects <https://www.glam.ox.ac.uk/procedures-for-return-of-cultural-objects-claims>.

Panesar, Sukhinder. 2000. 'Theories of Private Property in Modern Property Law' *The Denning Law Journal* 15: 113–138.

Paparrigopoulos Constantine. 1886. *History of the Hellenic Nation from Ancient Times to the Present* (tr. Mary Kitroeff) Hungary: OpenEdition Books.

Papa-Sokal, Marina. 2009. 'Beyond the Nationalist-Internationalist Polarisation in the Protection of Archaeological Heritage: A Response to Professor Merryman' *Art, Antiquity and Law* 14: 237–274.

Paterson, Robert K. 1996. 'The "Curse of the London Nataraja"' *International Journal of Cultural Property* 5(2): 330–338.

Paterson, Robert K. 2014. 'The Art of the Sale: Museums and Deaccessioning' in Valentina Vadi & Hildegard E.G.S. Schneider (eds.) *Art, Cultural Heritage and the Market* Heidelberg: Springer 273–295.

People's Republic of China, *National Report to UNESCO: Implementation of the 1970 Convention on the Means of Prohibiting and Preventing the Illicit Import, Export and Transfer of Ownership of Cultural Property 2011–2015* C70/11/National-report/China.

Prott, Lyndel. 2005. 'The International Movement of Cultural Objects' *International Journal of Cultural Property* 12(2): 225–248.

Rassool, Ciraj. 2015. 'Re-storing the Skeletons of Empire: Return, Reburial and Rehumanisation in Southern Africa' *Journal of Southern African Studies* 41(3): 653–670.

Report from the Select Committee of the House of Commons on the Earl of Elgin's Collection of Sculptured Marbles, 1816 London: W. Bulmer and Co.

Robson, James. 2003. 'A Tang Dynasty Chan Mummy [Roushen] and a Modern Case of Furta Sacra? Investigating the Contested Bones of Shitou Xiquian' in Bernard Faure (ed.) *Chan Buddhism in Ritual Context* London: Routledge 151–178.

Roodt, Christa & David Carey Miller. 2013. 'Stolen Cultural Property: Implications of Vitium Reale in Private Law and Private International Law' *Transnational Dispute Management* 10(5): 1–10.

Rosén, Frederik. *NATO and Cultural Property: Embracing New Challenges in the Era of Identity Wars, Report on Best Practices for Cultural Property Protection in NATO-led Military Operations 2014–2017* (NATO SPS project G4866) 2017.

Roth, Henry Ling. 1903. *Great Britain. Its Customs, Art and Horrors* Halifax: Smithsonian Libraries.

Rubin, Avi. 2011. *Ottoman Nizamiye Courts: Law and Modernity* London: Palgrave MacMillan.

Rudenstine, David. 2000. 'Did Elgin Cheat at Marbles?' *The Nation* 270(21): 30–34.

Rudenstine, David. 2021. 'Trophies for the Empire: The Epic Dispute Between Greece and England Over the Parthenon Sculptures in the British Museum' *Cardozo Arts & Entertainment Law Journal* 39: 377–505.

Schneider, Marina. 2016. 'The 1995 UNIDROIT Convention: An Indispensable Complement to the 1970 UNESCO Convention and an Inspiration for the 2014/60/EU Directive' Santander Art and Culture Law Review 2(2): 149-164.

Shapiro, Daniel. 1998. 'Repatriation: A Modest Proposal' *New York University Journal of International Law and Politics* 31(1): 95–108.

Sharf, Robert H. 1992. 'The Idolization of Enlightenment: On the Mummification of Ch'an Masters in Medieval China' *History of Religions* 32(1): 1–31.

Simpson, Moira G. 1996. *Making Representations: Museums in the Post-Colonial Era,* London: Routledge.

Smith, Arthur Hamilton. 1916. 'Lord Elgin and His Collection' *The Journal of Hellenic Studies* 36: 163–372.

Smithsonian Institution. 2022a. Shared Stewardship and Ethical Returns Policy, 29 April <https://ncp.si.edu/sites/default/files/files/Ethical%20Return%20Docs/shared-stewardship-ethical-returns-policy_4.29.2022.pdf>.

Smithsonian Institution. 2022b. Directive 600, 12 May <https://www.si.edu/content/pdf/about/sd/SD600.pdf>.

Smithsonian Institution, National Museum of the American Indian, Repatriation Policy February 2014 <https://americanindian.si.edu/sites/1/files/pdf/repatriation/NMAI-RepatriationPolicy-2014.pdf>.

Soirila, Pauno. 2022. 'Indeterminacy in the Cultural Property Restitution Debate' *International Journal for Cultural Policy* 28(1): 1–16.

Spitra, Sebastian M. 2021. 'The Administration of Culture in International Law Since the 19th Century: A New Historical Narrative' *University of Vienna Law Review* 5(1): 121–158.

Stahn, Carsten. 2022. 'Beyond "To Return or Not to Return" – The Benin Bronzes as a Game Changer?' *Santander Art and Culture Law Review* 8(2): 29–68.

Stahn, Carsten. 2023. *Confronting Colonial Objects: Histories, Legalities, and Access to Culture* Oxford: OUP.

Stamatoudi, Irini & Elena Korka. 2013. 'The Parthenon Marbles Issue: Legal, Ethical and Political Issues' in *Proceedings of the 3rd International Conference of Experts on the Return o*f Cultural property Hellenic Ministry of Culture and Sports, 23 Oct 2013–26 Oct 2013.

St Clair, William. 2006. 'Imperial Appropriations of the Parthenon' in John Henry Merryman (ed.) *Imperialism, Art, and Restitution* Cambridge: CUP 65–97.

Stewart-Harawira, Makere. 2005. *The New Imperial Order: Indigenous Response to Globalization* London: Zed Books.

Stuart, James & Nicholas Revett. 1762. *The Antiquities of Athens Vol 2* London: J. Haberkorn.

Supiot, Alain. 2007. *Homo Juridicus: On the Anthropological Function of the Law* London: Verso.

Theurer, Karina. 2023. 'Minimum Legal Standards in Reparation Processes for Colonial Crimes: The Case of Namibia and Germany' *German Law Journal* 24(7): 1146–1168.

Thielecke, Carola & Michael Geißdorf. 2021. 'Collections from Colonial Contexts: Legal Aspects' DMB *Guidelines for Care of Collections* Berlin: German Museums Association 153–164.

Thompson, Kenneth (ed.) 2005. *Readings from Emile Durkheim* Revised ed. London: Routledge.

Titi, Catherine. 2023. *The Parthenon Marbles and International Law* Switzerland: Springer.

Truth and Reconciliation Commission of Canada. 2015. Final Report, *Honouring the Truth, Reconciling the Future.*

Tuhiwai Smith, Linda.2021. *Decolonizing Methodologies: Research and Indigenous Peoples* (3rd ed) London: Zed Books

US National Intelligence Council. 2017. *Global Trends: Paradox of Progress.*

UN General Assembly, *Report of the Secretary General on the Implementation of the International Decade for People of African Descent* Doc. No. A/78/317, 18 August 2023.

Van der Walt, Johan. 2018. 'The Origins of Legal Obligations: Towards a Fundamental Phenomenology of Moral and Legal Obligation' in Daniel Matthews & Scott Veitch (eds.) *Law, Obligation, Community* London: Routledge 35–70.

Van Woudenberg, Nout. 2016. 'Adherence to the 1995 UNIDROIT Convention: Wider Than One Would Think at First Sight' *Uniform Law Review* 21(1): 120-128.

Veraart, Wouter. 2015. 'Between Justice and Legal Closure: Looted Art Claims and the Passage of Time' in Evelien Campfens (ed.) *'Fair and Just Solutions?' Alternatives to Litigation in Nazi-Looted Art Disputes: Status Quo and New Developments* The Hague: Eleven International Publishing 211–221.

Virdee, Satnam. 2019. 'Racialized Capitalism: An Account of its Contested Origins and Consolidation' *The Sociological Review* 67(1) 3–27.

Von Bar, Christian & Eric Clive (eds.). 2010. *Principles, Definitions and Model Rules of European Private Law: Draft Common Frame of Reference vol. 5* Oxford: OUP.

Von Bulow, Mathilde. 2016. *West Germany, Cold War Europe and the Algerian War* Cambridge: CUP.

Voudouri, Daphne. 2008. 'Greek Legislation Concerning the International Movement of Antiquities and its Ideological and Political Dimensions' in Dimitris Damaskos & Dimitris Plantzos (eds.) *A Singular Antiquity: Archaeology and Hellenic Identity in Twentieth Century Greece, 3rd Supplement* Athens: Mouseio Benaki 125–139.

Vrdoljak, Ana F. 2008. *International Law, Museums and the Return of Cultural Objects* Cambridge: CUP.

Wadsworth, Tanner J. 2023. 'The Advantages of Giving up: Greece and the Futile Quest to Force the Parthenon Marbles Home by Judgment' *Columbia Journal of European Law* 29(1): 129–151.

wa Thiong'o, Ngũgĩ. 1986. *Decolonising the Mind: The Politics of Language in African Literature* Nairobi: EAEP.

Weasel Head, Frank. 2015. 'Repatriation Experiences of the Kainai' in Gerald T. Conaty (ed.) *We Are Coming Home!: Repatriation and the Restoration of Blackfoot Cultural Confidence* Athabasca: AU Press 151–181.

Weil, Simone. 2002. *The Need for Roots: Prelude to a Declaration of Duties Towards Mankind (*tr AF Wills 1952) London: Routledge.

Weststein, Arthur. 2017. 'Provincializing Grotius: International Law and Empire in the Seventeenth-Century Malay Mirror' in Martti Koskenniemi, Walter Rech & Manuel Jimenez Fonseca (eds.), *International Law and Empire: Historical Explorations* OUP 21-38.

Wheaton, Henry. 1866. *Elements of International Law* (Eighth edition, edited, with notes by Richard Henry Dana, Jr.) London: Sampson Low, Son & Co.

Whitby-Last, Kathryn. 2011. 'Legal Advice for the Care of Human Remains' in *Scottish Museum Collections, Guidelines for the Care of Human Remains in Scottish Museum Collections*https://www.museumsgalleriesscotland.org.uk/wp-content/uploads/2023/06/guidelines-for-the-care-of-human-remains-in-scottish-museum-collections.pdf.

Winiger, Benedict. 2018. *Responsibility, Restoration, Fault* Cambridge: Intersentia.

Winkelmann, Andreas. 2020. 'Repatriations of Human Remains from Germany – 1911–2019' Special Issue on Sensitive Heritage: Ethnographic Museums, Provenance Research, and the Potentialities of Restitutions (in Philipp Schorch ed.) *Museum and Society* 18(1): 40–51.

Williams, Andrew J. 2014. *France, Britain and the United States in the Twentieth Century 1900–1940: A Reappraisal* London: Palgrave Macmillan.

Wood, Paul. 2012. 'Display, Restitution and World Art History: The Case of the "Benin Bronzes"' *Visual Culture in Britain* 13(1): 115–137.

Woodhead, Charlotte. 2023. *Caring for Cultural Heritage: An Integrated Approach to Legal and Ethical Initiatives in the United Kingdom* Cambridge: CUP.

Zeidler, Kamil. 2016. *Restitution of Cultural Property: Hard Case, Theory of Argumentation, Philosophy of Law* Gdańsk: Gdańsk University Press.

Zimmerer, Jürgen (Andrew H. Beattie, trans.). 2004. 'Colonialism and the Holocaust: Towards an Archaeology of Genocide', in A. Dirk Moses (ed.) *Genocide and Settler Society: Frontier Violence and Stolen Aboriginal Children in Australian History* New York: Berghahn Books 49–76.

Zimmerer, Jürgen. 2021. 'European Colonialism: Political, Economic, and Cultural Aspects of Early Globalisation' DMB *Guidelines on Care of Collections* Berlin: German Museums Association 94–104.

3 Overcoming fundamental fragmentation in the law

3.1 Introduction

The sacred is frequently understood in a limited sense. Its many forms exist within but also outside of institutionalised religions, and so it cannot be reduced to the specific beliefs of individual religions or confined to ritual as a phenomenon. Gaps continue to loom in the protective regime because needless and frivolous distinctions stand in the way of achieving a common conception of the sacred. The central proposition of this study is that a common definition and understanding of 'the sacred' in the context of colonial legacies brings with it pathways to overcome the fundamental problem of fragmentation within and between legal systems and norms which currently hampers restitution and repatriation efforts. A common conception of the sacred has inevitable implications for law reform, jurisprudence and policymaking that deserve systematic study. Legal barriers need to be crossed to begin the process of repatriation and cultural tensions between different legal traditions diffused. Girard's theory does not limit the 'sacred' to religious contexts in a narrow sense, nor does it confine its function and meaning to 'ritual.' The meaning of 'sacred' is collectively constituted in it and is not conferred indiscriminately nor arbitrarily. This makes Girard's theory a useful frame for the developments in the emerging field of restitution of intangible cultural heritage.

Commercial exchanges in global markets for cultural material interrupt the fluidity of knowledge exchange between past, present, and future. For instance, reducing the power of medicine bundles to heal and bless to mere manifestations of primitive forms of worship, fetishes, or objects with 'mysterious' or curious protective powers will see their spiritual significance disappear by the time they are restored back to where they belong (Parker 1990: 43; Simpson 1996: 200). Many types of sacred material harvested during expeditions make the rounds in exhibitions; however, the displaying of sensitive items to 'demystify' them for Western audiences are highly inappropriate for source cultures. Through the marketisation and commoditisation of cultures, oral traditions cease to transmit knowledge concerning the authority that material believed to be imbued with a life force and spiritual potency carries. The acceleration of the wheels of commerce distorts the universality of the 'sacred'.

After the disappearance of the Zhanggong Zushi statue its spiritual and cultural meaning was transferred onto a replica and the devotional rituals continued to be

DOI: 10.4324/9781003565314-3

practised by the community in the original location. The effect of ritual in building and sustaining community is truly 'universal.' Ritual persists where religion is in decline because it cultivates non-violent behaviours that decelerate the mimetic drive and nurtures 'values that privilege the interrelationships among the spiritual, the natural, and the self' (Greenwood and de Leeuw 2007: 48–53). The 'sacred' carries obligations to see its meaning fulfilled. When decontextualisation drains the material of meaning, these obligations prompt action. The parallel lawsuits instituted in courts in East Asia and Europe demonstrate that the replica of the Buddha Mummy replica could never replace the ancestor. The replica does not mirror all the intangible qualities of the physical object.

Science may clash with the sacred when democratic liberal orders embrace innovative technology and theocracies with antidemocratic tendencies turn against minority faiths. The dichotomy may also manifest on purely moral and legal planes. It makes sense to start by asking whether moral theory can provide any steer to restitution claims in the absence of a common definition for the 'sacred,' before moving to investigate the potential of the ethic of law in relation to the 'sacred.'

3.2 Moral clashes and moral theory

The best-known models of moral theory do not necessarily draw from a meta-conception of human nature framed around similar ideas about individual human agency or state command of their behaviour. Western models are located on an ethical scale, from consequentialist (utilitarian) to non-consequentialist (deontological). The contours of the best-known consequentialist theory were drawn by the 19th-century philosophers Jeremy Bentham (1748–1832) and John Stuart Mill (1806–1873). Their approach considers as the most important moral consideration in decision-making whether it promotes happiness for more people than it would cause suffering for. The greatest happiness of society—all those whose interests are at stake in a decision—is the morally correct and universally desirable end of human action in the business of government where functionaries exercise the powers of Government (Bentham 1988: 70). Bentham's felicific (hedonic) calculus compares the amount of pleasure and pain with factors like duration and intensity for each person affected. This type of calculus is used in law and economics approaches that seek to determine the 'highest-valued' location for sacred cultural material such as the Parthenon Marbles. The value of the number of people who may enjoy the aesthetic experience of viewing the Marbles in competing locations is weighed against the intensity of the desire for possession in locations that do not offer the same viewing experience. The utilitarian doctrine of happiness was supposed to be altruistic because the happiness of all was considered. Both Bentham and Mill favoured the 'higher' pleasures of the intellect and imagination which promote education, cultural awareness, and moral sentiments over the 'lower' pleasures inhering in mere sensations that are satisfied superficially and fleetingly.

Since utilitarianism is such a vast area of ethics, broad brushstrokes will not do. The weighing it requires to express the common good as the simple sum of narrowly focused individual interests, is over-simplistic and rights and duties are relegated to a secondary position. Given that public preferences change and are prone to contradictions, it is meaningless to keep citing polls to back one stance or another. As indicators of what is good, such polls are flawed (Zeidler 2016: 88). There is no empirical methodology that can accurately calculate the outcomes of pleasure or pain for countless stakeholders. Measuring and evaluating difference is vital in socio-legal research but attempts to create benchmarks from empirical study or quantitative surveys of restitution claims involving sacred cultural material or human remains from the colonial era stifle debate (Flanagan 2016: 133, 140). The educational contribution of western cultural institutions as high traffic tourist destinations cannot justify their role as the ultimate keepers of local and tribal knowledge. The pleasure of viewers in the British Museum is wholly incommensurate with the pleasure of Greek citizens having autonomy over their cultural heritage.

The DIVUM echoes a utilitarian approach with its assertion that museums serve not just 'the citizens of one nation but the people of every nation.' Elevated aims to link the whole of humanity together spurred researchers to fit objects into an all-encompassing worldview of peoples and their cultures. Institutions such as the British Museum could then be 'a global resource for the citizens of the world' (MacGregor and Williams 2005: 57ff). These claims collapsed along with claims that the safety and conservation of objects may be put at risk by repatriation in the wake of Hartwig Fischer's resignation as Director of the British Museum in August 2023 when it transpired that insider thefts had not been properly investigated. Arguments about which social order can provide the best level of care and conservation for objects, and comparisons between institutions in this respect, draw on the importance of the Eurocentric model of conservation. The risk of theft and black-market trade increases in periods of conflict and political instability, but a Eurocentric model equates political instability with the inability to preserve historical memory. Comparisons of care can regress into a mimetic race ifutilitarianism is the moral safety net, since it obscures the real concern of some museums to retain the largest possible collections. Not only have efforts to maintain purely Euro-American centric forms of knowledge become increasingly untenable as the dominance of the North Atlantic powers shrinks, but the diversity of society increases even in the 'old imperial centres.'

Deontology and teleology both make room for obligations, but the origin of those obligations differs fundamentally. In a teleological approach, the end is paramount; obligations arise to achieve it. Deontological ethics focus on the intrinsic nature of conduct and consider duty to be a basic orientation for existence. Moral action is necessary in and of itself and everyone should act in the same way because it is right (Holmes 1998: 20). A weaker deontological theory permits considerations to weigh in on what is considered right, such as fairness, truth, promises, and undertakings. Goodness is relevant to what is right, albeit not decisive. Turning to the categorical imperative of what is right and wrong, which Immanuel Kant conceived as wholly independent of what is good or bad, we see legality and morality remaining distinct. The Kantian instruction of a universalistic moral theory is threefold: (1) to 'act only according to that maxim by which you can at the same time will that it should become a universal law' (meaning that an act qualifies as a moral act if the person who committed it were willing for it to have general application); (2) act in such a way that you treat humanity never as a mere means to an end but always as an end; and (3) contemplate the will of every rational being as a universally legislating will (Kant 1983). The hierarchy of races which he proposed existed beneath white Europeans in texts published during the 1780s was supplanted by a more egalitarian view that did not espouse white superiority by the 1790s (Kleingeld 2007: 573). Neo-Kantianism was the dominant philosophical movement in Germany between 1870 and the First World War, but Hitler's rise to power caused it to become sidelined.

Non-consequentialist moral theory does not promote ethical decision-making concerning restitution in a consistent manner. No maxim can fix the attitude of a slave owner who is convinced that slavery makes the economy thrive and that the compassion of the slave owner suffices (Flanagan 2016: 156). Universal deontological maxims may conflict with some leading to actions that most would consider reprehensible and others failing to capture the urgency or significance of the situation. A universal law that sacred looted material must be restituted to a state museum, for instance, could deny the rightful owner or cultural community access to their cultural heritage. Maxims that elevate unrestricted movement and trade in, and non-restitution of sacred cultural material, to a universal praxis, may cement the normative effects of mimetism. Maxims underestimate the considerable emotional charge that accompanies disputes about sacred cultural treasures, both as resources and as ideologies. Targeting of cultural heritage and the removal and intentional destruction of cultural or religious monuments representative of the contribution of targeted groups to the cultural heritage of humankind invoke the cultural genocide foreshadowed in Lemkin's work (Vrdoljak 2008: 163). The dynamic of human behaviour at the meta-conception of human nature is more accurately captured by the description of the moral wrestler than by any maxim, for a person may face a conflict between the quest for pleasure and happiness of some kind and the quest to live up to their moral values or responsibilities that provide a sense of affirmation (Etzioni 2018: 4).

Neither consequentialist nor non-consequentialist moral theories provide constructive criteria for normativity. They are too closely identified with the Enlightenment (Flanagan 2016: 45). Analytic philosophy of the 20th century cannot have a stronger claim than the material philosophies and ethics as relates to Navajo cultural heritage, for instance, as thecriteria to select one over another are lacking. No centralised agency can reconcile the colliding value systems inculcated by philosophies embedded in everyday practice with philosophies emanating from abstract systems of academic thought emerging from specialised institutional structures associated with the European mould of education, industrialisation, and Kantian antinomies (Da Col and Graeber 2011: vi, xi n3).

Moral systems interact in a multicultural context. The virtues, values, and norms that define one worldview may be entirely incongruous with those informing another, with neither one being 'better' or 'truer.' Rather than contemplate a choice between 'principle' and 'consequence,' it is more constructive to acknowledge the difficulty inherent in translating and comprehending others' cultural positions (Flanagan 2016: 141). A form of life that has better resources to solve a problem or set of problems is likely to supersede the competition (Flanagan 2016: 46). The interaction of moral systems may also introduce novel possibilities leading to either radical change or incremental adjustments of norms, values, and practices (Flanagan 2016: 155). Radical shifts may follow when cultural restitution claims are shown to have moral benefits that outweigh other ideas of maximising benefit. German sociologist Max Weber (1864–1920) posited a normative ethics that offer an alternative to the formal ethical theory of late modernity (De Villiers 2017: 8). The Weberian ethic of responsibility has been interpreted exclusively as responsibility for consequences, but Weber understood 'responsibility' to be a moral principle that could be qualified not just by consequence, but also by necessity or feasibility. Such a responsibility arises when, through knowledge and acknowledgement, conditions are created that support reconciliation in the next generation. Weber's ethic of responsibility provides the next generation with the opportunity to resolve hatred instead of repeating cycles of atrocity. It renders the ethic of responsibility applicable to policymaking in respect of repatriation, and may also give direction to adjudication in which normative conflicts are resolved by having recourse to law. Girard's theory is not constructed around responsibility but is alive to the cyclical pattern of the mimetic drive which the sacred can break.

3.3 Normative conflicts (PrIL) against a backdrop of competition and the sacred

A heightened awareness of the ethical dilemmas surrounding museum collections could foster a drastic renegotiation of ownership of sacred cultural heritage. Values, obligations, duties, and rights will continue to invite contestation, but a wider understanding of 'normativity' and the 'sacred' will help curb the normative pressure which mimetic competition can generate for cultural heritage. It may also make meaningful law reform possible. At the level of the material alone, the 'sacred' adds more definition to the connections between Nazi spoliated art, stolen and unlawfully excavated archaeological material, and the colonial removals that are clearly unethical. For example, Jewish temples, ceremonial art, and Judaica could meet the definition just as unearthed and artefactual human remains and grave goods may.

Normative reform of primary legal rules and uniform law is not always feasible. For instance, reform is ruled out in respect of the process elements in genocide. While restitution models and solutions may become more identifiable and workable as political and legal frameworks adjust and change, no change is likely in respect of the distinction between physical–biological genocide and cultural genocide. The distinction is the result of a legal controversy, but it is also ascribable to the fragmentation caused by the conceptual priority claimed by the human body in the west. Against the backdrop of the unlikelihood of law reform, a common understanding of the 'sacred' that connects the aims and priorities of the study with its structure and method, becomes vital. The 'sacred' is the common ground on which a unifying model of the social and human sciences can emerge to support those who are struggling to articulate the conceptual basis of claims or to formulate policy frameworks and the structure of law and ethics argument for restitution. Inquiry into the common core of the 'sacred' dislodges fractious thinking and unifies approaches to claims for sacred heritage looted or trafficked during the colonial era. The 'sacred' also brings about a foundational shift in the discourse about the repatriation of the Parthenon Marbles as it dismantles the British colonial narrative while it connects with the Greeks' responsibility to re-interpret the Marbles as intangible heritage that belongs to the Athenians alone. Both narratives are light-years away from the popular dichotomous interpretations harking back to either 'cultural internationalism' or 'cultural nationalism.' The breadth of the scope of the 'sacred' has implications for normativity of law, moral theory, and ethical precepts, which European legal and policy frameworks have not yet worked out. They do not take account of depth perspectives on the 'sacred' and normativity, which bring greater coherence to ad hoc attempts to constrain the normative thrust of mimetism. Facts concerning the 'sacred' and the 'normative' are interdependent categories of thinking, but their interdependence produces moral and legal obligations.

In transnational disputes the law that can be established with certainty is typically considered to be the 'better' law to apply because the ready availability of information about its content, application, and interpretation makes it so. Cost–benefit analyses indicate that, in disputes involving cultural property, uniform law fares better than PrIL rules and approaches (Kono 2020). Yet uniform law does not provide much support for the return of sacred cultural heritage beyond objects used in ritual by a tribal or Indigenous community. The special rules regarding protections and returns of cultural heritage in these instruments are frequently unavailable and resort needs to be had to residual conflict rules. As such, PrIL's tools of legal reasoning and the ways in which the toolmakers have arranged them in different toolboxes for different purposes, deserve to be studied. If the interaction between PrIL and ethics can be better supported, pathways to repatriation may become more visible.

In transnational cases legal norms may be in symbiosis across space, but the level of legal diversity in the world may set competing regimes in opposition and 'at war.' The present state of PrIL in and of itself also conjures a battleground of competing ideas from across time where no grand objective has emerged from antithetical and opposing conceptions. Conceptual oppositions include the clash between territorialism and personalism (i.e., the territoriality of laws and the personality of laws); unilateral and multilateral choice-of-law methods; and national conflicts systems and aspirations towards a uniform conflict of laws system (Hatzimihail 2021: 78–79, 139 ff). The personality of the tribal personal laws of African and Asian colonies was considered to be different from PrIL in the 19th century; indeed, it has been claimed that 'intercustomary' law developed from the interpersonal laws regime (Hatzimihail 2021: 75). To place PrIL doctrines into their proper context, historicisation is desirable (Banu 2022: 385). 'Pedigree history' may be expressed as a quest, a dialectic, a narrative, or an opposition (Hatzimihail 2021: 79–92). It would be important to remain alert to the fact that the historical narrative can be deployed as an argumentative device. Medieval and Early Modern conflicts may yield insights on substantive policies pursued by colonial law and the international legal order that superimposed itself on the law of the forum. However, conceptual oppositions are bound to appear in the approach adopted to history. The historical narrative could gradually be weaponised (Hatzimihail 2021: 91). For one thing, the history of PrIL doctrine stands isolated from general European legal history and developments in jurisprudence, private law, the international system, or legal theory. For another, it is a very different undertaking to recreate the past with the eyes of the present than to use the past to explain the present (Hatzimihail 2021: 84, 110, 135). When historical approaches to the pedigree of PrIL start to vie for the upper hand in restitution claims, it would be vital to strive for balance. The factual circumstances of historical injustices and the voices of those affected must be remembered. A follow-up study investigates what PrIL could offer as lessons of history for restitution claims (*Restoration and the Law of Restitution: Complex Colonial Contexts*).

The ambiguity of legal norms in the restitution debate is brought to light by Girard's mimetic theory and the mechanism that hems in the mimetic drive within it. Using mimetic theory to frame normative uncertainty clarifies why one would-look to law as an ethic and a 'practical reason' and to secondary legal norms that determine the spatial and temporal scope of primary legal norms, found in PrIL. Concerned with secondary legal normsPrIL's methodology offers a theory and a method for thinking about the same perennial questions against the backdrop of an aspiration for 'global justice.' There is scope to clarify the contribution which PrIL's methodology can make, alongside its contribution in balancing formal rationality with value rationality, to reduce injustice and advance justice. The integration of primary and secondary legal norms with the juridical framework of exception based on PrIL's ethical dimension promises more benefits for the law of restitution. The contribution its common principles can make, must be clarified. PrIL's attunement to public policy and provenance research in the domain of restitution deserves to weigh in on an evaluation of its capacity to deliver a jurisprudence of power in complex colonial contexts. Clearer communication concerning its connectivity to other legal disciplines—public law, including criminal law and international humanitarian law—is another important component of the restoration of law and of the operation of legal norms in complex colonial contexts.

The 'sacred' may cast light on the recognition of foreign concepts and PrIL classification in adjudicating ownership claims It is only when the intangible qualities of the sacred are seen in the proper light that the legal norms that limit the time available for an original owner's claim for recovery of sacred material looted or trafficked during the colonial era can be put in a proper perspective. A more integrated law and ethics approach makes for a sturdier critical framework for the vexing legal questions about the extinction of a right that ceases to exist and the procedural barring of the remedy that precludes the claim from proceeding. This non-legal factor can indicate that the claim needs to be heard on the merits and that an alternate chronosophy is better suited for adjudication on time limitations. A common understanding of the sacred is also expected to help reframe the context in which technology is invoked in claims for restitution. Just as a copy cannot sustain the intangible qualities of the physical object, the transfer of sacred and intangible properties of cultural heritage into physical replicas and digital environments remain constrained; they cannot stop the interminable gaps left by colonialism in the legal and ethical framework for the protection of intangible cultural heritage.

3.4 Restoring the law of restitution, repatriation, and return

Disagreements arise in legal circles over the issue of ownership of cultural property and heritage that cannot be settled to everyone's satisfaction. These disagreements are not just about legal norms. They encompass the semantic, semiotic, and conceptual. Semantic ploys aim to secure semiotic advantage; they protect 'blind spots' in areas in which normative uncertainty prevails, such as technology. Conceptual disagreements occur at various levels. At the material level, e.g., complex objects may be described differently if one alters one's perspective or views on the significance of descriptions of their component features. The dichotomous divide between 'law' and 'ethics' promote polarised narratives and stale, circular arguments. Non-compliance with moral standards puts pressure on 'justice' yet is a by-product of formalist legal argument based on positivist notions of what 'law' is and what 'law' does.

The methodology of materiality and the anthropology of ideal formation refer to the 'sacred' in discussions about restitution, but legal debates over ownership only pay random attention to the unresolved question of its definition. At the level of systems of knowledge associated with the tangible and the intangible, fragmentation impacts cultural sectors including higher education. Fragmentation thrives also at the subtle level of language. Obscure language has grave implications for norm formation and the decoupling of 'private' and 'public' in law's subject specialisms add to the complications. The structure and method of international law and the invocation of technicalities in normative conflicts routinely draw a veil over 'sacred' cultural property and heritage in transnational litigation, obscuring their nature. Dichotomizing classifications between 'commercial' and 'non-commercial' have shaped legal argument in the colonial era but also imprinted on legal thought. Problems are noticeable at the interplay between historical events and the legal mechanisms premised on time as a gatekeeper that provides reasons for why the merits of a transnational case cannot be heard and an order for restitution cannot be issued.

Faced with the special social question raised by claims to cultural heritage looted and trafficked during the colonial era, adjudicators and policymakers must formulate novel responses. The success of restitutionary claims to sacred heritage depends on an understanding of the non-legal factor that drives claims. At the core of claims to sacred material lies their intangible heritage value but the legal tools are not in place to meet these demands. The main challenge is to find and define this factor in a way that integrates tangible and intangible, cuts across social sciences and humanities, surmounts the dichotomies the plague the field, and relaxes the unstinting belief that there is a single, unified chronology for complex colonial histories. Researchers are called to explore the taxonomic implications of intangible qualities of complex sacred material for law and ethics, and to work towards a common legal basis for claims. The most challenging questions are how a non-legal factor—the 'sacred'—affects the taxonomies of private and public law, and those posed by the time factor and by new technologies that encourage fragmentation. Focusing on the complex and contradictory relationship between human rights and religions is unlikely to provide adequate direction (Fagan 2017: 192–193). Among other things, cultural elements of genocide remain hidden inside the myths informing national identity, stoking ethnocentrism and ethnic prejudice. It is important that the questions we formulate are led by what nurtures human capabilities, promotes human development, and inspires ways of living based on more than just competitive self-interested pre-occupations.

Giving shape and substance to a vision of restoring the law of restitution is as urgent as restoring collections looted or trafficked during the colonial era. However, the different understandings that attach to different cultural conceptions of the 'sacred' affect how cases are dealt with and promote clashing outcomes. While the 'sacred' is all-encompassing in an Indigenous world view, secular circles do not always accommodate the 'sacred' in discussions about the return of cultural heritage. Focusing exclusively on national heritage inevitably produces gaps in conceptions of responsibility. The structure and 'ethic' of the law stands to be strengthened by a common definition and understanding of the intangible 'sacred.' Among other things, the 'sacred' invites the possibility that obligations and the nature of legal obligations may be conceived before conceiving of rights and without invoking a rights discourse. Issues such as standing, a common legal basis for claims, and alternate chronosophy in restitution claims, deserve consideration along with what PrIL is capable of.

Disputes for which the legal argument for restitution is in evident need of refinement will serve as valuable points of orientation. The Parthenon Sculptures dispute and the parallel transnational litigation in the Zhanggong Zushi Statue cases reveal what adjudicators and policymakers need to know about the troubling hurdles encountered by claimants who wish to pursue legal pathways and norms supporting restitution and repatriation. Thesedisputes are paradigmatic of the fragmentation in legal and ethical frameworks that envelop complex material, the systems of knowledge associated with that material, the structure and method of international law, and the split across subject specialisms.

Bibliography

Banu, Roxana. 2022. 'Teaching by Historicising Private International Law' *International Journal of Law in Context* 18(4): 383–392.

Bentham, Jeremy. 1988. *The Principles of Morals and Legislation (1823)* Buffalo, NY: Prometheus Books.

Da Col, Giovanni & David Graeber. 2011. 'Foreword: The Return of Ethnographic Theory' *HAU: Journal of Ethnographic Theory* 1(1): vi–xxxv.

De Villiers, Etienne. 2017. *Revisiting Max Weber's Ethic of Responsibility* Tübingen: Mohr Siebeck.

Etzioni, Amitai. 2018. *Happiness is the Wrong Metric: A Liberal Communitarian Response to Populism* New York: Springer.

Fagan, Andrew. 2017. *Human Rights and Cultural Diversity: Core Issues and Cases* Edinburgh: Edinburgh University Press.

Flanagan, Owen. 2016. *The Geography of Morals: Varieties of Moral Possibility* Oxford Scholarship Online.

Greenwood, Margo & Sarah de Leeuw. 2007. 'Teachings from the Land: Indigenous People, Our Health, Our Land, Our Children' *Canadian Journal of Native Education; Edmonton* 30(1): 48–53.

Hatzimihail, Nikitas E. 2021. *Preclassical Conflict of Laws* CUP online.

Holmes, Robert L. 1998. *Basic Moral Philosophy* 2nd edn. Belmont, CA: Wadsworth Publishing.

Kant, Immanuel. 1983. *Werke in zehn Bänden. Sonderausgabe,* herausgegeben von Wilhelm Weischedel ed., vol 6 Darmstadt: Wissenschafliche Buchgesellschaft.

Kleingeld, Pauline. 2007. 'Kant's Second Thoughts on Race' *The Philosophical Quarterly* 57(229): 573–592.

Kono, Toshiyuki. 2020. 'Impact of Uniform Laws on the Protection of Cultural Property – The 1995 Convention', Keynote delivered at the 1995 UNIDROIT Convention Conference on Cultural Objects at the Crossroads of Rights and Interests, Rome, 8–9 October 2020.

MacGregor, Neil & Jonathan Williams. 2005. 'The Encyclopaedic Museum: Enlightenment Ideals, Contemporary Realities' *Public Archaeology* 4(1): 57–59.

Parker, Patricia L. 1990. *Keepers of the Treasures: Protecting Historic Properties and Cultural Traditions on Indian Lands: Report on Tribal Preservation Funding Needs Submitted to Congress* National Park Service, United States Department of the Interior, The Branch.

Simpson, Moira G. 1996. *Making Representations: Museums in the Post-Colonial Era* London: Routledge.

Vrdoljak, Ana F. 2008. *International Law, Museums and the Return of Cultural Objects* Cambridge: CUP.

Zeidler, Kamil. 2016. *Restitution of Cultural Property: Hard Case, Theory of Argumentation, Philosophy of Law* Gdańsk: Gdańsk University Press.

Index

FSC
www.fsc.org
MIX
Papier | Fördert gute Waldnutzung
FSC® C083411

Kolibri 360 GmbH
Ferdinand-Jühlke-Straße 7
99095 Erfurt, Deutschland
produktsicherheit@kolibri360.de